# complete book of wood finishing

*Robert Scharff*

# complete book

**second edition**

**McGraw-Hill Book Company**

new york    st. louis    san francisco    düsseldorf
johannesburg    kuala lumpur    london    mexico
montreal    new delhi    panama    paris
são paulo    singapore    sydney
tokyo    toronto

# of wood
## finishing

Library of Congress Cataloging in Publication Data

Scharff, Robert.
Complete book of wood finishing.

1. Wood finishing. I. Title.
TT325.S26 1974      684'.084      73–22239
ISBN 0–07–055166–9

1 2 3 4 5 6 7 8 9 0   B P B P   7 9 8 7 6 5 4

The editors for this book were Tyler G. Hicks and Carolyn Nagy,
the designer was Naomi Auerbach, and its production
was supervised by Teresa F. Leaden. It was set
in Electra by The Book Press.

It was printed and bound by The Book Press.

To my daughters
Alpha Jay and Nan

# Contents

# Preface

**Y**our woodworking project will be as beautiful and durable as the finish you give it—whether it is a furniture project of your own, some built-ins, ready-made unpainted furniture, or an antique that needs refurbishing. With a really professional finish your project will be one of which you can be justly proud.

To achieve such a professional finish you will want easy-to-follow, step-by-step instructions that cover every step of the wood-finishing process. This is what we have tried to give you in this book. It is the result of years of practical experience, research, and experimentation in this field, combined with data from scores of professional wood finishers, material manufacturers, and other home craftsmen. The many radical changes that have taken place in finishing in recent years—new materials, equipment, and techniques—help to make this a truly practical guide on the subject.

Whether you are a home craftsman, professional finisher, carpenter, or student, you will find this an invaluable handbook which will give you all the sound, practical foundations of good wood finishing.

The author wishes to thank the following organizations for their technical assistance and the use of their photographs and material: Delta Power Tool Division, Rockwell Manufacturing Company; National Paint and Coatings Association; United States Plywood Corporation; Masonite Corporation; American Plywood Association; Wooster Brush Company; Baker Brush Company Inc.; Behr-Manning Corporation; Western Pine Association; De Vilbiss Company; Sherwin-Williams Company; William Zinsser & Company, Inc.; H. Bahlen & Brothers, Inc.; Minnesota Mining & Manufacturing Company; Carborundum Company; E. I. du Pont de Nemours & Company, Inc.; Valspar Corporation; Benjamin Moore & Company; Pittsburgh Plate Glass Company; Boyle-Midway, Inc.; Shellac Information Bureau; Perce & Stevens Chemical Corporation; Martin Senour Paints; Watco-Dennis Corporation; American Brush Manufacturers Association; Savogran Company; Wilson-Imperial Company; Glidden-Durkee Company; The Rez Company; McCloskey Varnish Company; Bridgeport Brass Company.

*Robert Scharff*

**complete book of wood finishing**

# CHAPTER ONE

# Woods and Their Accepted Finishes

The beauty of any wood depends on its finish. There are, however, no short cuts to obtaining a good finish. It takes time and patience. But remember, the finish applied will flatter or ruin the appearance of either a newly completed project or an old object which has been done over. Before any attempt is made to finish a woodworking project, you should first become acquainted with the structural differences of the many varieties of wood.

For all practical purposes, there are two broad classifications of wood—hard and soft. Hardwoods are cut from deciduous trees such as oak, maple, walnut, birch, cherry, and mahogany—trees that lose their leaves in the fall. Softwoods are the evergreens or conifers such as pine and spruce. The terms *hardwood* and *softwood*, however, are sometimes misleading, for some so-called softwoods are considerably harder than many hardwoods; and some so-called hardwoods—for example, cottonwood and basswood—are as soft as the softest conifers.

In the composition of wood there will be found hundreds of small cells called pores. In most hardwoods these pores are very pronounced and must be taken into account when the wood is finished so that the finish will not dry rough. Oak and mahogany, for example, have very noticeable pores and are called open-grained woods. Birch and maple, with small pores, are referred to as close-grained woods. The relative size and the arrangement of these cells are fairly constant in each species of wood, but vary among the different species. This variation is a reliable means of distinguishing one wood from another.

Just beneath the bark, a layer of wood is added each year outside the layer previously formed. In temperate climates, the cells formed at the beginning of each year's growth are considerably larger than those formed later in the season. This contrast forms a definite line of demarcation for each year's growth. In a cross section of a tree trunk, the layers are well defined and are known as annual rings.

The soft, open-celled wood formed in the spring is called springwood; the harder and denser wood formed later in the season is known as summerwood. In some types of wood, such as birch, maple, and gum, the distinction between springwood and summerwood is not clear. Some species, such as red oak, fir, and certain types of pine have wide annual rings, which means that they have a wide variety of hard and soft spots in their surface.

Because of their structure, some woods lend themselves

to the use of stain; others will have a more attractive appearance if left natural; still others are not adaptable to either of these treatments and should be finished with paint or enamel. Walnut, ash, birch, chestnut, cherry, cedar, gum, maple, mahogany, oak, rosewood, and hickory may be placed in the group whose beauty will be enhanced by the use of stain. Woods that will take a natural finish are walnut, cherry, cedar, oak, rosewood, redwood, and teakwood. (As you can see, some woods are included in both groups.) The third group—woods that should or can be finished with paint or enamel—are white and sugar pine, fir, spruce, basswood, and poplar. (See chart on pages 6 to 10 for a complete list of wood characteristics and finishes.)

The most important consideration is to use the finish that will bring out all the natural beauty of the wood, keeping in mind that the finish should not be too uneven in color. The function of stain is to color by penetration into the pores. The greater the penetration, the darker the finish. When a piece of wood has hard and soft spots, the stain penetrates more deeply into the soft portions, resulting in an uneven or contrasting effect. Thus, when working with open-grained or highly figured wood, don't overdo the finish. It might even be advisable not to use stain on these woods; or if stain must be used, choose one that does not have much penetrating power. Analine, or water stain, for example, with a little alcohol added, has considerable penetrating ability, while most oil stains have less penetration.

There are other factors to consider when a type of finish is being chosen. The surface as well as the color of the wood must be protected against two major enemies: (1) moisture, which is the cause of cracking and warping; (2) dirt, which causes a surface to become cloudy. Varnish, shellac, lacquer, or penetrating resin finish may be used for this purpose. Only by applying one or more of these materials will you achieve a durable finish. To produce colors that are clear, brilliant, and durable, it is necessary to do the work of finishing in a definite order. For a piece that is to be handled

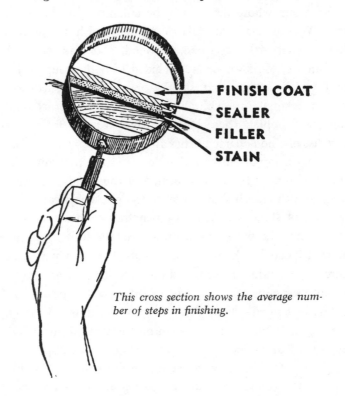

**FINISH COAT**
**SEALER**
**FILLER**
**STAIN**

*This cross section shows the average number of steps in finishing.*

very little, use a stain, filler, and wax. For a more durable finish: stain, filler, shellac, and wax. For pieces that will be in constant use, apply stain, filler, shellac, and at least three coats of varnish followed by a coat of wax. If a piece of wood is to be left natural, any of these procedures is in order—omitting the stain, of course.

An attempt to imitate expensive wood by staining a cheaper wood to match the color is not likely to be successful. A common error of the beginner is to put mahogany or walnut stain on pine and expect it to look like the costlier wood. This cannot be done, because a so-called "mahogany" stain will produce an entirely different color on two different woods. The mistake that is always made is to take the name of a stain literally. Because it is marked walnut, oak, or mahogany, it is a common belief that a stain will produce the color of the wood after which it is named. Actually the name implies only a color that has a certain tint of red, brown, or black. Mahogany stain may be used on many woods, of course, to produce a reddish color, and walnut stain may be used for a dark-brown finish. The point to keep in mind is that a stain may be used on any wood to obtain a certain shade, regardless of the name given to the stain.

Some woods require the use of fillers. These preparations are used on open-grained wood to close the pores—woods such as oak, walnut, and mahogany. A filler may be left natural, for natural finishes, or it may be tinted the color of the stained wood. A variety of finishes may be obtained by staining the wood one color and applying the filler in its natural condition or in a different tinted shade.

The final step in finishing is the protective coat of shellac, lacquer, varnish, and wax. All the details of wood finishing will be discussed in the following chapters.

**General wood-characteristic and finishing chart***

| Wood | Natural color | Grain figure | Stain | | Filler | | Natural finish | Bleach | Paint |
|---|---|---|---|---|---|---|---|---|---|
| | | | Type | Color | Weight† | Color | | | |
| Alder | Pink to brown | Plain or figured | Oil or water | Red or brown | None | None | Yes | Yes | Yes |
| Amaranth | Purple | Plain or stripe | None | None | 8 | Match wood | Yes | No | No |
| Ash | White to brown | Plain | Any | Any | 1.5 to 2 | White or brown | Yes | Yes | Yes |
| Aspen | Light straw | Plain or stripe | Water | Amber | None | None | Yes | No | Yes |
| Avodire | White to cream | Stripe | None | None | 8 | Match wood | **Yes** | Yes‡ | No |
| Basswood | Cream | Mild | Water | Red or brown | None | None | No | Yes‡ | Yes |
| Beech | White to brown | Mild | Water | Red or brown | 8 | Red or brown | No | Yes | Yes |
| Birch | Cream | Mild | Any | Walnut or mahogany | None or 7 | Natural or brown | Yes | Yes | Yes |
| Bubinga | Pale red to flesh red | Plain to figured | Water | Red or brown | 12 to 14 | Red or brown | Yes | No | No |

| | | | | | | | | |
|---|---|---|---|---|---|---|---|---|
| Butternut | Amber and cream | Like walnut | Water | Walnut or oak | 12 to 14 | Medium brown | Yes | Yes | No |
| Cedar | Red and cream | Knotty or stripe | None | None | None | None | Yes | No | No |
| Cherry | Red to brown | Fine | Water | Red or brown | 6 to 8 | Brown, red, or black | Yes | No | No |
| Chestnut | Gray-brown | Heavy grain | Oil§ | Red or brown | 15 | Red or brown | Yes | Yes | Yes |
| Cypress | Brown and cream | Plain or figured | Water or oil§ | Red or brown | None | None | Yes | No | Yes |
| Ebony | Dark brown to black | Plain or stripe | Water | Red or brown | None | None | Yes | No | No |
| Elm | Cream to brown | Heavy grain | Water | Red or brown | 12 to 14 | Dark brown | Yes | No | Yes |
| Fir (Douglas) | Cream | Wild | Oil§ | Brown | None | None | No | No | Yes |
| Gaboon | Golden to pinkish tan | Plain or stripe | Water | Red or brown | None | None | Yes | No | No |
| Gum (red) | Cream and red | Plain or figured | Any | Red or brown | None or 4 to 6 | Match wood | Yes | Yes | Yes |
| Hemlock | Light reddish brown | Plain | Water or oil§ | Red or brown | None | None | No | No | Yes |
| Hickory | White to cream | Straight | Water | Red or brown | 15 | Brown | Yes | Yes | No |

**General wood-characteristics and finishing chart (continued)**

| Wood | Natural color | Grain figure | Stain Type | Stain Color | Filler Weight[†] | Filler Color | Natural finish | Bleach | Paint |
|---|---|---|---|---|---|---|---|---|---|
| Holly | White | Mild | Water | Amber | None | None | Yes | Yes[‡] | Yes |
| Kelobra | Brown | Plain or stripe | Water | Dark brown | 12 to 14 | Dark brown | Yes | Yes | No |
| Korina | Creamy gray | Plain or stripe | Water | Red or brown | 12 to 14 | Red or brown | Yes | Yes | No |
| Lacewood | Light brown | Flake | Water | Oak | 12 to 14 | Dark brown | Yes | Yes | No |
| Lauan | Brown to red-brown | Stripe | Water or oil§ | Red or brown | 18 | Red, brown, or black | Yes | Yes | No |
| Locust | Golden brown | Wild | Water or oil | Brown | 12 to 16 | Brown | Yes | No | Yes |
| Magnolia | Light to dark yellowish brown | Plain | Water or oil§ | Brown | None | None | Yes | Yes | Yes |
| Mahogany | Brown to red-brown | Stripe | Water | Red or brown | 12 | Red, brown, or black | Yes | Yes | No |
| Maple | Cream | Varied | Water or oil§ | Maple | None | None | Yes | Yes | Yes |

| | | | | | | | | | |
|---|---|---|---|---|---|---|---|---|---|
| Oak (red) | Red to brown | Plain or flake | Water | Light green | 15 | Brown | No | Yes | Yes |
| Oak (white) | White to pale brown | Plain or flake | Water | Brown | 15 | Brown | Yes | Yes | Yes |
| Orientalwood | Light brown | Stripe | Water | Amber or brown | 12 | Brown | Yes | No | No |
| Padouk | Golden red to deep crimson | Stripe or mottle | None | None | 14 to 16 | Red or brown | Yes | No | No |
| Pine (white) | White to cream | Very mild | Water or oil | Brown | None | None | No | No | Yes |
| Pine (yellow) | Cream to yellow | Mild | Water or oil | Brown | None | None | Yes | No | Yes |
| Poplar | White | Mild | Water or oil§ | Red or brown | None | None | No | No | Yes |
| Primavera | White to yellow | Stripe | Water | Amber | 12 | Natural | Yes | Yes | No |
| Redwood | Red | Mild | Oil§ | Red | None | None | Yes | No | Yes |
| Rosewood | Red to brown | Stripe to varied | Water | Red | 12 to 15 | Dark red to black | Yes | No | No |
| Sapeli | Medium brown | Stripe | Water | Red or brown | 10 | Dark brown | Yes | Yes | No |

**General wood-characteristic and finishing chart (continued)**

| Wood | Natural color | Grain figure | Stain | | Filler | | Natural finish | Bleach | Paint |
|---|---|---|---|---|---|---|---|---|---|
| | | | Type | Color | Weight† | Color | | | |
| Spruce | White | Plain | Water or oil§ | Amber or brown | None | None | No | No | Yes |
| Sycamore | White to pink | Flake | Water | Amber or brown | None | None | Yes | Yes‡ | Yes |
| Teakwood | Golden brown | Plain or figured | Water or oil | Brown | 16 | Natural or brown | Yes | Yes | No |
| Tigerwood | Golden brown | Stripe | Water | Dark brown | 8 to 12 | Dark brown | Yes | Yes | No |
| Tupelo | Pale to brownish gray | Plain | Water | Brown | None to 7 | Brown | Yes | Yes | Yes |
| Walnut | Cream and dark brown | Varied | Water | Dark brown | 12 to 15 | Brown to black | Yes | Yes | No |
| Zebrawood | Tan with brown stripe | Heavy stripe | Water | Light oak | 12 | Natural | Yes | No | No |

* This chart is a general one and gives only the usual accepted finishes and uses of the wood.
† Weight designates number of pounds of filler plastic per gallon of thinner.
‡ Generally not necessary because of the light color of the wood.
§ Penetrating oil stain may also be used. Non-grain-raising stains may be substituted for water stains throughout.

# CHAPTER TWO

# Preparing the Surface for Finishing

**P**roper preparation of the surface is of first importance in wood finishing. The finish coat will not cover defects; it will magnify them. Scratches that may be undetected or seem slight in bare wood will stick out like sore thumbs under a bright finish.

In this chapter, the preparation of new wood surfaces is described. The detail of refinishing can be found in Chapter 14.

Successful finishing begins with the choice of wood. Pieces must be carefully matched as to grain and color. Surface must be clean and smooth. To obtain this smoothness, start the finishing process before the pieces are assembled. The rough edges left by the saw should be smoothed down with sandpaper until perfectly smooth. If the edges are too rough, touch them up with a rasp or plane, and then sand. Any other rough spots on the wood surface should be removed by sanding, planing, or scraping with a wood scraper or piece of broken glass. The latter, by the way, makes an excellent scraper, especially for spots that are small or difficult to remove with an ordinary wood scraper.

Small dents and hammer marks can generally be eliminated by placing several thicknesses of moistened cloth over the dent and then pressing with a hot iron. The steam swells the wood fibers, bringing them back to their original position. The process may have to be repeated several times to remove the dent completely. Sandpaper the surface when it is dry.

Nailheads should be driven below the wood surface with a nail set and the resulting hole filled with wood putty, spackle, or other type of filler. Screwheads that have been countersunk can be treated in the same manner. But a more professional method is to glue a wood plug on top of the screwhead. The wood plug is cut off flush with the wood surface after it is in place. Wood plugs, available at lumber yards and hardware stores, can be had in several types of hardwoods.

Joints between pieces of wood that are not as tight as they should be can be filled with a wood putty or filler. The seam should first be cleaned out and then packed with the material. After it is dry, shave down the excess with a razor blade, and then sand. Similarly, cracks in end grain and other spots should also be filled.

When smoothing is completed, don't be in a hurry to put on the paint, penetrating resin, varnish, lacquer, or shellac. Dust off the wood with a brush or soft cloth. Then remove all spots of dirt or grease. Usually such spots will come off by washing over them with benzine or naphtha. If the wood is oak, walnut, or another open-grained variety, be sure to remove dirt and grease from the pores by using special care with the cleaning liquid. When such spots are not properly cleaned, stain does not penetrate and the finish will be spotty in appearance.

Dark stains on new surfaces should be bleached before finishing in natural or stained colors. Bleaching methods are described on page 32.

## SANDING

Sanding is the most important operation in preparing the wood for a finish. It must be done to remove tool marks and to smooth the surface so that the reflective properties of the finishing materials will accentuate the full beauty of the wood grain. By taking time to do a good job of sanding, using correct procedures and selected grades of abrasives, you can produce a finish of professional appearance and quality.

The term *sandpaper* meaning paper coated with abrasive particles had its birth many years ago, probably when sand was actually used in that way. Today, four different mineral particles, of various degrees of hardness, are used. Two are natural, being mined or quarried, and two are artificially produced in electric furnaces. The latter are often called *synthetic papers*. The natural minerals are:

**Flint quartz** (commonly called flint), generally off-white in color. Flint sandpaper is commonly sold in hardware stores, but has almost no use in industry, as other particles are far superior in cutting ability and enduring sharpness. Flint sandpaper should be avoided, unless it is impossible to obtain any better, as it takes too long to get results because of the dull cutting edges of the crushed quartz grit. It should be used only for sanding paint or shellac.

*Garnet* (sharp and hard), of the same name as the semiprecious jewel and coming from the same source. This reddish abrasive paper, widely used professionally and industrially in wood finishing, is available in most hardware stores. It is well suited to sanding operations on wood and finishes.

The artificial minerals are:

*Aluminum oxide,* reddish brown, made in electric furnaces by fusing the mineral bauxite at very high temperatures. Its toughness and enduring sharpness make it a fine abrasive for both wood and metal. Aluminum oxide may be substituted successfully for garnet.

*Silicon carbide (or oxide),* also an electric-furnace product, produced by high-temperature fusing of silica sand and coke, much as nature makes diamonds. The result is a crystalline abrasive, very hard and sharp—in fact, it approaches the diamond in both respects. Silicon carbide or oxide may be used on lacquers, plastics, composition materials, and metals.

When selecting sandpaper, it is most important to obtain the correct grade for the job to be done. This means choosing the proper coarseness or fineness of the grit. Today, there are three principal methods of designating the grade. Some papers, usually the flint-coated ones, are labeled "very coarse," "coarse," "medium," "fine," and so on. Most garnet, aluminum oxide, and silicon oxide types list the grit numbers—80, 100, 240, 320, etc. These numbers are mesh sizes—the number of openings per square inch in each direction on sieves used in grading the grit. A few synthetic and flint papers—and most garnet ones—are labeled by the size of grit and carry designations of 2/0, 4/0, 7/0, 8/0, etc. In either of the last two cases, the larger the number, the smaller the size of the mineral particles and the finer the grit. While it makes no difference which system is used, it is important to know the comparisons of the three methods of grade designation. The following table should help you do just this:

### Sandpaper table

| | Aluminum oxide or silicon oxide | Garnet | Flint |
|---|---|---|---|
| Super fine | 12/0–600 | 10/0–400 | |
| | 11/0–500 | 9/0–320 | |
| | 10/0–400 | 8/0–280 | |
| Extra fine | 9/0–320 | | |
| | 8/0–280 | | |
| | 7/0–240 | 7/0–240 | |
| Very fine | 6/0–220 | 6/0–220 | 4/0 |
| | 5/0–180 | 5/0–180 | 3/0 |
| | | | 2/0 |
| Fine | 4/0–150 | 4/0–150 | |
| | 3/0–120 | 3/0–120 | |
| | 2/0–100 | 2/0–100 | 0 |
| Medium | 1/0–80 | 1/0–80 | ½ |
| | ½–60 | ½–60 | 1 |
| Coarse | 1–50 | 1–50 | 1½ |
| | 1½–40 | 1½–40 | 2 |
| Very coarse | 2–36 | 2–36 | 2½ |
| | 2½–30 | 2½–30 | 3 |
| | 3–24 | 3–24 | |

All abrasive papers, except those made of flint, come in two types of coatings—closed- and open-coat. Closed-coat papers have tightly packed abrasive particles of grit that cover their entire surface, while the particles on open-coat papers cover only 50 to 70 percent of the surface, leaving open spaces between them. The closed-coat paper cuts faster because of the greater number of particles. This type, however, is more likely to become clogged when used on soft materials that jam in between the particles. The open-coat paper which lets the clogged material fall out, should be used on soft or gummy woods or surfaces, paint, shellac, and other similar finishes.

Open-coat papers are usually made in grades 80 (1/0) and finer. Coarser grades tend less toward clogging because there is more space between the abrasive particles. There are special nonfilling papers available which permit smooth sanding and still have wide spacing between the particles. While these papers are more expensive, they do not tend to clog up as easily as regular papers of the same grade.

The backing to which the abrasive particles are glued may be paper, cloth, a cloth-paper combination, fiber, or a fiber-cloth combination. For home-workshop work, paper and cloth backings are generally used. The others are used mostly in industrial applications. Cloth and paper backings (except flint) also come in waterproof versions (sometimes called wet-or-dry) that permit wet sanding.

Paper backing comes in four weights, which are designated as A, C, D, and E. The A grade includes the fine-grit lightweight papers known as *finishing papers*. The C and D grades, known as *cabinet papers*, are medium-weight papers with abrasive particles of medium fineness. The E grade, known as *roll stock*, is heavyweight with stiff paper backing and is only occasionally used in handwork.

In cloth backings, the J grade, the lighter of the two commonly available cloth backings, is used for finishing shaped work. The X grade is heavier and stronger and is used for flat or shaped work in power tools. As a rule of thumb, use either cloth or paper backing in a weight light enough to bend as much as necessary without cracking. When cracking occurs, switch from paper to cloth or to the next heavier weight in either type. Remember that paper backing is the cheapest, so use it wherever it will stand up. A general classification and recommendation for grades to be used on various types of work is given in the following table.

| Handwork | Backing | Grit number | Grade number | Word description |
|---|---|---|---|---|
| Rough sanding and shaping | D | 60 or 80 | ½ or 1/0 | Medium |
| Preparatory sanding on softwood | A | 100 to 150 | 2/0 to 4/0 | Fine |
| Preparatory sanding on hardwood | A | 120 or 150 | 3/0 or 4/0 | Fine |
| Finish sanding on softwood | A | 180 or 220 | 5/0 or 6/0 | Very fine |
| Finish sanding on hardwood | A | 220 to 280 | 6/0 to 8/0 | Very fine to extra fine |
| Dry-sanding sealers and finishes between coats | A | 220 to 280 | 6/0 to 8/0 | Very fine to extra fine |
| Wet-sanding sealers and finishes between coats | J or X | 220 to 280 | 6/0 to 8/0 | Very fine to extra fine |
| Rubbing down after finish coat | J | 280 to 400 | 8/0 to 10/0 | Extra fine to super fine |

Sandpaper is available in many forms other than the common sandpaper sheets. Most abrasives can be bought in continuous rolls of various widths and backings for use with magazine hand sanders, for sanding in lathes, and for wrapping on special-purpose mandrels. They also come in disks, drums, and belts for use with the various types of power sanding tools.

## Power or hand sanding?

Sanding can be done by hand or by power. There are four basic power-type sanders: vibrating, belt, disk, and drum. The last, however, is seldom used as a wood-finishing device except on floors. The disk sanders which operate in a circular path are not used too frequently—except for rough sanding —because they create swirl marks which may show in the final finish. This type of machine, however, is fine when fitted with buffing pads for polishing a finished surface. Actually, between the belt and vibrator types, the latter is by far the most popular.

The vibrator type—often called a *finishing sander*— operates in one of three ways: straight-line, orbital, and dual-action. With straight-line or in-line action, the abrasive paper moves back and forth in the direction the sander is moving. It should only be used when sanding with the grain and is excellent for final sanding. The vibrator straight-line sander does not remove much material, or do it quickly, but it does it with perfect smoothness.

With an orbital-action sander, the abrasive moves in a flat, tight oval, rather than straight back and forth. But the cross-grain motion can cause swirl marks on the wood, which will usually be visible no matter how fine the sandpaper may be. The swirls must be sanded away with the grain, to complete the job. In other words, the orbital type of vibrating sander cuts first, making it ideal for first sanding, but should not be used for smoothing before applying the finish.

The so-called dual-action vibrating sanders combine both straight-line and orbital-action into the same machine. That is, you start the sanding operation with the orbital-action for heavy stock removal, then by flicking a switch or turning a key, the straight-line action takes over for finish sanding. A dual-action vibrating sander does not cost quite twice as much as a straight-line and orbital sander combined, but it approaches it.

When purchasing a vibrating sander, size of pad and weight of machine are two other important considerations. The larger the pad area, the quicker the job can be completed. But on small or irregular surfaces, a small pad performs best. Therefore, in most cases, the in-between size is the best bet. Standard size of sheet of sheet abrasive is $9 \times 11$ inches. Some sanders use one-half of a sheet, others use one-third of a sheet, still others one-fourth, one-fifth or less. Incidentally, the pad on which the abrasive paper goes may be either neoprene (synthetic rubber) sponge or felt. The latter usually has more firmness and works best on flat surfaces. The neoprene may adapt to uneven contours better and can be used for either dry or wet sanding. Some vibrating sanders are available with interchangeable pads.

Weight is an important consideration since no hand pressure should be applied to the sander. The weight of the sander, plus the natural weight of the hand, are all the pressure required in normal operation. If more pressure is exerted, its operation is slowed down, and the paper will clog more readily. A heavier sander smooths a surface quicker.

Power-type sanders provide the fastest straight-line sanding but require practice in handling for fine finishing. In fact, while power sanding does a good job in most cases, a great many wood-finishing experts recommend that the final sanding be done by hand.

For hand sanding, some form of backing other than the

fingers or hand must be provided. Sanding blocks can be purchased from hardware stores, or you can make one by tacking the abrasive on a wood block faced with a ½-inch-thick sheet of sponge rubber or felt. A blackboard eraser also makes a fine sanding block. Do not use unpadded blocks for finish sanding, because if a piece of grit or sawdust gets between the block and the sandpaper, it can make deep scratches in the finish. The felt or rubber padding also helps to disperse some of the heat caused by sanding action that would otherwise cause a clog or fill-up more rapidly.

Not all sanding surfaces are flat; therefore, not all sanding blocks are flat. For this reason, make several sizes of rounded blocks to handle the various diameters of concave curves that must be sanded. When working on a project where it is necessary to sand a great deal of molding or other shaped work, you should devise special sanding blocks to fit these specific curves. But don't forget the felt or rubber padding in such cases.

### Follow these steps in sanding

1. Begin sanding new wood with coarse paper at an angle with the grain. This will level the ridges and remove glue stains and other discolorations. The coarse abrasive will leave fine scratches over the entire surface of the wood.

2. Discard the coarse abrasive and follow with a medium abrasive, sanding with the grain. (If the wood is coarse and open-grained like chestnut or oak, sand at a slight angle to the grain to avoid enlarging the pores of the wood by rounding their edges. This should be kept in mind for all open-grained woods, as individual particles of the abrasive passing through the tiny elongated pores

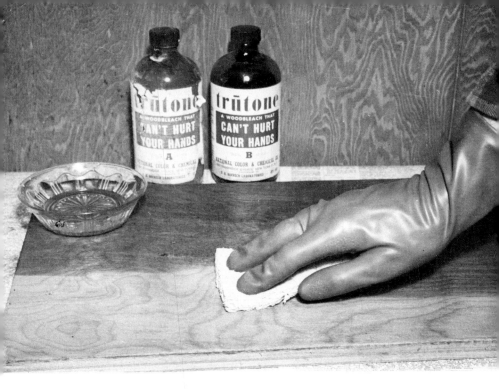

When applying a bleach, the first application of a two-solution commercial bleach is poured into a bowl and applied with a brush or cloth. Let it stand the designated time (follow manufacturer's instructions), then apply second solution (top). Before you apply any finish to unfinished furniture, fill nail holes and open joints with a nonshrinking wood putty. Butter them slightly more than full. Let the filler dry; then sand smooth (bottom).

*Four popular types of sanding blocks available at hardware stores.*

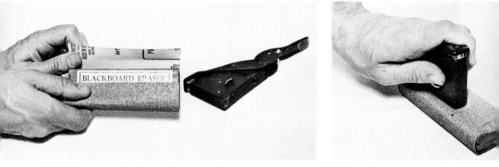

You can make the sanding block (above) by simply stapling the proper grade of sandpaper to a blackboard eraser. To cut the sandpaper to size, tear it against a metal straightedge or hacksaw blade. Never cut sandpaper with scissors or knife, as this will damage the cutting edge of the tool. Pictured below are three popular types of portable sanders. The disk (left) and belt (center) are good for rough sanding, while the vibrating type (right) is excellent for finished sanding.

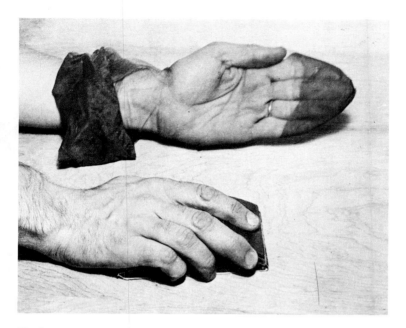

To locate rough spots, place a nylon stocking over the hand, and run it over the sanded areas. Any rough spots will snag the hose.

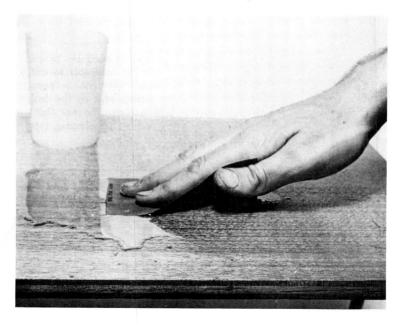

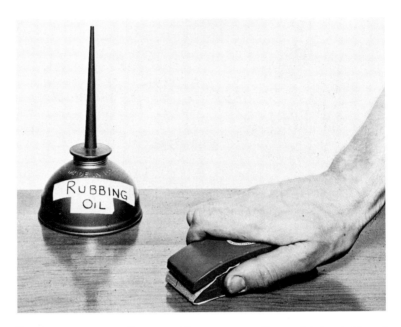

For *between-coat sanding, use either water or oil as a lubricant. Round work can be sanded with strip-type sandpaper.*

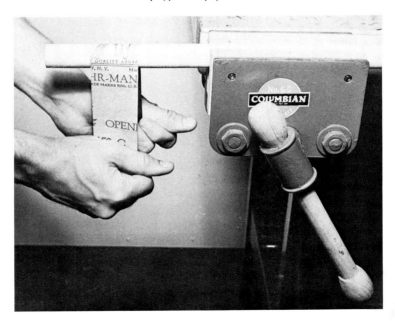

parallel to their length tend to enlarge them. This leaves the surface rough and, in some cases, even changes the pattern of the grain.) Continue the second step until all fine scratches produced by the first sanding have been eliminated.

3. Change to a fine grade of paper and sand directly with the grain. At this stage, the surface will be approaching a degree of smoothness capable of reflecting oblique light. Hold the work horizontally just below eye level, and look across it toward a light source. Minor ridges or other irregularities will show up quite clearly. Pencil mark the high points, and sand them down with the fine abrasive until the reflection of light is uniform over the whole surface.

4. Before the final sanding with very fine finishing paper, some experienced craftsmen prefer to apply a thin wash of shellac (see Chapter 7 for proper shellac proportion), a commercial sanding sealer (applied as directed by the manufacturer), or a nonsealing glue size. The last is preferred when planning to use a water stain, since it provides good stain penetration. To make a suitable glue size, mix ¼ cup of flake hide glue in a gallon of hot water. Brush it lightly and evenly over the surface, leaving no trailing film. Allow the surface to dry completely, and then sand with the same grade as last employed. If any glue stains should occur, they can be bleached out as described later in this chapter.

5. Some finishers dampen the wood during the final sanding with a sponge to raise the grain and wood fibers. The dampening of the wood also swells out any pressure marks or dimples made during construction. After drying, the

raised grain is sanded smooth and either sealed or shellacked with a very light wash coat before being given the final sanding with very fine or extra fine paper.

When working with open-grained woods that require staining and filling, many finishers apply stain and filler, allow it to dry, and then finish-sand the surface. In this procedure it will be necessary occasionally to apply a few drops of rubbing oil to the sandpaper to prevent clogging. (See Chapter 9.) Care must be used in this method to avoid cutting through the stain and exposing bare wood. Succeeding finishing maerials (shellac, lacquer, or varnish) are sanded lightly between coats.

The trick in producing a true, flat surface by hand sanding is to adopt a sanding stroke of uniform length and equalized pressure. When you stroke the sandpaper as far as you can reach in both directions on a large surface, the pressure falls off near the end of each stroke, resulting in an uneven surface. Some experienced finishers sand with short, straight strokes, and by moving back and forth along the length of the work the strokes are made to overlap continually. This technique produces a true, flat surface on large work, such as a table top.

When you are sanding to an edge, do not allow the sanding block to extend beyond the edge more than one-fourth its length on each stroke; otherwise, a rounded edge will result. When you are sanding either large or small work, your strokes should overlap about half the width of the sanding block and should progress uniformly in one direction at right angles to the direction of your arm.

To smooth heavy crack filler or paint undercoater, use a medium flint paper and replace it frequently or an open-coated silicon carbide paper with abrasive particles spread enough to retard clogging. If the sanded material cakes on the paper, slap the paper against a hard surface, or use a stiff scrub brush to clean it out.

To sand the edges and ends of such items as the tops of tables and cabinets, use only very fine abrasive papers, regardless of the step in finishing. Use a sanding block on any top surface of edge or end. As a guide for sanding an end grain, clamp two pieces of wood, flush with the end to be sanded, to the top and bottom of the board and to the workbench top. The two guides should be longer than the width of the board, to avoid chipping the ends and to give clamping room. This will ensure a nice square edge.

For sanding curved work, fold a strip of fine grit sandpaper over the end of a stick sharpened to a chisel edge. To crease sandpaper for sanding into a sharp, deep crevice, pull the paper, grit face up, once or twice over a sharp corner. This will impart great flexibility even to the heaviest abrasive paper, and will enable it to take almost any form without cracking. A rubber sanding block, obtainable at hardware stores, is valuable in rounding corners and edges. Sanding the corners slightly helps the finish to stick.

When sanding with the finer grits of paper or when it is desirable to increase the flexibility of backing, moisten the backing with warm water, making certain not to allow the sponge or rag to touch the grit face. This greater flexibility, in most cases, gives a faster and cleaner sanding job.

Never cut sandpaper with a knife, scissors, snips, or other sharp tool, as this will dull or damage the cutting edge of the tool. Instead, use a metal straightedge or an old hacksaw blade. Fold a sheet in straight-lined quarters; hold the folded paper flat on the workbench with one hand; slip the blade be-

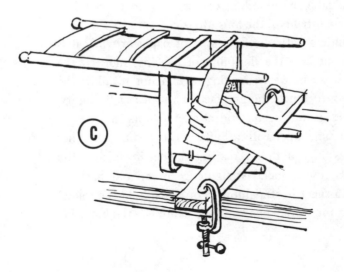

(A) *To prevent movement when sanding a flat surface, place work between two pieces of wood that are clamped to a table top.* (B) *To sand edge grain, use vise or clamp it to the side of an up-turned box.* (C) *To sand round chair legs, clamp it to a table top as shown.*

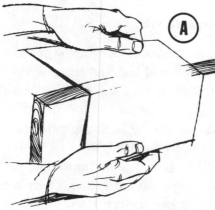

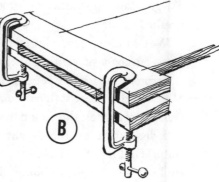

(A) To crease sandpaper—for sanding into a sharp, deep crevice—first pull the paper, grit face up, once or twice over a sharp corner. This will make even the heaviest abrasive paper flexible and enable it to take almost any form without cracking. (B) For a flat end with square corners, clamp two pieces of wood flush with the end of work. This will keep sandpaper from rounding off edges. (C) Before edge-joining and gluing two boards together, slip a piece of folded abrasive paper between the two edges and sand off high spots that prevent the boards from meeting evenly. (D) To sand intricate carving or molding, fold a strip of fine sandpaper over the end of a stick sharpened to a chisellike edge. Hold stick like a pencil, and work it along the surface.

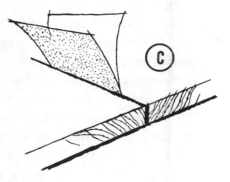

tween the folded sheets, and cut with a sweeping motion. Change the saw to the opposite fold line, and tear the paper into quarters. This is the best size for sanding most wood surfaces.

After sanding, clean the surface by brushing and wiping with a clean, soft cloth. It is good practice to clean the surface with a lint-free cloth moistened with turpentine. Remember that stray pieces of No. 80 grit getting under the 320-grit sanding block can groove its way across a smooth finished surface.

Wet sanding generally gives best results when you sand between coats of varnish, shellac, lacquer, and enamel. Use waterproof abrasive papers, either garnet or aluminum oxide. Wetting the paper softens the abrasive action and helps prevent clogging, as the liquid tends to wash away the chips, and dissipates heat that might alter or discolor a finish. Use water (but never on shellac), kerosene, mineral spirits, or rubbing oil. A good rubbing oil can be made of 3 parts of golden paraffin oil plus 1 part gasoline.

In some cases these versatile waterproof papers will replace the slower pumice and water or pumice and oil. For the final rubbing, use extra fine paper with rubbing oil. (For details on rubbing, see Chapter 9.)

Sandpaper that has been used for removing old finish and is clogged with the gummy residue of this finish can be cleaned for reuse by dissolving it from the abrasive surface. Simply soak the paper in a solvent that will dissolve the particular finish being removed. For example, turpentine will clean varnish out of the paper, alcohol will dissolve shellac, and lacquer thinner will remove lacquer.

Many experts prefer to employ "aged" abrasive papers for

fine-polished finishes. That is, they like to use well-worn paper—those that most people would throw away—because most of the grit clumps, a problem with new papers, have been eliminated. True, old abrasive papers work much slower. You can age paper quickly by scuffing together two papers with identical grit sizes, thus removing any oversized grit or grit clumps.

### Treatment of veneers

Veneers require careful sanding to avoid cutting through to the core stock. Medium paper is coarse enough to cut off the tape if the work is a built-up pattern with sand-off taped joints. This should be followed with very fine garnet or aluminum oxide abrasive paper, using fresh stock to ensure clean cutting. On veneers it is often impossible to follow the grain of the wood, and it is best to disregard it entirely. Always back the paper with a wood, cork, or felt block in order to ensure cutting to a level surface. Veneers, particularly mahoganies, will often stain from using too thin a glue or too much pressure in clamping. Do not try to sand out these marks; the only way to correct them is to paint the area with a bleaching solution. Proper veneering technique will eliminate staining.

### Power sanding

Machine sanding should always be done with the grain. To work across the grain or in sweeping oval or circular patterns is to invite disaster, for scratches caused by such poor sanding practices are difficult to remove. The belt sander is used for the first stages of rough sanding, and the grade of paper is determined by the condition of the surface to be sanded. Belt sanders cut very rapidly, even with the finer grits of paper, and therefore should never be used on veneered surfaces where there is danger of cutting through the veneer.

The finishing sander, which works on a vibrating principle, is more suited to working on veneered surfaces and putting the final touches of smoothness to belt-sanded surfaces. It can be used with all the finer grits of paper to prepare the surface for painting or varnishing.

When starting a power sander or when turning it off, don't turn the switch on or off with the sander in contact with the wood surface. Starting or stopping while the sanding surface is in contact will make marks that will be most difficult to remove. Once the sander has been turned on and is in contact with the surface, keep the tool moving. If you stop in one spot too long, a rut will quickly form. With a straight-line sander, should you go across the grain you will tear the wood fibers. With an orbital-action sander, grain direction is not quite so critical. Of course, the orbital sander should be used for such jobs as removing an existing finish, smoothing wood down to size, and other preliminary rough and medium sanding. The straight-line-action sander should be employed for fine-finish sanding and always in the same direction as the wood grain.

As in hand sanding, start with a grit coarse enough to accomplish the rough work, then move on to a finer grit and a still finer grit until the desired smoothness is obtained. For a finer finish with a minimum amount of sanding effort, start with the finest grit that will remove the surface defects. It is wise, when proceeding from coarse to fine paper, never to skip more than two grit numbers at a time.

Power sanders create a great deal of dust. This problem,

however, can be quickly solved by using a sander with a vacuum dust-collector system. Many sanders are available with their own vacuum bag. Some have a hose which can be attached to most kinds of tank-type vacuum cleaners. While tank-type arrangements may offer a stronger vacuum than the integral back pickup, the bag is much handier to use. It is important to remember that the bag should be emptied— no more than half full keeps the machine running at full efficiency.

Speaking of efficiency, be sure to follow the manufacturer's instructions for care and maintenance. Keep the sander clean. It is especially important that the ventilating holes never become clogged. Overheating can reduce the life of the motor. Should the motor overheat while sanding, remove the sander from the work, and run it at no-load speed to cool it off.

**Steel wool**

Pads of steel wool may be used to smooth off the sanded surface or for light sanding between finish coats. There are six grades of steel wool for woodwork:

NO. 3   The coarsest grade, rarely used in finishing work
NO. 2   Should be used on rough lumber only
NO. 1   The coarsest grade that should be used on furniture
NO. 1/0   The most commonly used of all grades for general cleaning and smoothing
NO. 2/0   Used for rough smoothing
NO. 3/0   The fine grade, often used for final smoothing
NO. 4/0   The very fine grade, used for between-coat smoothing
NO. 5/0   The extra fine grade, used for top-coat rubbing
NO. 6/0   The super fine grade, used for top-coat rubbing

For smooth-off operations, use the finer grades 2/0 and 3/0. Avoid too much rubbing at any one spot, or you will cut through the surface. Use only light pressure, and clean off all particles of steel wool with a damp cloth. This abrasive is best on hardwoods and is particularly good for smoothing turnings and carvings. On long turned surfaces (like table or chair legs) it will work rapidly and will not disturb marks or ridges left from the old, slow-turning lathes. Steel wool will put a smoother finish on end grain surfaces after they have been sanded. The major disadvantage of steel wool is its tendency to discolor some woods. For instance, it should not be used on oak.

Steel wool is also useful, in refinishing, to mop up or clean off the messy residue left after paint and varnish remover have been removed with a putty knife or burlap. Use grade 1 for this work. It will not scratch when the surface is wet, and it may be used to advantage when dipped in denatured alcohol. This steel-wool method is sometimes advisable in removing paint from softwood, where there is danger of scarring the wood with a scraper.

## PATCHING

Holes, cracks, and other imperfections can be filled with stick shellac, wood plastic, hardwood putty, or one of the patching vinyl materials. Actually, the selection depends on the top finish. If the work is to receive an opaque finish, any of these commercial patching compounds may be used. Neither stick shellac nor wood plastic will take water stain or oil stain, and either must be the same color as the final finish. In the case of stick shellac, it is a simple matter of buying the color you need; wood plastic can be colored with colors in oil. In addition to the so-called "natural" shade, wood plastic also comes in various colors. You can use one that is close to the desired final finish, and then blend the shade, if necessary.

Rock-hard wood putty or crack filler contains real wood flour and takes both oil and water stains well. Mix with water to a smooth paste and spread over the imperfection with a putty knife, pressing the filler down into the crack. Because most wood putties dry white, most experts prefer to color the patch to match the natural or stained wood. This can be done with water-mix colors, analine wood stain dyes (see page 83), household dyes, or food coloring such as used for cake frostings. Put the color in a glass of water, and add color or increase water until you get the right shade; then use this water in mixing the wood putty powder. Mix colors and wood putty somewhat darker than a true color match, as the dried patch is usually lighter than the color of the wet filler.

While vinyl patching compounds are easy to apply and sand, they are difficult to spot-stain and are usually only used with opaque finishes. If you plan to use a wiping stain, frequently it is possible to blend the vinyl patch into the overall wood finish.

If the work is to receive an opaque finish, patching is best done between coats. Some workers also prefer this method on brightwork, although it should be remembered that sanding the patching material to a smooth surface is much simpler on bare wood than over the stain coat.

Instead of a commercial patching compound, plaster of paris or a prepared cabinetmaker's cement that is soluble in hot water can be used for crack filling. Plaster of paris putty is used on new wood that is to be finished with stain, since it will absorb the stain color where wood plastic and stick shellac will not. Plaster of paris putty is made simply by submerging a handful of dry plaster of paris in water. As long as it remains below the surface of the water, it will not set. A small amount should be lifted with the putty knife and kneaded with the fingers. Press it into place, and clean off the surface around it. Be sure to fill the cracks and holes full and level with the surrounding surface.

Another wood putty sometimes used with success is made of glue and sawdust. This can be applied before or after staining. It will absorb water stain fairly well, but it is usually best to add stain to the mixture. To make this putty, apply a little hot glue to the end grain of a piece of wood, and then scrape the wood with a chisel. This will give you a fine mixture of sawdust and glue which must be applied immediately, before the glue has time to set. Use a piece of the same kind of wood that you are repairing, and scrape with the chisel so as to produce as fine a powder as possible. The stain can be applied directly to the end grain of the wood, or it can be mixed with the glue.

Although most patching can be said to be "nonshrinking," it is usually wise to fill large voids with two or more layers, permitting each to dry before applying the next. With all filling jobs, make the patch a little high, and then, after the material has dried, it should be sanded smooth and clean. Then the surface should be cleaned up around the repair.

## BLEACHING

Bleaching is the process of lightening the color of wood by the use of chemicals. It plays an important part in so-called blond finishes such as harvest wheat, honey maple, and amber walnut. The name simply describes the color of the wood.

Apart from the bleaching process, the various steps in finishing do not differ in any way from ordinary practice.

Not all blond finishes are secured by bleaching. Maple, birch, and other light-colored woods are successfully blonded by the use of a pigmented undercoater. This subject is treated in Chapters 11 and 14.

## Bleaching solutions

*Oxalic acid*  Used in a saturated solution, generally about 12 ounces per gallon of hot water. A mild bleach when used alone, it is more effective in combination with sodium hyposulfite (photographer's type) as a second application. It should be neutralized by sponging with clean water or borax in water.

*Sodium perborate*  A crystalline powder of considerable bleaching action when made into a saturated solution.

*Sodium bisulfite*  An inexpensive bleach in a saturated solution. This bleach is more effective when preceded by a wash of potassium permanganate (1 ounce per gallon of water). The sodium bisulfite solution is applied while the first coat is still wet. When dry, the surface is sanded smooth.

*Hydrogen peroxide*  A concentrated commercial grade which should not be confused with the 3 percent solution used as an antiseptic. This is a high-power expensive bleach.

*Commercial wood bleaches*  Ready-prepared. Many of these are based on commercial hydrogen peroxide and are fairly expensive. They are very powerful and are the only satisfactory bleaches for light tones on dark wood. The best and most thorough-working wood bleaches are the so-called "two-solution" bleaches, although one-solution commercial bleaches are available.

Sometimes chlorinated liquid laundry bleach is effective for such woods as gum, walnut, and maple. Such a laundry bleach is also good to remove chemical, dye, ink, and water stains from wood surfaces. Household ammonia is a fair bleaching agent on all but dark woods. It is, however, very good for spot work.

Knowing the characteristics of the wood to be bleached is important. Some woods bleach easily; others do not. Here are bleaching qualities of the more common woods:

| Wood | | Wood | |
|---|---|---|---|
| Ash | Fairly easy | Lauan (Philippine | Fairly easy |
| Basswood | Difficult | mahogany) | |
| Beech | Fairly easy | Locust | Difficult |
| Birch | Easy | Magnolia | Easy |
| Cedar | No | Maple | Fairly easy |
| Cherry | Difficult | Oak | Easy |
| Chestnut | Difficult | Pine (white) | No |
| Cypress | Difficult | Pine (yellow) | No |
| Ebony | Difficult | Poplar | Difficult |
| Douglas fir | No | Redwood | No |
| Gum | Fairly easy | Rosewood | Difficult |
| Hemlock | No | Spruce | No |
| Holly | Easy | Sycamore | Easy |
| Korina | Easy | Teakwood | Fairly easy |
| Lacewood | Fairly easy | Walnut | Fairly easy |

## Applying homemade bleaches

Simple homemade bleaches are 100 percent effective on light-colored woods and will lighten any dark wood to a considerable extent. The simple oxalic acid bleach is inexpensive and the easiest to make and use. Three solutions are required:

1. Three ounces of oxalic acid crystals dissolved in 1 quart of water

**2.** Three ounces of hypo in 1 quart of water

**3.** One ounce of borax in 1 quart of water

All these chemicals can be obtained from any drugstore at a nominal cost. The oxalic acid is poisonous. It is not deadly, but it will scuff the skin from your hands through prolonged contact, and is slightly irritating to the throat when inhaled. The hypo is not poisonous. The first two solutions act as bleaches; the borax solution is simply an alkalizer which destroys traces of acid remaining in the wood after bleaching. All solutions are made with hot water but are used cold.

The oxalic acid solution is applied first with a brush or rubber sponge. When this coat has partly dried, the second solution (hypo) is applied, after which the work should be allowed to dry thoroughly.

If the color of the wood is not light enough, the process can be repeated. If any unevenness should occur as a result of some areas being bleached lighter than others, apply the bleaching solution to these concentrated spots. When the color is right, the surface should be flushed with the borax solution and followed with a clear water wash. (White vinegar, used full strength, can also serve as the neutralizing agent.) Allow the wood to dry 24 hours before sanding. The work is then ready for any varnish, shellac, or lacquer finish.

### Applying commercial bleach

All commercial bleaches are concentrated chemical solutions and will burn flesh or clothing with which they come in contact. Therefore wear rubber gloves, and protect clothing with a rubber or heavy cotton apron. Under all circumstances keep these liquids away from mouth and eyes. Never intermix commercial bleaches or add other materials to them unless so directed.

Bleaches can be applied with a spray gun, a rubber sponge, or a fiber (not bristle) brush. If the solution is sprayed on, you should afterward rub it into the wood with a brush or sponge. The procedure for two-application bleaches will vary with the brand being used, some types requiring complete drying of the first solution before the second is applied, whereas other types call for the second solution 5 minutes after the first. Follow the maker's instructions.

Single-application bleaches are applied in one coat after mixing the two solutions together. It is not necessary to flush the surface with water in either case. Complete drying must be allowed, preferably overnight. As long as the bleach is damp, it is effective and may break down any finishing coat applied over it. Some types of commercial bleaches require neutralization just as the oxalic acid solution does. Check the manufacturer's directions carefully since there are frequently small variations in applicable techniques between brands.

When using household bleaches, they should be used in much more concentrated proportions that those given on the container for bleaching of clothes. A little experimenting with various degrees of concentration will help determine the best proportions for the specific piece you are working on. These bleaches are also good for spot work, where they should be used in even greater concentration than in surface bleaching. After applying these bleaches, they should be allowed to dry and followed by a borax neutralization as previously described.

After the work is completely dry, it should be sanded lightly with very fine paper to remove any chemical residue and to clean up wood fibers lifted by the bleaching solution. A bleaching solution is much like a water stain in raising the grain; if you sponge with warm water and sand smooth before using a bleach, there will be a tendency to whisker when the bleach is applied.

The surface to be bleached must be absolutely dry and clean. Apply all materials in the direction of the wood grains to prevent spotty bleaching. Apply these materials evenly; do not saturate or flood the surface to be bleached. Unused bleach must be disposed of and not returned to original containers. These solutions must not come in contact with metal. Use only glass or earthen jars, storing them in a cool place away from sunlight.

## PRECAUTIONS on the use of bleaches

1. *Bleaches have a caustic effect on the skin! Wear rubber gloves to protect your hands. If you spill any bleach on your skin, flush with generous quantities of water. Apply boric acid to the affected parts.*
2. *Use a nylon brush to apply commercial-type bleaches.*
3. *Bleaches must never be intermixed, except on the surface being bleached. This precludes the use of the same sponge for applying, unless it is thoroughly cleaned with water.*
4. *Never pour bleaches into metal containers, or they may stain the wood rather than bleach it!*
5. *Avoid too much bleach on the edges of veneer panels, as it may loosen the plies.*
6. *Bleaches will deteriorate if left standing for any length of time. They should be stored in a dark, cool place, with caps loose.*

### Bleaching old finished wood

Before you bleach old finished wood, remove completely all old coating with the usual removing materials (see Chapter 14). Then wash thoroughly with a water solution of trisodium phosphate (1 pound to a gallon of warm water), followed by a vigorous scraping and sanding in order to expose the natural wood surface. Bleaching may then proceed as recommended for new wood.

# CHAPTER THREE

# Methods of Applying Finishes

Finishing materials may be applied by brushing or spraying. Brushing is the commonest and most economical method. It is a slow method as compared with spraying, but it has advantages in simplicity of equipment and ease of application. With paint, varnish, and other brushing mediums, the quality of the brushed finish, as judged by durability and appearance, is equal and in some cases superior to the same finish applied by spraying.

## BRUSHING

### Selecting brushes

Quality is a very important factor in selecting a brush

regardless of the size or style needed for a particular project. A good brush will hold more finishing material and enables one to apply the material more smoothly and with less effort. In almost all types of brushes, quality depends on four points.

1. The bristles should be resilient. Test for "bounce" by brushing bristles against back of hand. In a good brush, bristles will feel springy and elastic. When the brush is gently pressed on any surface, the bristles will not fan out excessively. If a brush is too coarse or fans out too greatly, it will not spread the finish well.

2. Examine the bristle ends by fanning them out between the fingers. All good brushes have bristles that are "flagged," a term denoting splits on the bristle end. The more flags the better, as they help retain paint. Hog bristle is naturally flagged; synthetic bristle is artificially flagged. The type of bristle is a matter of personal preference. Some finishers swear by natural bristle and some by nylon bristle.

3. Check the setting. Bristles should be solidly set to prevent chance of fallout while painting. Jar the brush, by hammering against the paint can or some other object, and fan the bristles—any loose bristles will be apparent. The metal band is called a *ferrule*. Stainless steel and aluminum are generally used on better grade brushes for greater resistance to corrosion.

4. Look at the filler block. Cheap brushes have a large block which robs them of additional bristles. A good brush has a small block and the bristles are set closer within the ferrule.

**5.** The bristles should be long enough to flex well. A quick
rule of thumb for selecting a paint brush is that the
bristles should be approximately 50 percent longer than
the width. For instance, a brush that is 2 inches wide
should have bristles that are about 3 inches long. However, this rule does not hold for small brushes. A 1-inch
brush with bristles only 1½ inches long would be too
stubby. The following table gives typical widths, lengths,
and thicknesses of quality brushes as suggested by the
American Brush Manufacturers Association:

| Width, inches | Grade of brush | | | |
| | A | | B | |
| | Length, inches | Thickness, inches | Length, inches | Thickness, inches |
| --- | --- | --- | --- | --- |
| 1 | | | $2\frac{3}{16}$ | $\frac{7}{16}$ |
| 1½ | $2\frac{11}{16}$ | $1\frac{1}{16}$ | $2\frac{3}{16}$ | $\frac{1}{2}$ |
| 2 | $2\frac{15}{16}$ | $\frac{3}{4}$ | $2\frac{7}{16}$ | $\frac{9}{16}$ |
| 2½ | $3\frac{3}{16}$ | $1\frac{3}{16}$ | $2\frac{11}{16}$ | $\frac{5}{8}$ |
| 3 | $3\frac{7}{16}$ | $1\frac{3}{16}$ | $2\frac{15}{16}$ | $\frac{7}{8}$ |

Most finishers prefer a full chisel brush; that is, one in
which long and short bristles are arranged to form a true
chisel edge. In other words, when looking at the edge of a
good brush, you will note that the center bristles are longest
and they are increasingly shorter on the flat sides. (A cheap
chisel edge is sometimes made by trimming the bristles.)
The chisel shape permits the bristle tips to be in contact
with the surface as you stroke in either direction.

Most wood-finishing work is best done with brushes
ranging in size from 1 to 3 inches. The 2- to 2½-inch brush
is the best for general work. Carvings and turnings can

frequently be worked better with a 2-inch brush than with a narrower one. It is also a good idea to have one or two sizes of small, fine-pointed artist's brushes for touch-up work.

### Preparing a new brush for service

A new brush usually has some loose bristles which must be removed before the brush is used. This may be done by rolling the brush rapidly between the hands, and then beating it lightly across your spread fingers. This will also remove any dust.

Many wood finishers prepare their new brushes for use by suspending their bristles in raw linseed oil for about 12 hours. Before using, squeeze out the surplus oil with the fingers, and then brush clean on a lintless cloth.

### Brushing technique

The proper handling of a brush is largely a matter of common sense coupled with a little practice. Use the tip or edge of the brush to work into corners or to a line or edge. Cross-brush all large areas for good coverage and to eliminate any skipped places, or "holidays." Brush turnings round and round, and then use light lengthwise strokes where possible.

For general brushwork, the bristles should be dipped to a little over one-third their length. Surplus paint or varnish should be wiped off against a strike wire (a wire fastened across the top of the can) or against the edge of the can. Materials that permit brushing, such as paint, should always be brushed until the surface film is level and uniform. Other materials, such as varnish and shellac, work best if flowed on and allowed to level off. In finishing flat surfaces, brush out toward the edges. This will prevent drips, which invariably occur when a loaded brush is pulled over a sharp edge.

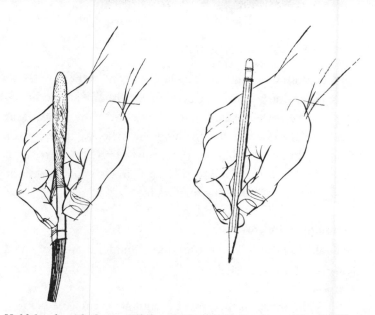

Hold brush with fingers lightly gripping metal ferrule, and let handle rest between thumb and first finger. The position is similar to that used in holding a pencil. Then paint on with long, steady strokes. Lift brush gradually at end of stroke to assure an even finish. Never press bristles hard against surface, but stroke lightly and smoothly.

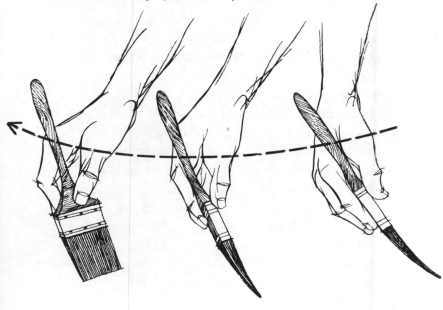

When using stain, shellac, lacquer, and other materials where a uniform coat must be applied without undue brushing, exercise care to prevent double-coating any areas. This can usually be done by brushing into the lap left by the previous brushful—that is, the loaded brush is started on bare wood and carried into the lap. This is good technique in applying any finishing material.

### Cleaning paintbrushes

A quality brush is a fine tool and should be properly used and cared for. Always clean a brush while the finishing material is still soft.

Soak the brush in the proper cleaning solvent (see below), and remove the surplus fluid out of the bristles by pressing the flat side of the brush against a strike wire or by squeezing out the liquid with the fingers. Then hold the brush by the handle between the palms of both hands, and twirl it inside an empty paint pot to throw off the remaining solvent. Straighten the bristles with a steel comb, and with the back of the comb smooth the bristles to their original shape to remove the comb marks.

Brushes used in oil stain, enamel, oil paint, or varnish (oil-base) should be cleaned in turpentine, followed by naphtha or mineral spirits. Latex, or water-base enamel or paint, can be easily removed by dissolving the excess material in water. Denatured alcohol should be used on brushes after applying shellac or alcohol-base (spirit) stains. Cleaning should be followed by washing the brush in soap and water.

Brushes used in lacquer should be cleaned with lacquer thinner, preferably a thinner made by the manufacturer of the lacquer in which the brush was used. Synthetic varnish and similar materials should be cleaned from a brush as directed on the can for thinning. If no directions are given, try turpentine or mineral spirits. Paste wood fillers can be removed from bristles with mineral spirits.

Brushes used in water stains should be washed thoroughly in warm running water and then dipped in a solution of vinegar or vinegar and cold water. Comb the bristles straight, and, to dry, hang the brush up by the handle so that the brush does not rest on the flag end of the bristles. Allow sufficient time to dry thoroughly before putting into service again. Do not place on a hot radiator or stove to dry.

If, after thorough cleaning, the finishing material still clings to the bristles, lay the brush on a flat surface and, with a worn-down, stubby, flat sash brush, scrub the bristles with a downward stroke only, working from the heel of the brush toward the flag end.

The best way to keep brushes overnight or for short periods of time is in a brush keeper. Three simple styles are shown. The bristles should be completely submerged in the fluid. The fluid should be the same as that used for cleaning the brush.

### Storing of brushes

If a brush is to be stored for any length of time, clean and oil it as follows, in preparation for storing:

1. Clean thoroughly, in accordance with the detailed instructions already given.
2. Remove all the cleaning fluid by the spinning method mentioned previously.
3. Comb the bristles straight, to return them to their original shape.
4. Rewrap the brush in heavy paper, as outlined in the illustration.

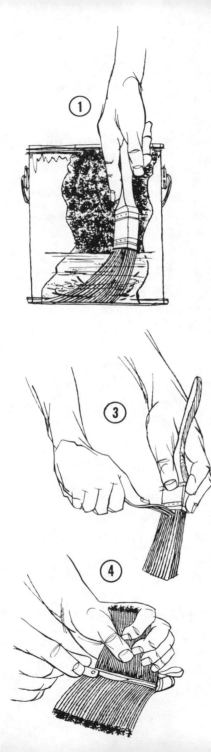

**Cleaning of brush** (1) Press brush, flat side down, into a couple of inches of the proper solvent, working it well up into heel of brush. (2) If paint clings to bristles, lay brush flat on a piece of paper, and scrape it loose with a blunt putty knife. (3) An ordinary kitchen fork is a good tool for combing out loosened, gummy pigment close to binding. Work with gentle downward motion. (4) Scrape loose pigment from center of brush with a blunt knife. Hold bristles firmly while exposing center. Use same operation on both sides of brush. (5) Rinse frequently during cleaning operation to free brush of paint residue. (6) Fan-dry the brush by twirling or rolling the handle between the palms of the hands. To straighten bristles, comb with wire or fiber brush. Never beat

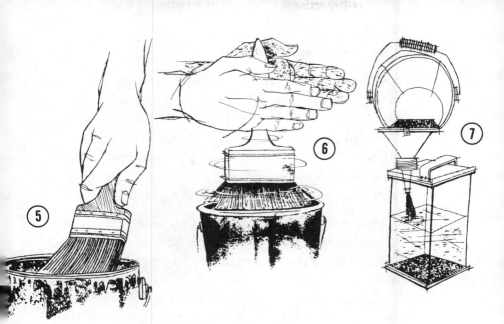

a brush against a hard surface to remove loose paint or solvent. (7) After cleaning, pour solvent solution into a container and allow pigment to settle to the bottom of the container. Save the solvent for next cleaning. (8) To store a brush for a period of time, cut and crease heavy wrapping paper or aluminum foil to fit the brush. (9) Fold the covering over the bristles. (10) Then tie the covering to brush, and either store the brush flat or hang it on a nail.

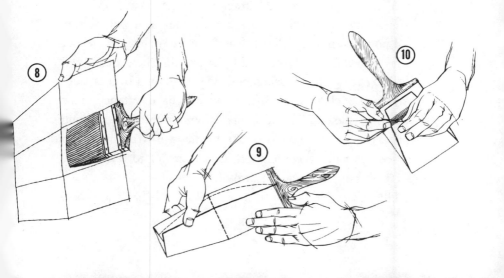

5. Stand the wrapped brush in the pot containing raw linseed oil, having sufficient oil in the can to overflow into the wrapper. Allow brush to remain in the oil for at least 72 hours.

6. Remove the brush from the oil, place additional wrapping paper over the oiled wrapper, and store the brush in a cool place, resting the brush on its flat side.

When a brush has been stored for a period of time, it is a good practice occasionally to apply a fresh coating of oil.

Artist brushes and stripers should be washed in the proper solvent until thoroughly clean; then a small amount of petroleum jelly should be applied to even out the hair. Lay the brush away flat. When it is to be used again, wash out the petroleum jelly thoroughly; otherwise it will prevent the finishing material from drying.

**Reclaiming old brushes**

Discarded brushes, no matter how old they may be, can be washed and revitalized for further use. When the bristles in a brush have hardened, do not attempt to apply finish with it. You must remove the hardened material first.

To clean hardened brushes, place them in a pot or tray and pour the proper solvent over them—liquid brush cleaner or turpentine over paint and varnish brushes, denatured alcohol over shellac brushes, and lacquer thinner over lacquer brushes. Let them soak until the bristles have softened. This sometimes takes 24 to 48 hours. From time to time during this softening process, work the bristles with the fingers to loosen the paint accumulation. Use a scraper to remove the paint, working it from the heel of the brush to the tip.

Then place the brush in a pail filled with hot water and

soap powder. The water should be hot, but not so hot that it will burn your hands. Use 1 cup of soap powder to 1 gallon of water.

The washing is done on an old-fashioned washboard placed in a tub. Sprinkle some soap powder on the washboard, and, while holding the brush firmly by the handle with the narrow side toward the body, rub it across the washboard, using the same motion as is used in washing clothes. First rub the brush at both corners to free the bristles at those points. After the material has been loosened at the corners, place the brush with the bristle part flat on the washboard, and with the other hand pressing down firmly on the bristles continue the rubbing motion. Then reverse the brush and repeat the rubbing process, from time to time dipping the brush into the hot water and sprinkling fresh soap powder on the board. Continue the rubbing operation until the bristles are clean; then rinse the brush in cold water until all traces of material and soap have been removed from the bristles and the rinse water remains clear. (If the bristles are stubbornly hard, sprinkle some fine sand on the washboard with the soap powder during the rubbing operation; this will help loosen the paint more rapidly and hasten the cleaning process.)

After the brush has been washed, comb the bristles straight with a steel comb, wrap the brush in heavy wrapping paper, and set it away to dry thoroughly. When the brush has dried, dip it in linseed oil, rewrap it in an oil-coated wrapper, and put it away until it is needed.

### Cause and effect of abuse or misuse of brushes

*Fingering* results when the brush is used edgewise or when it is pressed edgewise against the paint pot or the wire across the top of the paint pot to remove the excess paint. Thus the corners become worn off and rounded, destroying one of the essential features of the brush—ability to cut in properly. Fingering is also caused by soaking the brush in water, pounding it or dabbing it into small corners, or allowing it to stand on the flag end for any length of time. To avoid fingering, use and clean your paintbrushes properly.

*Flaring* results from allowing the finishing material to accumulate and harden at the heel of the brush. This can be avoided by daily cleaning, and by dipping the brush in the paint pot to only one-half the length of the bristle.

*Shedding* may result from improper cleaning methods such as twisting and wringing the bristles to remove paint or cleaning fluid. This causes the bristles to break off at the setting. To avoid this, follow the cleaning procedure suggested on page 44. Shedding also results from using brushes in paints or other materials which contain chemicals harmful to the bristles and which cause them to deteriorate and break off. A good example of this occurs when a nylon brush is used in shellac, for in most cases the action of the shellac on the bristles will cause shedding.

*Floppy brushes* are caused by using the wrong cleaning fluids (see page 44), which leave the bristles soft and flabby. It is essential that brushes be thoroughly dried before being used again.

*Loose handles and dented ferrules* will result if the metal or leather binding of the handle is hammered against the paint can or some other object to jar out the soft paint or other finishing material. Soaking the brush in water will swell the handle, which, when dry, may loosen the ferrule.

## SPRAY-GUN FINISHING

Application of paint, varnish, enamel, lacquer, and other finishes by means of a spray gun has many advantages. Speed of application, economy of time and labor, and simplicity of operation have made the spray gun a good tool for the painter, finisher, or handyman.

### Spray-gun types

Spray guns are of two types—suction-feed and pressure-feed. A mouth spray is a simple example of suction feed, and some inexpensive guns use suction feed in exactly this form. In more expensive guns, the suction is created at the nozzle, and air from horn holes on the cap blows the paint out to form a fan pattern. Since the air and paint mix outside the cap, this kind of construction is called *external mix*.

The illustration shows the principle of pressure feed. Since the paint is under air pressure, it is possible to spray heavy-bodied materials such as enamels and plastic paints. The nozzle pictured is the one commonly used on the pressure-feed gun. Air and fluid mix inside the cap; hence it is called *internal mix*. Internal mix always means pressure feed, but pressure feed can be used with either internal or external mix. A pressure gun can be recognized by the fact that the paint-cup lid is solid, whereas the lid of a cup for suction feed must have a hole in it to admit air as paint comes out.

Either suction- or pressure-feed guns can be of the bleeder or nonbleeder type. A bleeder gun passes air at all times, the trigger controlling the flow of fluid only. A spray gun used with a portable air compressor should be a bleeder in order to keep the compressor from overloading. On the other hand, a commercial tank outfit takes a nonbleeder gun, since a

Mouth spray is simplest type of suction feed. With this type the fluid is pulled upward by vacuum.

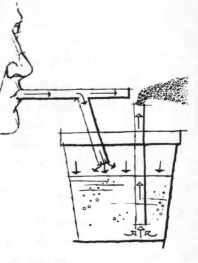

In the nonbleeder type, the fluid is under air pressure.

In the nonbleeder type, the air is shut off inside the gun.

In the suction-feed gun, external mix, the air and fluid are mixed outside the cap.

In the pressure-feed gun, internal mix, the air and fluid are mixed inside the cap.

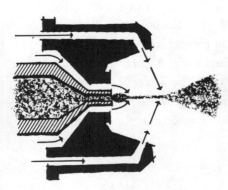

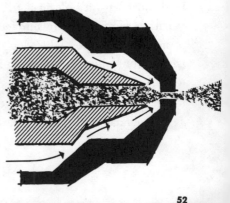

Shown on this page are several ways to store paintbrushes. Brushes in the large jar in the photograph at the right are held in the solvent by means of brush clips available at hardware stores. For small brushes, you can drill holes in their handles and pass a large nail through the holes. In the photograph at the bottom of the page, the brushes are suspended by means of clip clothespins.

Strain paint or similar surface materials through window screen, cheesecloth, or old nylon stocking before applying them with either a brush or spray gun.

Three common types of spraying equipment are illustrated here. The electric vibrator sprayer (above) is very easy to use and does a fairly good job for most finishes. The aerosol spray can is inexpensive and reduces the mechanics of spraying to its simplest form. The built-in compressor type (lower right) is the most inexpensive of better-type units.

The gun that will give the best results is the type with a separate compressor. This is also the most expensive type of gun. For more details on spray guns see text.

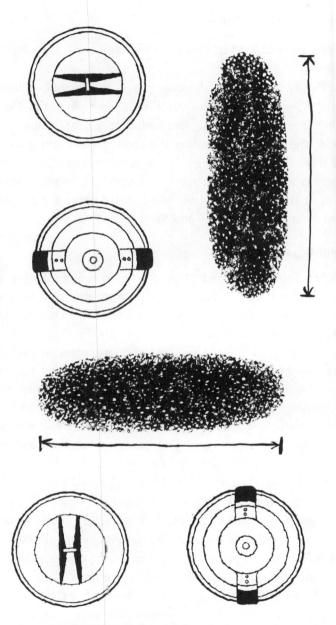

*Close-up of nozzle of both internal- and external-mix types. Arrows show the way to measure the width of both vertical and horizontal pattern.*

bleeder would exhaust the air in the tank even when not in use.

The cheapest type of spray gun is the electric vibrator sprayer, which is a self-contained unit—just plug in and use. On these units, a sliding spray adjuster on the handle provides the means of adjusting the spray pattern and amount of flow. Pressing the trigger in the pistol-grip handle sets the unit in action. Another type of sprayer, while not a spray gun in the true sense of the word, is the aerosol unit spray can described on pages 75 and 81.

### Which gun is best?

When you buy just one spray gun for spraying all types of finishing material, it should be a pressure-feed gun, because only pressure feed will spray heavy paints and enamels. On the other hand, internal mix, which is usually a part of pressure feed, prohibits the use of fast-drying material such as lacquer, because the paint dries inside and around the cap opening. If you want to spray lacquer, you must use a suction gun. A suction gun is advantageous because it can be used with a variety of glass jars, whereas the pressure gun requires a metal cup. Suction-feed guns can be cleaned from any open container, but the pressure gun can be cleaned only from the standard metal container. (For cleaning instructions, see page 73.) Thus the suction gun is easier to clean and more convenient to use, but will spray only lacquers and light-bodied materials. The pressure gun, although a little less convenient, will spray any weight of material used in brush painting except fast-drying lacquer.

The air-compressing unit is commonly of the piston, diaphragm, or rotary type. The piston type consists of a metal piston working inside a cylinder—like the piston in an automobile motor. When the piston goes down, air is sucked into the cylinder; when the piston goes up, the air is compressed. The metal-piston type is the only one suitable for heavy-duty use.

The diaphragm compressor is much the same except that a rubber diaphragm substitutes for the metal piston. Obviously, metal will outwear rubber. However, the diaphragm will last hundreds of hours, and replacement is inexpensive and simple. The rubber diaphragm is excellent for light duty. Unlike the moving metal piston, it requires no oil and is less expensive and lighter in weight. So far as air delivery is concerned, the two are about equal.

The rotary type is used with direct electric drive. This type has less capacity than piston or diaphragm, but has the advantage of direct drive and compactness.

Any compressor needs a motor to run it, and the horsepower of the motor gives the name and size of the whole unit. A motor of from ¼ to ⅓ horsepower is the smallest that can be used for satisfactory spray finishing. For best results, a spray gun and compressor should be purchased as a unit—the gun should suit the capacity of the compressor.

Spray equipment is sometimes available at paint stores and tool-rental shops for daily or weekly rental fees.

### Spraying hookups

The commonest setup is the direct connection from compressor to spray gun. Another setup, used only with a pressure-feed gun, involves disconnecting the pressure-feed cup and substituting a much bigger "cup" with a suitable hose connection to the gun. With a setup like this, you can put a whole gallon can of paint in the paint tank and spray away without the bother of refilling the cup and without the weight of the cup. Of course, it is more bother to set up and to clean, and hence is usually confined to big jobs of wall and house painting. In a setup ideal for home shop use, the air goes from compressor to transformer and then to the spray gun. The transformer consists of two parts: a regulator, which can be used to set any pressure within the capacity of the compressor, and a condenser, which filters out moisture and oil in the air supply. Actually, there is very little need for the regulator, since most spray jobs require the full air supply. However, it does provide a handy check to see if the compressor is performing as it should. The condenser is invaluable when spraying lacquer in muggy weather—it eliminates that possible drop or two of water from spitting from the gun and spoiling the job. A condenser can be purchased without the regulator if desired.

### Spray-shop booth

The paint-spray booth is something you will want as you become more and more of a perfectionist in finishing. The ideal home shop installation is the separate finishing room, equipped with a turntable, paint cabinet, and an exhaust fan. Second choice is a spray booth located near a basement window to accommodate an exhaust fan. The spray booth need not be large—a 5 × 5 foot area will handle most projects. A shower curtain hung in a corner will make a fine spray booth. For safety in paint-spraying operation, the curtain should be fireproofed. This is how: To 100 ounces of water add and dissolve 6 ounces of borax and 5 ounces of boric acid. Thoroughly soak the curtain in the warm solution several times in order to get maximum protection. The flameproofing solution is water-soluble; therefore after each

washing it must be impregnated again for its further protection.

The turntable is an important piece of equipment, since it
eliminates a lot of dancing around the job. A backstop is a
handy auxiliary. It can be used as a backstop for the turntable, or it can provide a complete spray setup in itself. A
good exhaust fan is expensive, so many home craftsmen get
along without this piece of equipment. Spraying without a
fan is best done with two basement windows open to provide
ventilation. It is convenient to work directly under a window
since the gun cleaning can be done through the window
opening if desired.

### Preparation of the finishing material

The first step in preparing the material to be sprayed is to
mix thoroughly the pigment, vehicle, and thinner or solvent.
When a fresh can is opened, you will notice that some
portion of the pigment has settled to the bottom and that
some vehicle-thinner fluid is at the top. To attempt the mixing
of the pigment when the container is full will result in spilling a great deal of the vehicle and thinner and will make
proper mixing next to impossible.

To mix a full container of paint, pour off a portion of the
vehicle into a clean container; then the remaining pigment
and vehicle can be mixed with a paddle without spilling.
After the pigment has been mixed thoroughly with this
portion of the vehicle, mix further by pouring the material
from one container to another. Do this several times until
the consistency of the material is uniform.

Next, add thinners as indicated on the container label.
Most materials in common use will spray readily if thinned

according to the manufacturer's directions for brushing. However, if the material still appears too thick, add a little more thinner, determining the amount by testing the mixture in a gun. A good general rule is to thin materials to the consistency of SAE-20 motor oil.

To be sure that the material used for spraying is clean and free from lumps, strain it through a fine-mesh wire screen (60 mesh). An excellent substitute for a fine screen is an old silk stocking.

## Materials guide

Most finishing materials formulated for brush application can be sprayed at can consistency with a pressure-feed gun. Always follow label directions on can.

**Lacquer**   Reduce clear lacquers about 25 percent and pigmented lacquers 100 to 150 percent, depending on manufacturer's recommendations. A suction-feed, external-mix gun gives cleanest pattern and least clogging, and is preferred for all lacquer work. Material can be thinned to any extent, since almost instant drying eliminates sags and runs which would occur with other thinned materials. Must be sprayed wet (enough thickness) to retain gloss. Use a fairly small pattern of 5 to 6 inches, holding gun about 6 inches from work.

**Water-mix paint**   Pressure-feed only. Use at maximum weight that the gun will handle (about three-fourths of the amount of water recommended for brushing). Use maximum fluid flow. Spray pattern 8 to 12 inches with gun 6 to 8 inches from work. Always flush gun with turpentine or lacquer thinner, after cleaning with water, to prevent rust.

**Oil-mix paint**   Pressure-feed only. Spray at can consistency; avoid thinning unless specified. Some types formulated especially for spraying are exceptionally free from misting.

**Synthetics**   Suction- or pressure-feed at can consistency or reduced as specified. Usually applied in a medium-weight first coat, followed by a second full coat after first has set up slightly. Also practical to apply in single coats with full drying between.

**Varnish**    Most clears can be sprayed with a suction or pressure gun at 70° F. or higher. Stains and flats are usually heavier and may require thinning. Gun distance, 6 to 8 inches. Avoid heavy coats.

**Shellac**    Reduce four parts normal 4-pound cut shellac to three parts alcohol. Spray-pressure or suction. Shellac picks up moisture from the air and should not be sprayed in humid weather.

**Stain**    All types can be sprayed suction- or pressure-feed. Best work, however, can be done with a suction gun, external mix. NGR stain is preferred type for spraying.

## How to spray

The technique of successful spraying involves

1. The use of correct atomizing air pressure and volume
2. Correct fluid pressure, if a material pressure cap or material pressure tank is used
3. Correct air cap and fluid tip for the materials to be sprayed (see table below)
4. Correct triggering and stroke of the gun
5. Proper position of the gun in relation to the surface being sprayed

### Pressure and tip size

| Material | Pressure (pounds) | Fluid tip (inches) | Drill size (equals tip size) |
|---|---|---|---|
| Stain | 25 | 0.040 | 60 |
| Shellac (2-lb cut) | 30 | 0.040 | 60 |
| Shellac (4-lb cut) | 40 | 0.060 | 52 |
| Varnish | 40 | 0.040 | 60 |
| Lacquer | 30–40 | 0.060 | 52 |
| Synthetics | 40 | 0.060 | 52 |
| Paint | 40 | 0.060 | 52 |
| Enamel | 40 | 0.060 | 52 |

**Use of spray gun**

Although handling a spray gun is simple, it is wise to spray a few practice panels before undertaking actual work. Practice spraying can be done on old cartons or on sheets of newspaper tacked to a carton or box. Ten or fifteen minutes of practice work will give you the feel of the gun and enough know-how to tackle an actual job. If possible, do a few simple jobs before attempting anything complicated or anything that necessitates skillful gun handling and flawless results.

Fill the cup about one-quarter full with the finishing material. Start the electric motor. Have the sprayer near enough to the work to allow a full movement of the gun at 6 to 10 inches from the surface to be painted.

PRECAUTION in use of spray gun

*Be sure that spray or fumes cannot reach any flame and that there is plenty of ventilation.*

Experiment with the full range of fluid adjustment, starting with the fluid needle screw backed off from the closed position just far enough to obtain a small pattern an inch or so wide when the trigger is pulled all the way back. With this small pattern, practice the "stroke" and "triggering" as suggested later in this chapter. After you get the feel of the gun, gradually back off the fluid adjustment screw to spray more material and widen the pattern. With the increased flow of material through the gun, you will find that the breakup, or atomization, becomes coarser. Test patterns should be sprayed in both vertical and horizontal positions, the required adjustment for pattern direction being made by

*Standard fan and round spray patterns.*

Right

*Right and wrong fan patterns.*

Wrong

rotating the nozzle or air cap. A small round pattern is preferred for small irregular surfaces, and a flat, fan pattern for large areas.

The spray-gun stroke is made by moving the gun parallel to the work and at a right angle to the surface by flexing the wrist at each end of every stroke. Never allow a stiffly held wrist to "arc" the stroke. This is a fault common to beginners. Arcing causes poor distribution of materials, with too much at the center of each stroke.

The speed of stroking should be about the same as that of brushing.

The distance from gun to work should be between 6 and 10 inches. The closer the gun is held to the work, the more paint is deposited on the work surface; the more paint applied, the faster the gun must be moved to prevent sags. When the gun is too far from the work, the stroke must be slowed down to a speed that is beyond average patience; the distant position is also undesirable because of excessive dusting, as shown in the illustration.

Use straight, uniform strokes, moving back and forth across the surface so that the pattern laps 50 percent on each pass. In other words, the aiming point for each stroke is the bottom of the preceding stroke, as shown. This system gives double coverage and assures a full wet coat without streaks. The full half-lap is especially good for lacquer. It is sometimes practical to use less lap, but until you are experienced, it is best to use the half-overlapping stroke for all work.

In order to reduce overspray and to assure full coverage, many sprayers use a banding technique. The single vertical stroke at each end assures complete coverage and eliminates the waste of material that results from trying to spray to the very edge with the usual horizontal strokes. At the top and bottom of the panel, the stroke is aimed at the edge and is an automatic banding stroke. Do not skimp the surface near the edges.

A long panel can be sprayed with vertical strokes. This is sometimes the best system, since stroke-end laps are avoided. However, most sprayers have better control with the more natural horizontal stroke. With a spray gun it is easy to make perfect, invisible overlaps. Spraying surfaces that require overlapping involves the same triggering as in spraying a small panel, the only difference being that each area is sprayed like a separate panel.

When a panel is to be sprayed on the edges as well as on the face, a modified banding technique is used. One stroke along each edge coats the edge and bands the panel. The center is sprayed like an ordinary panel. An outside corner, such as the corner of a box, is treated in the same manner.

When an inside corner is sprayed square-on, the coating may not be uniform but the technique is fast and practical. Use this system for all paints and enamels. When you spray furniture with stain or clear top coats, the preferable method is to spray each side separately. After you make the single vertical stroke at the corner, use short pull strokes to cover the area adjacent to the corner. The idea here is control—do not overspray or double-coat the adjoining surface.

Always start level surfaces on the near side and work to the far side. This is a must in lacquer work, since lacquer overspray that lands on wet work will dry sandy. Paint and synthetics are also peculiar in this respect. Level surfaces require more or less gun tilting. A tilt of about 60 degrees, with the cup half or two-thirds full, is recommended. When it is practical, tilt the work a little to lessen the amount of gun tilt needed.

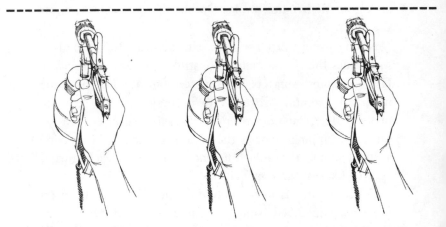

**RIGHT.** *Move gun parallel to surface of work keeping wrist flexible. Hold gun 6 to 10 inches from work.*

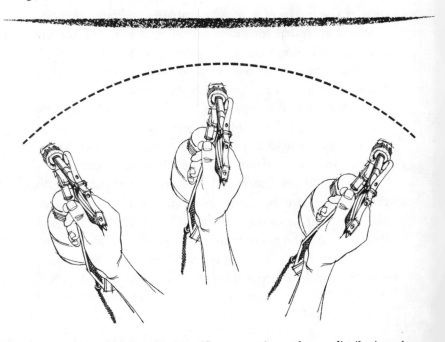

**WRONG.** *Keeping the wrist too stiff causes arcing and poor distribution of the finish.*

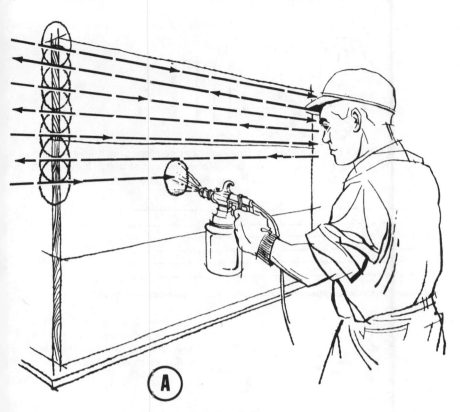

*Spraying strokes.*

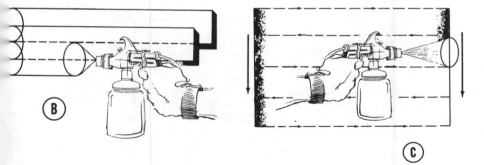

*Overlap strokes one-half.*

*Spray band at ends.*

*A long panel can be sprayed with up-and-down strokes. When you are spraying horizontally, most long work requires overlap.*

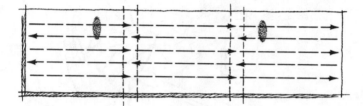

*On level surfaces start at the near edge to avoid overspray on coated work. Any overspray then falls on uncoated work.*

*On an inside corner spray each side separately to give an even coating.*

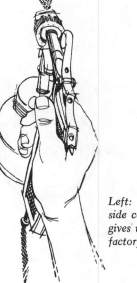

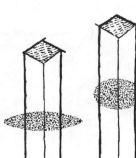

*Left: outside corner. Right: inside corner. Spraying into corner gives uneven coating but is satisfactory for most work.*

*Slender work. Avoid excessive overspray—make pattern fit center example, which is best for most jobs.*

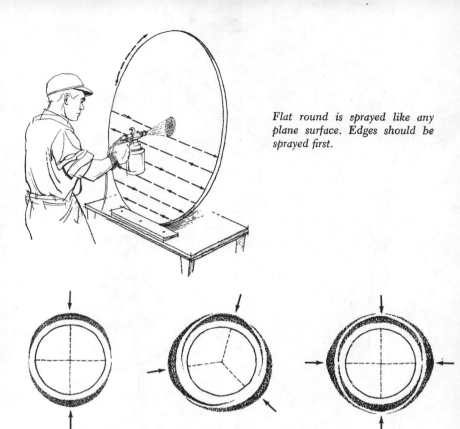

*Flat round is sprayed like any plane surface. Edges should be sprayed first.*

*Cylinders can be sprayed crosswise or up and down.*

*Small round needs at least three strokes to cover. Strokes should overlap.*

For slender work such as table legs, the rule is to make the spray pattern fit the work. Do not use a big horizontal pattern on a slender leg. A smaller horizontal pattern or a big vertical fan gives complete coverage without excessive overspray. On the other hand, do not try to work too small a pattern.

When a job requires gun tilting, use the fluid cup half full. Then the gun can be tilted up to 60 degrees without getting the finishing material on the lid. Although it is not generally recommended (an angle head should be used), the tip of a pressure gun can be tilted a full 90 degrees when necessary. A limiting factor with regard to the suction gun is that excessive tilt will cause paint to clog the vent in the cup lid. When spraying upward or downward with a half-full fluid cup, you may find it necessary to reverse the fluid tube to get proper fluid feed. This is easily done on a suction gun by turning the lid around, but on a pressure gun the nut holding the fluid tube must be released and the tube itself given a half-turn.

A flat, round surface is sprayed in the same way as a plane surface, by banding the edge and then spraying the center. Large to medium cylinders are usually sprayed like a flat panel except that the strokes are shorter. A small cylinder is more efficiently sprayed with a lengthwise stroke, as shown in the illustration. Very small rounds, such as table leg turnings, are sprayed with a vertical stroke, using three or four lapping strokes to get full coverage.

Simple masking may be done in three ways: (1) metal straightedge, (2) masking tape with cardboard shield, (3) masking tape with skirt. Tape-and-shield masking is most popular. Masking tape outlines the dividing line where finish material is to stop, and the cardboard shield catches the overspray. The adjustment of the pattern can reduce the need for masking, as shown in the illustration for slender work. A vertical fan on a horizontal line is practical but requires a heavy overspray. A horizontal fan gives the least overspray. When you are using a short shield, it is usually simpler to pull separate strokes away from the tape rather than use a single run-in stroke. A vertical line is the perfect case. The cut-in with the vertical fan gives the least overspray, and at the same time the adjoining surface is sprayed with the same pattern and with the horizontal stroke which most sprayers favor. In any system, if the shield is held close to the edge of the tape, the tape can be used several times.

The taped skirt offers complete protection, making it ideal for all exacting spray jobs. Make up the taped skirts to suit the job. For straight-line work, prepare the skirting on a clean board or varnished floor. Masking with a metal shield or straightedge is the fastest system and is often practical for rough work. The spray should be directed slightly away from the edge. Whatever method is used, cutting in is cleaner and easier if you use a small spray pattern.

### How to spray furniture

Expert spraying of furniture requires a systematic routine which gets the job done with the least amount of effort and without overspraying parts already coated. Most work is best done with a small spray pattern, 3 to 5 inches wide. The small pattern is dense to the edges, permitting close control of overspray.

Place chairs and tables on a pedestal turntable. The illustration suggests a small wood table fitted with a ⅜-inch pipestem that fits inside a larger pipestem attached to the base of the pedestal.

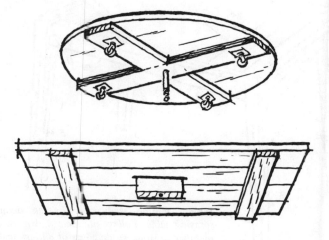

*A simple turntable is an excellent aid to good spray work.*

There are three common systems used for table and chair spraying. Most beginners like the four-square method, in which the operator stands opposite each of the four sides in turn and sprays everything facing him. A faster method is the diagonal system, which is done from two opposite-corner work positions. If the work has round legs, the usual system is to spray the inside of all legs first and then spray each leg complete.

The illustration shows a typical motion study of the spraying of a small table. The work is supported on a pedestal turntable. A vertical fan pattern is used throughout. The jib is started by spraying all legs on the inner edges, one surface at a time, followed by the four-square method on outer surfaces and edges. The top is sprayed last. If you are using lacquer, you may reverse the spraying direction to prevent overspraying the edges of the top, since they are already coated and nearly dry. One-direction spraying of the top is

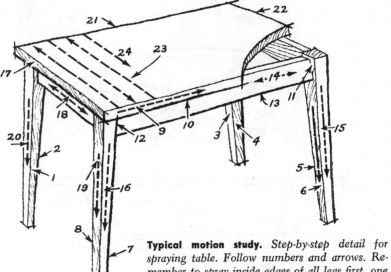

**Typical motion study.** *Step-by-step detail for spraying table. Follow numbers and arrows. Remember to spray inside edges of all legs first, one at a time, one complete stroke to each surface. Spray the top last.*

**Spraying outside of legs.** *Technique for spraying square or rectangular legs. Hold gun at an angle a little to avoid overspray on inside of legs.*

practical if you are using a slow-drying finish, since overspray on a wet coat absorbs readily. A faster system of spraying legs on two sides at a time is to use a horizontal fan for good coverage. In this case, spray the legs inside and out, and then change to the vertical fan required for the rest of the job.

In casework and cabinet jobs, the inside is always sprayed first. Then the outside is worked four-square, doing the right end first, followed by the front, left end, and top. On some jobs it is practical to leave drawers in place, although the usual practice is to remove them to be sprayed separately.

### Cleaning the gun

Cleaning a spray gun is an easy operation. If done systematically and thoroughly after each job, it will pay dividends in better spraying and trouble-free gun performance. Cleaning should be done promptly after the spraying job is finished. The time element will vary with different materials, but the main objective is the same in all cases—never give the material a chance to harden inside the gun.

Before starting to spray, fill an extra cup about one-quarter full with suitable solvent. Use water for water paint, turpentine for paint and varnish, alcohol for shellac, and lacquer thinner for lacquer. If the gun has suction feed, the cleaning fluid can be held in any open container, such as a tumbler. Pressure feed requires a spray cup, since this type of gun will not pull from an open container.

General cleaning involves only the spraying of solvent through the gun. Follow these four steps:

1. With the compressor off, let the fluid tube drip a few seconds, and pull the trigger to release fluid trapped in the fluid tube.

**2.** Wipe the tube.

**3.** Spray the solvent, using four or five pulls of the trigger for a period of about two seconds each. Spray at a sheet of newspaper or at a rag placed over a pan or into an old carton—anything that will catch the spray.

**4.** Hold a rag over the nozzle, and give the trigger a few quick pulls. This will surge the fluid violently within the cup and fluid tube. Remove the rag, wipe the cap, and then take a final squirt. Lift the gun from the solvent, and pull the trigger to release any solvent trapped in the fluid tube. Hang up the gun so that the fluid tube points down.

Sometimes it is necessary to wipe smudges from the gun with a wet rag. Empty the solvent into the paint cup, and clean the paint cup. Wipe the cup dry with a rag. About every second or third cleaning, remove the cap and fluid tip, and immerse them in a solvent. Then go over the inside of the cup lid with a toothbrush. Wipe the needle. Sharpen a match and push it through the fluid tip. Clean out any paint at the end of the fluid tube. If the gun has suction feed, push a broomstraw through the horn holes.

Fluid tips are often made of steel. In order to prevent rusting after spraying water-mix paints, clean the gun first with water and finally with turpentine or lacquer thinner.

Never use a metal object such as a wire or nail to clean out the fluid or air holes in the spray tip. Such practice may damage these precision-machined openings and result in a distorted spray pattern.

### Spraying defects

The spray gun, if not adjusted and manipulated properly, will apply a defective coating to the surface. Fortunately, defects from incorrect handling can be tracked down quite readily and corrected without much difficulty. The most common spraying troubles, with their possible causes and suggested remedies, are listed in the table on page 76.

## SPRAY-CAN FINISHING

For small wood-finishing tasks, the throwaway and refillable aerosol spray cans can be an extremely handy method of applying the top finish. Today, you can buy both types of spray can in a wide variety of finishes: varnish, shellac, lacquer, enamels, glazes, metallic, and so on.

There are four basic parts to an aerosol spray can: the container, the valve, the propellant which produces the necessary pressure, and the finishing material itself. The working principle of the can is a simple one, too. With the injection of the propellant, the pressure within the container becomes greater than that in the atmosphere. Thus, when the valve is opened, the pressure produces a fine spray of material. To keep the material stirred, most spray cans employ small balls within the container. When the can is shaken, the ball moves about and stirs the contents, mixing in any heavier particles that may have settled at the bottom of the container. Therefore, shaking the can is a very important step in the pre-application period. Without a thorough shaking, the finishing material may come out too thin, or you may use up the pressure before using up the material.

When using a spray can, hold the container at least 10 to 12 inches away from the surface you are painting, keeping the nozzle parallel with the piece. Press the button all the way down, and move the can evenly over the surface. Release pressure on the button before reaching the end of each stroke

**Common spraying troubles**

| Trouble | Possible cause | Suggested remedies |
|---|---|---|
| Sags or runs | 1. Dirty air cap and fluid tip | 1. Remove cap and fluid tip and clean. |
| | 2. Gun manipulated too close to surface | 2. Hold the gun 6 to 10 in. from surface. |
| | 3. Not releasing trigger at end of stroke (when stroke does not go beyond object) | 3. Release trigger after every stroke. |
| | 4. Gun manipulated at wrong angle to surface | 4. Work gun at right angles to surface. |
| | 5. Material piled on too heavy | 5. Learn to calculate depth of wet film of material. |
| | 6. Material thinned out too much | 6. Add correct amount of solvent by measure. |
| | 7. Fluid pressure too high | 7. Reduce fluid pressure. |
| | 8. Operation too slow | 8. Speed up movement of gun across surface. |
| | 9. Improper atomization | 9. Use larger air cap (internal mix); increase volume of air through horns (external mix). |
| Streaks | 1. Dirty air cap and fluid tip | 1. Same as for sags. |
| | 2. Not overlapping strokes correctly or sufficiently | 2. Follow previous stroke accurately. |
| | 3. Gun moved too fast across surface | 3. Take deliberate, slow strokes. |
| | 4. Gun held at wrong angle to surface | 4. Same as for sags. |
| | 5. Gun held too far from surface | 5. Stroke 6 to 10 in. from surface. |
| | 6. Air pressure too high | 6. Use least air pressure necessary. |
| | 7. Split spray | 7. Reduce air adjustment or change air cap. |
| | 8. Tripping gun | 8. Spray pattern should strike surface at right angles. |

| "Orange peel" (surface looks like orange peel) | 1. Material not thinned out sufficiently | 1. Add the correct amount of solvent by measure. |
| | 2. Not depositing a wet coat | 2. Check solvent; use correct spread and overlap of stroke. |
| | 3. Gun stroke too rapid | 3. Take deliberate, slow strokes. |
| | 4. Insufficient air pressure | 4. Increase atomizing pressure or reduce fluid pressure. |
| | 5. Using wrong air cap | 5. Select correct air cap for the material and feed. |
| | 6. Gun stroked too far from surface | 6. Stroke the gun 6 to 10 in. from surface. |
| | 7. Overspray striking a previously sprayed surface | 7. Spray detail parts first; end with wet coat. |
| | 8. Poor thinner | 8. Use better grade of thinner for material. |
| | 9. Gun too close to surface | 9. Gun should be worked 6 to 10 in. from surface. |
| | 10. Material not thoroughly dissolved | 10. Mix material thoroughly. |
| | 11. Drafts (synthetics and lacquers) | 11. Eliminate excessive drafts. |
| | 12. Humidity too low (synthetics) | 12. Raise humidity of room. |
| Excessive spray fog | 1. Atomizing air pressure too high | 1. Use least amount of compressed air necessary. |
| | 2. Spraying past surface of the product | 2. Release trigger when gun passes target. |
| | 3. Wrong air cap or fluid tip | 3. Ascertain and use correct combination. |
| | 4. Gun stroked too far from surface | 4. Stroke the gun 6 to 10 in. from the surface. |
| | 5. Material thinned out too much | 5. Add correct amount of solvent by measure. |
| | 6. Fluid pressure too low | 6. Increase fluid pressure. |

## Common spraying troubles (continued)

| Trouble | Possible cause | Suggested remedies |
|---|---|---|
| Excessive material | 1. Not triggering the gun at each stroke | 1. It should be a habit to release trigger after every stroke. |
| | 2. Gun at wrong angle to surface | 2. Hold gun at right angles to surface. |
| | 3. Gun held too far from surface | 3. Work gun 6 to 10 in. from surface. |
| | 4. Wrong air cap or fluid tip | 4. Use correct combination. |
| | 5. Depositing material film of irregular thickness | 5. Learn to calculate depth of wet film of finish. |
| | 6. Air pressure too high | 6. Use least amount of air necessary. |
| | 7. Fluid pressure too high | 7. Reduce pressure. |
| Material won't come from spray gun | 1. Out of paint | 1. Add paint. |
| | 2. Grit, dirt, paint skin, etc., blocking air cap, fluid tip, fluid needle, or strainer | 2. Clean spray gun thoroughly and strain paint; always strain paint before using it. |
| Material won't come from pressure tank or pressure cup | 1. Lack of proper air pressure in pressure tank or cup | 1. Check for air leaks or lack of air entry; adjust air pressure for sufficient flow. |
| | 2. Air intake opening inside pressure tank or cup lid clogged by dried-up paint | 2. This is a common trouble; clean opening periodically. |
| | 3. Leaking gasket on tank cover or pressure-cup lid | 3. Replace with new gasket. |
| Material won't come from suction cup | 1. Dirty air cap or fluid tip | 1. Remove air cap and fluid tip and clean thoroughly. |
| | 2. Clogged air vent on cup cover | 2. Remove obstruction. |
| | 3. Wrong air cap | 3. Ascertain and use correct setup. |
| | 4. Leaky connections on fluid tube, air cap, or fluid tip | 4. Check for leaks underwater and repair. |

| Trouble | Cause | Remedy |
|---|---|---|
| Gun sputters constantly | 1. Fluid tip not tightened to spray gun | 1. Tighten securely, using a good gasket. |
| | 2. Leaky connection on fluid tube or fluid-needle packing (suction gun) | 2. Tighten connections; lubricate packing. |
| | 3. Lack of sufficient material in container | 3. Refill container with material. |
| | 4. Tipping container at an acute angle | 4. If container must be tipped, change position of fluid tube and keep container full of material. |
| | 5. Obstructed fluid passageway | 5. Remove fluid tip, needle, and fluid tube and clean. |
| | 6. Material too heavy (suction feed) | 6. Thin material. |
| | 7. Clogged air vent in cup lid (suction feed) | 7. Clean. |
| | 8. Dirty or damaged coupling nut on cup lid (suction feed) | 8. Clean or replace. |
| | 9. Fluid pipe not tightened to pressure-tank lid or pressure-cup cover | 9. Tighten; check for defective threads. |
| Material leaks from spray gun | 1. Fluid-needle packing nut too tight | 1. Loosen nut; lubricate packing. |
| | 2. Fluid-needle packing dry | 2. Lubricate needle and packing frequently. |
| | 3. Foreign particle blocking fluid tip | 3. Remove tip and clean. |
| | 4. Damaged fluid tip or fluid needle | 4. Replace both tip and needle. |
| | 5. Wrong fluid-needle size | 5. Replace fluid needle with correct size for fluid tip being used. |
| | 6. Broken fluid-needle spring | 6. Remove and replace. |
| Material leaks from fluid-needle packing nut | 1. Loose packing nut | 1. Tighten packing nut. |
| | 2. Dry fluid-needle packing | 2. Remove and soften packing with a few drops of light oil. |
| Spray pattern top-heavy | 1. Horn holes partially plugged (external mix) | 1. Remove air cap and clean. |
| | 2. Obstruction on top side of fluid tip | 2. Remove and clean. |
| | 3. Dirt on air-cap seat or fluid-tip seat | 3. Remove and clean seat. |

## Common spraying troubles (continued)

| Trouble | Possible cause | Suggested remedies |
|---|---|---|
| Spray pattern bottom-heavy | 1. Horn holes partially clogged (external mix)<br>2. Obstruction on bottom side of fluid tip<br>3. Dirt on air-cap seat or fluid-tip seat | 1. Remove air cap and clean.<br>2. Remove and clean tip.<br>3. Remove and clean seat. |
| Spray pattern heavy to right | 1. Right side of air holes partially clogged<br>2. Dirt on right side of fluid tip | 1. Remove air cap and clean air holes.<br>2. Remove fluid tip and clean. |
| Spray pattern heavy to left | 1. Left side of air holes partially clogged<br>2. Dirt on left side of fluid tip | 1. Remove air cap and clean air holes.<br>2. Remove fluid tip and clean. |
| Spray pattern heavy at center | 1. Spreader adjustment valve set too low<br>2. Atomizing pressure too low<br>3. Material of too great viscosity<br>4. Fluid pressure too high for air cap's normal capacity (pressure feed)<br>5. Fluid tip too large for material used | 1. Increase volume of air by opening spreader-adjustment valve.<br>2. Increase pressure.<br>3. Thin material with suitable thinner.<br>4. Reduce fluid pressure.<br>5. Use smaller fluid tip. |
| Spray pattern split | 1. Air and fluid not balanced<br>2. Air cap or fluid tip dirty | 1. Reduce width of spray pattern.<br>2. Remove and clean. |
| Pinholes | 1. Gun too close to surface<br>2. Fluid pressure too high<br>3. Use of too heavy material | 1. Work gun 6 to 10 in. from the surface.<br>2. Reduce pressure.<br>3. Add the correct amount of solvent by measure. |
| Blushing or a whitish coat of lacquer | 1. Absorption of moisture<br>2. Too quick drying of lacquer | 1. Avoid spraying in damp, humid, or too cool weather.<br>2. Correct by adding retarder to lacquer. |

—the trick is to follow through. That is, work across the piece starting before its left edge and stopping beyond its right edge, as with a spray gun. Overlap the first stroke with at least one-third of the next. Keep your distance equal always, the angle 90 degrees. Be sure to use rapid, smooth strokes. Should you stop the movement of the can or go too slowly, streaking can result. Most of the other gun-spraying techniques mentioned earlier in this chapter hold good for spray-can applications too.

Label instructions on aerosol products have safety hints as well as instructions for the user. Remember, these products have been tested and tried by their manufacturers, and instructions are well-founded and should be followed. Aerosol finishes are inflammable mixtures, so perhaps one of the most necessary safety precautions is keeping these products away from open flames, particularly during use. The nature of the container also requires the user to store the aerosols in areas which are not too sunny and warm. Absolutely *never* keep them where temperatures are warmer than 120°F —even when empty. And do not incinerate these products.

Puncturing containers is also another don't, but *do* find a spot with good ventilation when applying the paint. If, by now, you are wondering how one does safely discard these products—without incinerating or puncturing—there is a way. Turn the can upside down, press the nozzle, and allow every bit of the propellant to be released. When nothing further comes out, the can is empty and you may discard it. Incineration is still a hazard, however, so let the community sanitation service deal with them.

# CHAPTER FOUR

# Stains

Stain gives color to wood and enhances the beauty of the grain. No other step in finishing brings about so radical a change in the appearance of the wood. This change in hue or tone is caused by a chemical reaction of a liquid penetrating the surface of the wood and by coloring matter changing the color of a layer of wood near the surface but at the same time allowing the grain to be seen clearly. Staining should leave a transparent effect and should not obscure the surface with opaque material such as pigments.

You have considerable latitude in the selection of stains, for there are hundreds of types and colors. A convenient classification can be made by grouping the stains according to the solvent used in their manufacture, namely, water, oil, alcohol, and lacquer thinner. The stain color or dye can be purchased in dry powder form or in ready-mixed liquid form. Two exceptions are water stain and non-grain-raising stain, which, because their solvent is water, are generally sold in a powder form.

### Types of stains

*Water stain* Water aniline stain is inexpensive, brilliant, and nonfading. It dyes the wood fibers in much the same manner as cloth is dyed. It has deep but even penetration and gives the most even and the clearest tone of all stains. It is very easy to obtain a lighter or darker tone; all that is necessary is to dilute the stain with water or add more powder. An ounce of dry powder added to hot water (just off the boil) will make a quart of stain. Some aniline powders are labeled "water- and alcohol-soluble," and, as the name suggests, these dyes may be dissolved in either water or wood (denatured) alcohol or both. Incidentally, the dyes do not produce the same color in water as in alcohol. For instance, when mixed in water a dye may produce a warm, reddish tone, but if mixed in alcohol, the powder will give a cold, greenish stain. Some very interesting color stains can be had by varying the proportions of water and alcohol in aniline dyes that are soluble in both vehicles.

While some dyes are available in straight colors—red, yellow, green, etc.—most manufacturers use wood hue names —dark oak, walnut, maple, etc. With about four or five different colors or wood hues, you can blend almost any shade of stain you desire. In other words, do a little experimenting on scrap wood of the same type you are planning to stain. Employ careful measuring processes, and record proportions carefully so that you will not have any problem repeating the color. Remember that the aniline stain, after it is mixed, will keep indefinitely. It may be applied with brush or spray, and wiped to an even tone. This stain dries for recoating in 12 to 24 hours, but can be force-dried with a heat lamp in from 2 to 6 hours. Water stain, however, has one bad fault— it raises the wood grain, which must then be resanded smooth. The water in the stain may also loosen glued joints.

***Non-grain-raising stains (NGR)*** Because water-soluble colors offer the best types of stain except for their grain-raising qualities, finishing manufacturers have developed raising qualities, finishing manufacturers have developed stains in which powders are dissolved in a solvent other than water. Stains of this kind are known by various descriptive trade terms such as non-grain-raising, fast-to-light, and non-sand. They are, of course, more expensive than water stains because of the solvent used, but offer one of the best types of stain for new work. Their rapid drying makes brushing difficult, but smooth coats are easily applied by spraying. Strictly non-bleeding, they can be used under any type of finish coat. They dry for recoating in from 10 minutes to 3 hours, depending on the manufacturer's recommendation. Ready-mixed colors are numerous, but if you wish, you may obtain concentrated primary colors and mix tints to suit your individual taste. It is possible to mix the stain powder and the solvent, but the cost is about the same as for the ready-mixed product.

NGR stains (sometimes called NFR, for "non-fiber-raising") are generally not recommended for fir, spruce, pine, and other woods which have a great variation in density between spring and summer growth, because the resulting grain pattern will probably be too wild.

***Penetrating oil stain*** Stain powders of this type can be disolved in any light oil such as benzol, naphtha, turpentine, or gasoline. A small amount of asphaltum or varnish—enough to make it brushable—can be added for body. Straight colors are referred to as oil black, oil red, oil yellow, and so on. This stain can also be purchased ready-mixed in liquid form. Oil stain has good penetration, but it strikes deeper into soft spots in the wood. It is moderately fade-proof, but it is not equal to water stain in this respect. Its good points are ease of application and the fact that it does not raise the grain of the wood. Oil stains are bleeding colors; that is, they tend to dissolve and to mix with later filler coats as well as varnish and lacquer. This is largely corrected by sealing the stain with a wash coat of shellac. This stain dries to recoat in 24 hours and can be either brushed or sprayed.

Oil stains are extensively used because they are convenient and very easy to apply. They dry slowly enough to permit brushing and rebrushing and show no laps or joints. If the color is too dark after the staining is done, some of the stain can be wiped off to make a lighter finish. Oil stains can be mixed to produce any desired color. Since the introduction of colored penetrating resin sealers (see page 163) in recent years, oil stains are not commonly used today.

**Pigment oil stain** This stain consists of finely ground color pigments, such as are used in coloring paints, in solution with such agents as linseed oil, turpentine, and naphtha. Pigment oil stain is really thin paint. A good pigment stain can be made by thinning any paint or enamel with turpentine. The ready-mixed stain can be purchased in paint stores; it is usually called *oil stain, wood stain,* or occasionally, *pigment wiping stain* and *uniforming stain.* The colors are nonfading and nonbleeding and are easy to apply with brush-on, wipe-off techniques (see page 93). They are made in slow-and-fast-drying types, the slow type requiring 12 hours to dry before recoating, the fast 30 minutes. This type of stain must be stirred constantly to assure even distribution of the pigments.

Pigmented wiping stains, or stain-sealers, are available in a wide range of color tones which can be intermixed to offer an even wider variety. They are effective in giving the wood a uniform appearance or in staining a piece of furniture made from different woods. Wood must be smoothly sanded to secure a uniform appearance. Unlike other stains, the coloring matter of pigment oil stains consists of pigment instead of dyes, which, being opaque, tend to cover up the grain pattern to a greater degree than dyes. Soft, porous woods darken heavily, since they soak up more of the color, while harder woods absorb less stain. But if used on open-grained hardwoods, the larger, wider-spaced pores tend to clog up with finely ground color pigment, producing a more or less muddy appearance. For this reason, pigmented wiping stains generally perform best on white pine and other softwoods. They also furnish a good method by which to create a "distressed" effect to a finish, since they help accentuate cracks, dents, and scratches.

Pigmented oil stains in a penetrating resin help seal the wood, to a degree. Places such as paneling which do not get much abuse can be finished with a topcoat of wax or a coat of shellac or varnish. And, on problem areas, which usually require three coats of varnish, you will need to apply only two.

**European oil-type stains** In recent years, the so-called European types of stains, such as Danish oil, have become popular with wood finishers. Most of them are rather clear stains with added synthetics which build up a smooth, tough surface. The oil colors the wood only slightly; it is clear enough to let the beauty of the grain come through. On lighter woods, most of the clear stains have a slightly yellow color—many people like it—but on darker woods such as walnut, they are an excellent stain.

**Spirit stains** Stain powders soluble in alcohol make penetrating spirit stains. They are also available in ready-mixed liquid form with various blended solvents. Spirit stains have the advantage of drying quickly. When you use them, a surface can be stained and filled or shellacked and varnished all on the same day. Because they dry rapidly, they are generally not suitable for brushing but can be sprayed. Spirit stains bleed and will strike through almost any type of finishing coat, including shellac. Bleeding causes a slight muddiness in the finish but is not a serious defect. Since spirit stains will penetrate an old varnish finish, they are often used for refinishing. Other uses include touch-up work and staining sap streaks. Spirit stains fade quickly when exposed to strong light unless well protected with finishing coats. They dry to recoat in 10 to 15 minutes.

**Wiping stains** These are merely concentrated oil pigment stains. They are used for shading, the surplus stain being wiped off to expose the highlights, hence the name. They may be purchased ready-mixed in various colors, or you can make them by adding naphtha to colors in oil or japan.

**Shading stains** These are ordinary powder stains mixed with a binder in addition to pure solvent. Since they dry very fast, they are intended primarily for application with a spray gun. The solvent is either alcohol or lacquer thinner, to which is added alcohol-solvent or lacquer-solvent dry powder at the rate of 1 ounce per quart. A small amount of white shellac (enough to make it brushable) can be added to an alcohol stain for body; clear lacquer is added to a stain made with lacquer thinner. Shading stain dries ready for a following coat in 5 minutes. This type of stain is used between finishing coats to produce shaded effects or to correct sap streaks. Shading stains are available ready-mixed in stock brown and red colors that are suitable for most work, or they may be purchased in powder form and mixed with the proper solvent. Shade staining is done mostly with spray equipment. Today, however, shade stains are giving way to color toning and glazing techniques (see page 222).

**Padding stains**   This type of stain has long been used as an overglaze when doing antique restorations. It can also be applied over existing finishes to obtain specific local effects. Usually a so-called "padding" lacquer or shellac is used as vehicle for these stains. Since these vehicles are not of great durability or resistance to moisture, alcohol, etc., they require topcoating of varnish or other protective surface.

**Varnish stains**   These are not often used for fine wood finishes. However, there are occasional quick, cheap, temporary, or repair jobs where a varnish stain may be used to advantage. Varnish stains are simply varnish to which coloring matter has been added in sufficient quantity to produce a decided color, but not enough to completely obscure the surface. Transparent colors are used. These stains fill, color, and add a gloss to the surface all in one coat. They do not penetrate the surface to any extent; they dry in from 3 to 12 hours; and they do not fade when exposed to strong light.

For really high-grade finishing, skilled craftsmen do not use this kind of stain. When a project is made from the cheaper grades of lumber, varnish stains may be used successfully because they give a uniform coloring to wood streaked with very soft and porous parts. This result is impossible with other stains unless you do a great deal of expensive preliminary work. If varnish stains are made too dark in color, they completely hide the wood grain and give the appearance of an enameled surface. (See Chapter 6 for instructions on application.) However, when the surface you are finishing is an inconspicuous one (such as the backs of chests, the bottoms of chairs and tables, or inside cabinets), using a varnish stain can be quite a time-saver.

**Vegetable stains**  Stains belonging to this group are extracted from roots, bark, and other vegetable matter. At one time they were used extensively but have now been replaced by water-soluble analine stains. Vegetable stains are mixed and applied in the same way as water stains but have a tendency to fade when exposed to sunlight. The following are some of the vegetable stains: dragon's blood (red); alkanet (red); madder (red); logwood (black); indigo (blue); fustic (yellow).

## How to mix powder stains

**Water stain**  1 ounce of water-soluble powder will make 1 quart of strong stain. Rain or distilled water is best. The water should be hot (165° F.) but not boiling. Stir thoroughly. Bichromate of potash or picric acid can be added (⅛ ounce per quart) for increased brilliance and penetration, but is not essential. Keep in glass jar.

**Non-grain-raising stain**  Add to 1 ounce of water-soluble stain powder 1 quart of Carbitol or Cellosolve. Keep in glass. Dilute as used with denatured alcohol, but not over 3 parts alcohol to 1 part stain.

**Oil stain**  Mix 1 ounce of oil-soluble powder with 1 quart of light oil (turpentine, benzol, naphtha, gasoline, toluol, xylol). A blended solvent gives best results. A typical blended solvent can be made by mixing 4 parts benzol, 4 parts turpentine, 1 part gasoline, 8 parts varnish. Heat the solvent in a double boiler, and stir in the stain powder. Let cool before using.

**Spirit stain**  Mix 1 ounce of alcohol-soluble powder with 1 quart of hot denatured alcohol or 1 quart of cold wood alcohol. The denatured alcohol can be heated by placing the can in a pail of hot water away from the fire. One pint of white shellac should be added if the stain is to be used as a shading stain.

**Pigment oil stain**    Mix 4 ounces of any color pigment ground in oil with 1 part of turpentine, benzol, or naphtha and boiled linseed oil in equal parts. Under lacquer, use colors ground in japan and mix with turpentine.

**Wiping stain**    Same as above.

**Shading stain**    Can be made with powders soluble in alcohol, as described above. Can also be made from powder stains soluble in amyl acetate or lacquer thinner. A stock solution can be made by adding 1 ounce of powder to 1 quart of lacquer thinner. Add to clear lacquer to produce strength desired, keeping the mixture about one third as heavy as ordinary lacquer.

## Mixing stain colors

Although all standard colors are obtainable in powder form, you may wish to mix your own color or modify the color of a commercial mixture. Water-solvent stains are most commonly used. All types can be obtained in a variety of colors. Some finishers prefer to use five straight colors—orange, red, black, yellow, and blue—intermixing these in varying proportions to produce any desired color. The usual method, however, is to purchase a specific shade intended for a certain kind of wood. All types of stain powders can be purchased in quantities as small as one ounce. An ounce of stain powder will make one quart of stain when mixed with the proper solvent. Some manufacturers mark the mixing ratio on each package. However, remember that every stain manufacturer has his own concept of wood colors. As stated previously, powder stain colors are available in both conventional color and wood-hue names. The common wood-hue or wood-tone colors are as follows:

*Mahogany*—mahogany (red); dark mahogany (brownish red)

*Walnut*—variation of brown to blackish brown

*Oak*—light oak (yellow); dark oak (brownish yellow); golden oak (dark oak lightly reddish)

*Maple*—maple (orange); honey (reddish brown); Vermont (brownish red)

Six colors will make almost every wood color you desire. Starting points for proportions are given in the following table:

| Color* | Yellow (Oak) | Orange (Maple) | Red (Mahogany) | Brown (Walnut) | Dark Blue† | Black† |
|---|---|---|---|---|---|---|
| Sheraton mahogany (light red) | | 12 | 5 | | 3 | |
| Medium-red mahogany | 2 | 6 | 6 | | | 3 |
| Red mahogany | | 9 | 7 | | 4 | |
| Brown mahogany | 2 | | 2 | 11 | | 1 |
| Dark-red mahogany | 2 | 6 | 7 | | | 4 |
| Light walnut | | 8 | 1 | 4 | | 4 |
| Medium walnut | | 10 | | 4 | | 6 |
| Oriental walnut | | 3 | | 1 | | 2 |
| Modern walnut | 5 | | | 8 | | 1 |
| Light oak | 1 | 10 | | | 2 | |
| Dark oak | 2 | 10 | | | 5 | |
| Golden oak | | 22 | 1 | | 3 | |
| Maple | 4 | 10 | | | 1 | |
| Honey maple | 4 | 11 | | 1 | 1 | |
| Red cherry | | | 12 | 8 | | 1 |
| Brown cherry | 2 | | 2 | 3 | | |
| Fruitwood | 8 | 2 | | 1 | | |
| Antique brown | 2 | 8 | | 11 | | 1 |
| Antique pine | | | 2 | 9 | | 1 |

\* Lighter tints of same color can be obtained by diluting with proper solvent.

† Add dark colors last.

Mixing is easy if you have a stock solution of each of the required colors on hand. The unit or part for mixing can be any convenient measure—a drop for very small test runs, a cubic centimeter (1 cc) for accurate tests, and liquid ounces for final measuring. Liquid stain is drawn by using a small syringe or rubber-bulb battery filler. The final selection should be made on the basis of a completely finished panel.

A simple method to determine the final appearance of a stain is to apply a sample to a piece of wood of the same type to be stained. Then take a piece of clear glass, about 8 x 4 inches, and coat half of one side only with a thin coat of orange shellac and the other half of the same side with white shellac. Simply hold the glass over the stained sample, first the end with white shellac, then the end with orange; in this way you can see, before staining the project, how your color or stain is going to look under either white or orange shellac.

Stains of the same type can be intermixed to produce different color tones. In fact, most color variation needed for staining wood surfaces can be obtained by intermixing three colors of stain—maple (brownish yellow), walnut (true brown), and mahogany (reddish brown).

| To stain woods | Start with base of | Add to base |
| --- | --- | --- |
| Brown (reddish) | Walnut stain | Reddish brown mahogany stain |
| Brown (yellowish) | Walnut stain | Brownish yellow maple stain |
| Yellow (brownish) | Maple stain | Walnut stain |

If the maple contains too much brown, it will be necessary to add the light oak to the list, and should the walnut contain too much black, raw umber or burnt umber may be needed. To lighten the other colors, add gum turpentine to oil stains.

Unusual color effects can be achieved by diluting various

colors in oil with linseed oil or turpentine until the mixture is thin enough to be absorbed into the wood. Here are several proportions that give standard wood colors:

| Colors | Yellow Ochre | Raw Umber | Burnt Umber | Raw Sienna | Burnt Sienna |
|---|---|---|---|---|---|
| Red mahogany | | | 1 | | 2 |
| Brown mahogany | | | 3 | | 2 |
| Walnut | | 3 | 2 | | |
| Oak | 1 | 3 | 6 | | |
| Maple | | 2 | | 3 | |
| Red maple | | | 3 | | 5 |
| Cherry (light) | | | | 1 | 3 |
| Cherry (dark) | | | 1 | | 3 |
| Fruitwood | 1 | | 4 | | 5 |
| Antique pine | 5 | 1 | 5 | | |
| Honey pine | 5 | | | 3 | |

Mix together:  3 parts boiled linseed oil
1 part gum turpentine
½ part japan drier

### General technique of staining

Surface preparation is the most important step in the staining process, since a stain merely highlights and accentuates the surface to which it is applied. Use sandpaper of the same grade for the *entire* area to assure a more uniform penetration of the stain. That is, do not sand one area with 3/0 paper and another with 6/0. As a rule, the relatively rougher 3/0 area will stain darker. As stated in Chapter 2, the final sanding should be done with paper at least as fine as 6/0. Smooth down any rough spots—unless, of course, you want them to remain and contribute to a "distressed" effect. Remember that staining will accentuate any rough spots, including even the minor scratches of crossgrain sanding. Sanding should remove any grease, dirt, and wax spots. However, you can make sure the surface is clean by wiping the entire area with denatured alcohol or lacquer thinner.

Although a surface that has gone through a planer or jointer may appear smooth and ready for stain, keep in mind that these tools have a burnishing, polishing effect on the wood. Since this effect tends to seal wood and prevent absorption of the stain, the surface must be lightly sanded.

Stains can be applied with a sponge, a cloth, a brush, or a spray gun. Most finishers prefer to use a brush or spray gun. It is always best to test a stain first on a scrap piece of the type of wood you are finishing—or on a portion of the furniture that will not show. If the object you are staining is composed of more than one type of wood, remember to test the stain on each of these woods. To test the color, apply the same number of coats you are planning to use, and then apply the number of finishing coats (varnish, shellac, etc.) you will be using—even the "colorless" coatings will impart some color change to your final finish. If there is an uneven or blotchy distribution of stain on the test area, it may be wise to apply a "wash coat" of a clear penetrating sealer or shellac before staining. This will result in a lighter but more uniform color.

When starting a job, plan a systematized procedure that will carry you over all the surfaces of the furniture in the most convenient order. A good rule to follow is to start on the areas that are least seen when the piece is standing in its normal position and end with those areas which are most seen.

Before applying stain, you should study the shape of the object and plan the way to do the work. Do one section at a time so as to eliminate, as far as possible, laps or double coats of stain. When you are doing a tabletop, for instance, start at one end and work toward the other end. In this way, it will not be necessary to apply stain to a part that has already dried.

Some wood finishers coat soft, porous woods with very thin shellac before staining; this stops the suction in the porous streaks when oil, water, or spirit stains are used. Others prefer to brush on a coat of oil (about one-fourth boiled linseed oil and three-fourths turpentine) before staining. The oil should dry before the stain is applied. Sometimes the whole surface is treated with the shellac or oil size, sometimes only the excessively porous boards.

For a uniform color on the entire piece, the stain must be applied evenly on all surfaces. This is easy to do on a smooth flat surface, but on the end grain it is often difficult to control the color. The ends of boards are more porous than the flat sides and will absorb more stain and become darker than the rest of the wood. This can be controlled by applying a thin coat of glue size or a very thin coat of shellac to the end grain before it is stained. Do this carefully, as too much glue or shellac will prevent any stain from being absorbed. In any case, use a fairly dry brush when staining the ends of boards or carved parts.

Some experienced wood finishers advocate that a wash coat be used on a wood surface before a stain is applied, while others do not. A wash coat is a ½- to 1-pound cut of white shellac (see page 140). Of course, no wash coat should be applied if it is going to lessen the penetrating characteristics of the stain, for without penetrating a stain will not last. For instance, it is recommended that no wash coat be applied when water stains or spirit stains are to be used, and it is not needed for a varnish stain or a penetrating sealer, for these materials both seal and finish. A wash coat is often beneficial when oil stains are employed. The wash coat should be applied with as few strokes as possible.

Resinous knots and streaks of sapwood sometimes do not take stain, or they will color much lighter than the balance of the wood. To overcome this, brush these areas two or three times with a 1 percent solution of water and potash (1 ounce of caustic potash to 99 ounces of water). After this treatment, wash the area a few minutes later with clear water. When this treatment is not successful, one or more coats of denatured alcohol may be brushed onto the surface to cut through the resin of pitch. Pine pitch can be made to take a stain more uniformly if washed over with a soda and water solution (4 ounces of sal soda and 1 ounce of yellow laundry soap to 1 gallon of warm water). Sponge the surface with this solution, let dry, and then clean with clear warm water.

Inlays are frequently coated with white shellac to protect them from finger marks. If the inlays are to be stained, remove the shellac with denatured alcohol. If different stains are to be used on different parts of the inlay, you can use shellac or tape to mask off for a two-tone effect.

The time to wipe off oil stains is when the surface begins to dry or get dull. This will minimize the danger of streaks resulting from premature wiping. The final wiping strokes should be done with the grain. Wiping across the grain can cause streaks, particularly if done when the stain has become too dry.

Two light coats of stain are better than one heavy one, because one heavy coat is likely to brush on unevenly. Dilute the stain with the proper solvent to make it light enough to require two light coats. Allow at least 24 hours' drying time between coats.

When staining carvings and similar raised places, it is usually wise to gently wipe these high spots so they are lighter. This dramatizes the carvings and gives them the proper antique or period look.

In most cases, apply the stain sparingly at first, following the grain whenever possible. Cover areas in such a manner as to allow succeeding strokes to butt against still wet edges. Butting strokes against dry edges may cause dark overlap marks. Don't try to cover too much of the object at once— instead, try to work a single surface at a time—back, sides, top. Always try to apply the stain with the surface horizontal. Where vertical surfaces are unavoidable, apply the stain from the bottom up with continuous edge-to-edge strokes, paralleling the grain of the wood. This procedure will minimize drips and overlap marks. To prevent the stain from bridging or spanning the pores of some open-grained woods which will give a spotty, light-pored effect, make certain to work the stain into all the pores.

Generally, it is best to start with a lighter rather than a darker stain, since it is much easier to add color than it is to lighten a stain. But do not allow a stain to remain on one section of the wood for too long a time while you try to cover the entire surface. The longer a stain is allowed to stand before wiping, the more it penetrates into the wood, and the darker the shade of the finish will be. If you want a lighter color, be ready to wipe it off quickly to pick up the excess stain before it is absorbed into the wood. In addition to the label directions, you must exercise your own judgment according to the depth of tone that suits you best. Keep track of the staining time when you are practicing on your test stain. Avoid overpenetration into the end-grain by brushing and wiping almost simultaneously. As a rule, two light coats of stain are better than one heavy one, because one heavy coat is likely to brush on unevenly. Dilute the stain with the appropriate solvent, as recommended by the manufacturer, to make it light enough to require two light coats.

Occasionally a piece of wood will stain lighter in one place than in another. In such cases there are two ways to obtain a more uniform finish: (1) Allow the stain to remain longer on the less absorbent wood, which you will recognize by its not taking the stain as quickly. And where the stain soaks in rapidly, wipe it off quickly. (2) Apply a bit of diluted stain to the light areas, and blend them into the darker surrounding wood. After this has dried, stain the entire surface. This method of obtaining a more uniformly stained surface is easiest with water stain. Pigmented wiping stains tend to seal the wood and prevent the second stain coat from penetrating.

If you find that more stain is soaking in than you want, don't panic. The degree of stain coloration can be lightened slightly with an extra hard wiping with clean rags or with a bit of fine steel wool. The surface can be lightened considerably by wiping it with a rag saturated in a solvent such as mineral spirits or turpentine. But when sanding is necessary on stained work, it should be only of the light touch-up type, because even a partial cut-through will show up light. If a mistake is made in the wood coloration, the surface can usually be bleached (see page 32) and the staining process started over again.

### Application of water stain

Water stain can be sprayed or brushed. The amount of hot water added to the stock solution determines the richness or deepness of the color. It is often difficult to predict what the finished color will look like, since these stains are strong and woods vary in their ability to absorb stain. It is wise to experiment carefully with these dyes on pieces of the wood you are working with. In experimenting to determine the desired color, always coat the sample of stained wood with a coat of clear varnish or lacquer—this shows what it will look like when finished. Be sure to follow the manufacturer's label directions when diluting and applying a water stain. Since, as previously stated, water stains will usually cause the grain of wood to raise, it is best to take preventive measures first. Do not slop the water on; simply dampen the wood, using a sponge, brush, rag, or gun. Sand with fine (6/0 to 8/0) garnet paper in 1 hour.

Apply the stain in a sweeping stroke with the grain of the wood, keeping all surfaces horizontal if possible. Work back and forth with the brush, without lifting, until your brush becomes too dry to cover the surface well with stain. Then dip the brush halfway into the stain solution and apply as before, with the grain of the wood, back and forth, from the farthest edge toward you, until the surface is covered. Apply stain freely and rapidly. Better penetration is obtained if the stain is used warm, but this is not essential.

After the surface has been stained, shake out the brush and lay off (brush out) the stain in long smooth strokes with the grain. Wiping with a cloth is seldom satisfactory but can be used to advantage on end grain to prevent darkening. Other methods used to prevent darkening of end grain include: (1) previous treatment with a thin glue size; (2) sponging with water immediately before staining; (3) using a separate light stain. Similar treatment is necessary in order to even the color in sapwood. (See page 95.)

Sap streaks in walnut must be gone over twice with stain.

The exact effect of stain on sap streaks is best observed when you are water-sponging, since this is a direct indication of how the wood will later absorb the stain. If the work has considerable sap, two coats of weak stain permit better blending.

Water stain will dry in 12 to 24 hours. A wash coat of 7 parts alcohol to 1 part shellac can be applied when the stain is dry. A light sanding will then remove any remaining traces of raised grain.

Hard, close-grained woods such as maple and birch will not absorb stain as readily as softer woods. When using water-soluble aniline stains on these woods, add a little potassium bichromate or vinegar to assist the penetration. Certain softwoods contain rosin or oils that make it very difficult to apply a stain evenly. Before staining these woods, remove the rosin from the surface by sponging with alcohol or benzine.

When you stain carvings or recesses of any kind, use a little less stain than customary, so that no surplus will be left when you are through brushing. If you get a surplus on any recess, pick it up quickly with waste or some absorbent material; otherwise it will penetrate too deeply and be darker than the flat surfaces.

Brushes that are to be used with water stains should be rubber-set with hard rubber or brass ferrules. Stain should be applied with a soft camel's-hair or synthetic bristle brush. If the brush has been used as a varnish brush for several months, all the better, for then the bristle butts will be well sealed with varnish against moisture and the wooden butt of the handle will not be inclined to absorb moisture from the water stain and swell or crack the ferrule. Before using such a brush, clean it in turpentine and then wash it with soap and water.

Water stains should be used under lacquer finishing coats. Wood finished with spirit stain should not be exposed to strong sunlight until coated with varnish. These stains dry for recoating in 10 to 15 minutes.

Water stains usually dry to a lighter shade than the shade they appear to be when applied. Therefore, let your test piece dry thoroughly before using the mixture on the wood. When blending lighter areas to match darker wood, it is a good idea to dilute some of the water stain to the proper intensity so that it makes the lighter wood the same color as the darker. Thus, when the entire piece is stained, the lighter wood disappears completely.

### Application of non-grain-raising stains

NGR stains are best applied by spraying. Because of their quick-drying nature (some of them are ready for recoating in 10 minutes), brushing is difficult. Also, because of the wetness of a brush coat, the stain tends to raise the grain of the wood, although it is strictly non-grain-raising when sprayed. These stains can be slowed down a bit with the addition of about 10 percent Carbitol or Cellosolve.

Use a large brush and apply the stain in a very wet coat. The cutting-in technique with a small brush is perfect for varnish top coats (see Chapter 6), but with NGR stain the edges will be dry before you get over the surface. Always break up the job into convenient areas; do the legs, rails, and top of a table in separate operations. If it is impossible to do a lap-free job, dilute the stain to half strength with an equal amount of solvent. Apply two coats of this weak stain. Another way is to wash the work quickly with the stain solvent and then apply full-strength stain immediately.

When you spray NGR stains, apply a moderate coat, not too wet. Shoot all inside edges first; do the top last. Use a small spray pattern but fan it out by holding the gun a fair distance from the work. Always have a good light on the work, so that the color density can be properly evaluated. By spraying more heavily on light wood and less on dark wood, it is easy to obtain a uniform color on mixed or off-color wood.

## Application of penetrating oil stain

This stain is non-grain-raising and does not require previous sponging as in water staining. It can be brushed on or sprayed. The main difference in technique is that the oil stain is wiped with a rag to remove surplus and equalize the color. Wiping is done while the stain is wet, but time should be allowed to ensure good penetration. Quick wiping of an end grain will eliminate darkening. Sap streaks may or may not require double coating. The slow drying of oil stains appeals to most finishers, and for that reason this stain is used in many places where water stain would be better. Little care is necessary in the application of oil stain. You need only to guard against slopping the stain over surfaces where it is not wanted or allowing the stain to run. If you spray it on, any surfaces not needing the stain can be avoided by sloping the gun. If you use a brush, you must exercise care at abutments or corners and the insides of drawers or cabinets.

To ensure a uniform shade over all the work, wipe each

piece uniformly and at about the same time after staining. The last wiping strokes with the pad should be parallel to the figure of the wood. Wiping across the grain may leave streaks, especially if the stain is too dry. However, very little instruction is necessary to get a uniform shade with oil stains, as application of a second coat will often tone up a surface that appears too light. Wiping time may vary from 3 to 30 minutes. Remember, the longer the stain is left on the wood, the darker the finished color. Most finishers claim that the time to wipe off oil stains is when the surface begins to dry or get dull. This will minimize the danger of streaks resulting from premature wiping. The final wiping strokes should be done with the grain. Wiping across the grain can cause streaks, particularly if done when the stain has become too dry.

### Application of pigmented stain

Follow the manufacturer's label directions when applying pigmented wiping stains. If you are going to use more than one can of stain, mix the cans together in a large container to ensure uniformity of color.

Pigment oil stains should be stirred well before using, because, unlike the other stains which contain dyes, the pigment coloring in these stains tends to settle on the bottom of the container when stored. The stain can be applied with a rag or brush, spreading it liberally over the surface and allowing it to set for 5 to 10 minutes or until the stain starts to flat; then wipe with a soft cloth, with the grain, until a uniform tone is obtained. If wiped too soon, or too briskly, the color will be lightened considerably. If wiped too late, the stain will be gummy and stick to the rag. If this happens, moisten the rag with turpentine or naphtha. While it is

**Characteristics of various types of stains**

| | Water stain | Non-grain-raising stain | Penetrating oil stain | Pigment oil stain | Spirit stain |
|---|---|---|---|---|---|
| Coloring matter | Water-soluble aniline powder | Water-soluble aniline powder | Oil-soluble aniline powder | Pigment colors in oil | Alcohol-soluble aniline powder |
| Solvent | Water | Carbitol or Cellosolve plus alcohol | Benzol, turpentine, etc. | Benzol, turpentine, naphtha | Denatured alcohol |
| Cost | Low | High | Medium | Medium | High |
| Application | Brush or spray | Best sprayed, but can be brushed[a] | Brush and wipe with cloth | Brush and wipe | Spray only |
| Grain raising | Bad[b] | Very little[c] | None | None | Very little[c] |
| Clarity | Excellent | Excellent | Fair | Excellent | Poor |
| Bleeding | None | None or very little | Bad[e] | None | Bad[d] |
| Permanence of color | Excellent | Excellent | Fair | Excellent | Poor |
| Effect on top coats | None | Possible slight bleeding | Bleeds; must be sealed with shellac[e] | None[f] | Bleeds[d] |

| | | | | | |
|---|---|---|---|---|---|
| Mixes with lacquer | No | Yes | Yes | No | Yes |
| Mixes with varnish | No | Yes | Yes | Yes | Yes |
| Drying time | 12 hr | 10 min. to 3 hr | 24 hr[g] | 3 to 12 hr[g] | 10 to 15 min |
| Principal use | Staining quality hardwoods | Same as water stain also for refinishing | Staining softwoods | Softwoods; also as a glaze coat or wiping stain | Patching and quick work |

[a] Some types, factory mixed in liquid form, dry very quickly and are difficult to brush smoothly.
[b] The only fault of water stain: water solvent causes wood fibers to lift. Work must be resanded smooth when dry. The addition of up to 25 percent Carbitol or Cellosolve will help correct this fault.
[c] Alcohol solvent absorbs moisture from air, causing slight grain raising in muggy weather.
[d] Refers to own-mix stain. Some factory-mixed stains of the alcohol series are strictly nonbleeding.
[e] Seal with shellac when used under varnish. Do not use under lacquer.
[f] Refers to factory-mixed product, made with specially treated oils to work under lacquer.
[g] Use benzol as solvent for fast drying. Retard drying with turpentine or turpentine substitute.

almost impossible to remove all the pigment from the surface, you should try. That is, wipe the surface clean. If after you have wiped it completely the color is darker than desired, dampen the cloth with turpentine or other paint thinner, and carefully wipe some more. This same procedure can be used to blend color areas, that is, lightening certain areas which may go darker than the rest of the wood.

After wiping, let the stain dry 12 to 24 hours, and then apply the desired top finish. It is not necessary, however, to seal it with shellac as many finishers seal oil stains, since pigmented wiping stains have no tendency to bleed.

### Application of spirit stains

Because the average stain of this type dries almost instantly, the best method of application is with a spray gun. If applied by brush, the work must be done rapidly and without backtracking. A small amount of shellac added to the stain will make it easier to brush evenly. Do not apply a coat of shellac over spirit stains because shellac, which is also soluble in alcohol, will lift the stain and cause a muddy appearance.

Penetrating spirit stains always bleed and will strike through any number of finishing coats. Wood finished with spirit stain should not be exposed to strong sunlight until coated with varnish. These stains dry for recoating in 10 to 15 minutes.

### Application of padding stains

Padding stains should be applied only over an old finish—never on bare wood. After moistening a pad of cheesecloth or other lint-free cloth with the padding vehicle—either thinned shellac or padding lacquer—dip the pad into the dry, powdered padding colors, and then rub it into the wood surface to produce the color, pattern, or marking effect desired. Padding stains are widely employed to liven the color of old finishes when complete removal and refinishing is not desirable.

# CHAPTER FIVE

# Fillers and Sealers

In fine work, a filler should be used after the stain has dried. The purpose of a filler is to close the cells or tiny crevices in open-grained woods. Close-grained woods are often finished without the use of fillers.

Fillers can be obtained in two forms—paste and liquid. Paste fillers, used on open-grained woods, are either semitransparent or opaque; liquid fillers, normally used on close-grained woods, are transparent. In general, fillers should be as transparent as possible so as not to hide the natural color and beauty of the wood. However, opaque fillers have their place in wood finishing when special effects such as two-tone finishes are desired.

If fillers are not used, finishing materials such as

varnish, shellac, paint, or lacquer will sink in and produce a rippled effect. Even though several coats of finishing material are applied and rubbed down, the rippled effect is likely to remain. The rubbing down of each coat serves as a substitute for a filler, but this operation is slower than filling the surface before applying the finish.

### Filler mix required for various woods

| No filler needed | Thin filler | Medium filler | Heavy filler |
| --- | --- | --- | --- |
| Aspen | Alder | Amaranth | Ash |
| Basswood | Beech | Avodire | Bubinga |
| Cedar | Birch | Butternut | Chestnut |
| Cypress | Cherry | Korina | Elm |
| Ebony | Gum | Mahogany | Hickory |
| Fir | Maple | Orientalwood | Kelobra |
| Gaboon | Sycamore | Primavera | Lacewood |
| Hemlock | Tupelo | Rosewood | Lauan (Philippine |
| Holly | | Sapeli | mahogany |
| Magnolia | | Tigerwood | Locust |
| Pine | | Walnut | Oak |
| Poplar | | Zebrawood | Padouk |
| Redwood | | | Teakwood |
| Spruce | | | |

### Paste fillers

Paste fillers are made of various formulations. They can be purchased in many stain colors as well as in natural (semi-transparent) and white. Paste fillers are sold usually under the name of "wood fillers" and in cans of 1, 5, 10, and 25 pounds. One pound will fill about 40 square feet of surface.

Before use, paste fillers should be thinned to the desired consistency with gum turpentine or naphtha, the amount of dilution depending on the size of the pores to be filled. Obviously, large pores require a thicker mix than small ones. Mix only enough filler for the job at hand, as the thinned filler thickens after a few hours and becomes useless. Mixing by exact weight is always good practice. Refer to the table on page 111 for mixing proportions for various quantities of heavy-mix filler. The term *heavy mix* does not mean a heavy-bodied material; actually, the consistency is no thicker than varnish.

The first step in mixing is to spade the unmixed paste with a putty knife. Then add a very small amount of thinner and stir. After the first mixing, add increasingly larger amounts of thinner and stir until the mix is the proper consistency. Do not add a lot of thinner at the start, as this makes mixing much harder. Use naphtha for thinning when the filler is to set up quickly for wiping; use turpentine to hold the coat open longer. A small amount of boiled linseed oil can be added to hold the coat open for 30 to 40 minutes. The reverse of this—a very quick-setting filler—can be obtained by adding a small amount of japan drier.

The natural paste filler, which is usually light gray, may be colored by adding a small amount of oil stain, or colors-in-oil. For changing natural filler to walnut, for instance, add a little raw umber ground in oil or japan drier. Vandyke brown will give a slightly redder color than raw umber. For mahogany, add lampblack and a little raw and burnt sienna. To test tinting, apply the filler to a scrap of stained wood and then a lacquer or varnish coat over it to get an idea of the color obtained when the surface is finished. For green, gray, white, and other colors, follow the same general procedure, except use colors-in-oil. Dry powder colors mixed in turpentine, and oil-soluble aniline colors thinned with turpentine, are sometimes used for colors in paste fillers, and a shade of color may often be had by using a pigment stain or a penetrating wood stain as it comes from the can. Remember that

## Proportions for mixing various quantities of filler

| HEAVY MIX (16-lb. base) | | | MEDIUM MIX (12-lb base) | | | THIN MIX (8-lb base) | | |
|---|---|---|---|---|---|---|---|---|
| Approx. amt. needed* | Paste | Thinner | Approx. amt. needed* | Paste | Thinner | Approx. amt. needed* | Paste | Thinner |
| 2 gal | 16 lb | 1 gal | 1 gal 3 qt | 12 lb | 1 gal | 1½ gal | 8 lb | 1 gal |
| 5 pt | 5 lb | 2½ pt | 3 qt | 5 lb | 3 pt 5 oz | 1 gal | 5 lb | 5 pt |
| 2 qt | 1 qt | 1 qt | 2 qt 10 oz | 1 qt | 2 pt 10 oz | 3 qt | 1 qt | 2 qt |
| 2 pt | 1 pt | 1 pt | 1 qt 5 oz | 1 pt | 1 pt 5 oz | 3 pt | 1 pt | 2 pt |
| 1 pt | 1 lb | ½ pt | 1 pt 20 oz | 1 lb | 10½ oz | 1½ pt | 1 lb | 1 pt |
| ½ pt | ½ lb | 4 oz | 9 oz | ½ lb | 5¼ oz | 12 oz | ½ lb | ½ pt |

* One pint thinned filler covers approximately 36 square feet.

it is best that the filler be approximately of the same color as the surface to which it is applied, except when the final finish is opaque. Otherwise, the filler might show through a transparent finish, if the filler is not correctly applied or properly wiped off.

Filler can be used to stain and fill in one operation by adding a little oil stain to the filler. However, the results will not be as good as those obtained by the two-system procedure and should not be used where high-quality results are desired.

On most surfaces it is desirable to have the filler a trifle darker than the wood itself, to emphasize the grain pattern. Exceptions are the lime-oak filler, which is almost white, and the blue and green fillers used for special effects.

### Standard filler colors

**Black**  Add drop black (a tint of black) to natural filler. Suitable for blackwood or dark mahogany.

**White**  Color natural base with zinc oxide. Used for limed oak and similar effects on chestnut and ash.

**Amber**  Tint natural base with yellow or orange oil colors. Suitable for ambered walnut, harvest wheat mahogany, and other bleached finishes.

**Light brown**  Tint with Vandyke brown to required shade. Can be used on any light-brown wood.

**Dark brown**  Vandyke brown with a touch of drop black. For walnut, mahogany, etc. Suitable for any medium- to dark-colored wood.

**Walnut**  Half and half Vandyke brown and burnt umber.

**Light red**  Use any red color (Indian red) in oil or japan, toning darker or lighter with drop black or zinc white.

**Dark red**  Equal parts of burnt umber and rose pink. Add drop black for darker shade. Use for Sheraton mahogany or any other red finish where dark pores are desirable.

If you wish to try your hand at preparing your own filler, obtain some silica, a finely ground white sand which is made by crushing quartz rock. It is ground so fine that it will float on water. If the filler is to be colored, it will be necessary to obtain colors ground in oil. Boiled linseed oil, japan drier, and turpentine also will be needed.

One much-used formula for preparing a paste filler consists of ½ pint of boiled linseed oil, 4 ounces of japan drier, and 1 pint of turpentine. Mix these liquids and then add fine silica until you have a very thick paste that is well mixed. Put the paste through a paint mill, or mix it thoroughly with a paddle and strain through a wire screen. Thin with naphtha or turpentine to a thick brushing consistency. It should be just thin enough to pour out of a pot. Tinting colors should be broken up with turpentine or benzine and strained before adding them to the filler. While in use, the filler should be stirred every few minutes, because the heavy pigment settles rapidly to the bottom. To overcome this, add cornstarch (10 to 20 percent of the weight of the silica used), or add up to 25 percent of asbestine (silicate of magnesia). These materials will keep the filler pigment suspended in the oil.

### Liquid fillers

For close-grained woods like maple and birch, use liquid filler or paste filler thinned to a liquid consistency. Transparent liquid fillers are available in pint, quart, half-gallon, and gallon cans.

Commercial liquid fillers composed of glass oil, hard oil, or other cheap varnishes are not dependable. Some of the cheap fillers bleach out white in time and make a mottled, cloudy appearance under the varnish. Some are brittle and crack easily. However, when made of first-class varnish by a well-known manufacturer, they are excellent.

For those who wish to mix liquid filler for themselves, the following formula may be used; 1 gallon of good rubbing varnish; I quart of turpentine; I pint of japan drier; and 2½ pounds of silica. Mix the silica well with a little of the varnish. Then add the other liquids and mix them thoroughly. Grind the whole batch through a paint mill, if one is at hand, or mix it with a paddle. After it is thoroughly mixed, let it stand for 2 or 3 days, and then strain through muslin. Then thin the mixture to easy brushing consistency with turpentine. Stir the filler occasionally while you are using it to keep the silica in suspension; it may settle to the bottom. It should dry flat, but not dead flat. Use less silica to avoid the dead-flat appearance.

Shellac makes a good liquid filler. White shellac is best for natural and light-colored finishes, and orange shellac is best for dark colors. For medium-dark finishes, mix white and orange shellac. As a filler, thin the shellac with shellac solvent or denatured alcohol. Shellac is usually a 4-pound cut (4 pounds of shellac dissolved in 1 gallon of alcohol). For use as a filler, shellac should be a 2-pound cut (2 pounds of shellac dissolved in 1 gallon of alcohol). By adding 1 gallon of alcohol to a gallon of 4-pound-cut shellac, a shellac suitable for filling can be obtained. Apply one or two coats and allow each coat to set hard before applying the next coat. Sandpaper each coat when dry, and clean dust from the surface before applying the next coat of filler.

## Application of filler

Paste filler should be applied liberally and worked well into the wood with a stiff brush. (Use an old, short-bristled paint brush or a heavy but cheap brush with about one-fourth of the length of its bristles cut off.) The loaded brush should be brushed first in the direction of the grain and then worked into the pores by brushing across the grain. Properly prepared filler will lose its wet appearance in 2 to 5 minutes. If thinned too much, it will take longer; if too heavy, it will show signs of drying in less time.

When the filler starts to take on this dry appearance, usually in 5 to 20 minutes, it is ready for rubbing with excelsior or burlap. Rub across the grain so as not to lift the filler out of the pores. This will roll off the excess and work the remaining filler down into the pores. This operation pads the powdered silex particles into the wood pores and smooths the wood surface.

Continue the wiping-off operation, across the grain only, with clean pieces of burlap squares followed by fresh rags, until all the surplus filler is removed and the surface is clean and free from smears and fingerprints. Be sure to use cross-grain motion only. Never wipe the filler with the grain, or you will surely wipe it out of the grainwise pores. Wipe as clean as possible. Remember that the filler must not be left on the surface of the wood, as it will produce a cloudy finish after shellac or varnish is applied. The final wiping is done lightly with a clean lint-free rag in the direction of the grain.

Another excellent material for padding in and wiping paste filler is ordinary oakum or tow such as is used by plumbers for calking joints. Professional finishers often use medium-fine excelsior or even wood shavings, but the amateur must be careful to avoid materials that might scratch the surface.

Narrow moldings, edges of cabinets, and similar surfaces are more difficult than flat surfaces to cover with a uniform thickness of filler. It is sometimes necessary to put two coats on these. Let the first coat set flat before you brush on the second; then wipe both coats after the second has set flat. Delicate carvings sometimes are not filled because the filler tends to round the edges and fill the recesses too much, and it is difficult to wipe out such places. If carvings are not filled, they must have at least one coat of shellac.

Filling works better on a horizontal surface. Wherever possible, lay the work down to bring the work surface into a horizontal position. Drawers can be removed and their front surfaces held level for filling.

To remove filler from corners and moldings, picking sticks are used. These are short ¼-inch, ⅜-inch, or ½-inch dowels sharpened to a point at one end and to a chisel edge at the other. Even better picking sticks can be made from old toothbrush handles. To pick up the filler cleanly, a rag is folded around the end of the stick; if the filler has hardened, the rag can be moistened with turpentine.

Surplus filler that has been allowed to remain on the surface will show up as blotches or smears when the filler has dried. Remove these by carefully wiping them with a cloth moistened with thinner or a 2-to-1 mixture of white gasoline and pure turpentine. If this fails to remove the dried filler, sand the spots carefully with very fine paper dipped in white gasoline. If this lightens the area in color, blend it back to the original shade by rubbing it with a rag dipped in filler.

If the filler is allowed to set too hard before it is rubbed, the wood surface will have to be washed with benzine to soften the filler for rubbing in. If the filler should lift out of the grain as it is being rubbed, it is an indication that too much oil was used.

Before applying filler, try a sample coat on a small

Oil stains can be brushed on with the grain. They are wiped with a rag to remove the surplus and equalize the color. Wiping is done while the stain is wet, but time should be allowed to ensure good penetration. The longer the stain is left on before wiping, the darker the finish.

Brush thoroughly a liberal quantity of filler in direction of grain. Padding-in (center) is done with a felt pad. Use circular motion to pack filler tightly into pores of the wood. Cut surplus filler from wood surface by towing-off as soon as filler starts to dry (bottom).

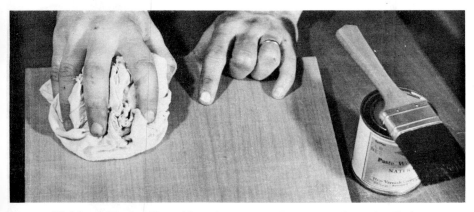

*Finish wiping the filler with a clean rag, stroking across the grain. If the filler sets too hard for easy wiping, moisten the wiping rag with benzine. If the pores are not filled level, apply a second coat of slightly thinner filler immediately, wiping off in the same way.*

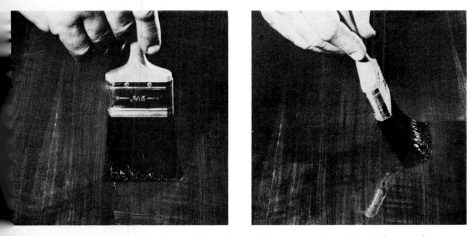

*Brush varnish on evenly and liberally, stroking across the grain of the wood first (left); follow immediately with light strokes with the grain (right)— always in the same direction. Finish a small area at a time and proceed quickly to the next area before edges have a chance to set; then brush from the dry area into the wet area.*

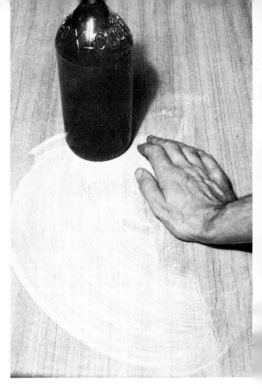

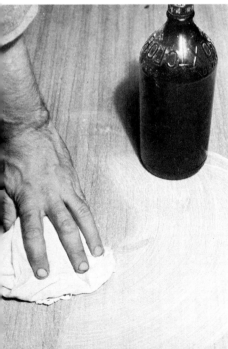

A varnished, lacquered, or shellacked surface can be rubbed with pumice or rottenstone. Mix with either water or oil (paraffin or mineral oil). Use a felt pad to rub the paste over the finished surface (left). Rub with the grain. On a shellac finish use pumice with oil, not water. Rub until desired finish is obtained. Expert finishers often simply rub the surface with the palm (right) instead of a pad. Clean the surface thoroughly with a soft rag after rubbing (bottom). Rottenstone is much finer than pumice and is used in much the same way.

piece of the same kind of wood to determine if the filler has been correctly prepared. Wipe the sample coat after it has set. When dry, examine the wood carefully. If pinholes are present, the mixture was either too thin or was not brushed thoroughly into the pores. If the pores are not well filled, the filler was wiped off too soon, or insufficient benzine was added. A cloudy surface indicates that rubbing was delayed too long or that the surface was not rubbed enough.

Paste filler should dry at least 12 hours unless it is a fast-drying type which is ready for coating in 3 to 4 hours. The slow-drying type is generally the best, and 24 to 48 hours is not too much time to allow for drying. In any case, it is of the greatest importance that the filler be bone dry before any other coating is applied. The surface that has been filled should be sanded lightly with fine garnet. Dust is removed with a cloth dampened with benzine.

Liquid fillers are applied in the same way as paste fillers. Check manufacturer's instructions for specific method.

### Staining filler

Wood fillers are sometimes used for staining as well as filling the pores; this is especially true in regard to walnut. Since this wood is dark, it requires only a little stain to give the desired shade. For two-tone finishes, use a transparent or natural filler with just a little color for the lighter shade, and a darker filler for the dark portion. Oil stain, usually brown or black, can be added to the filler to darken it.

### Sealing the filler

Whether or not you should seal the filler is largely a matter of preference. The same is true with regard to sealing the stain coat before applying filler. Generally, it is a good practice to seal both stain and filler on first-class work. A wash coat of shellac is the old standby; white shellac is used for light finishes and orange shellac for browns and mahoganies. Other materials are somewhat superior to ordinary shellac as sealer coats. Popular in small shops is shellac mixing lacquer. The shellac is first reduced with alcohol (4 to 1 for filler sealer; 7 to 1 for stain sealer), and is then poured slowly into an equal amount or less of mixing lacquer. This mixture brushes easier than straight shellac, is almost waterproof, and dries to recoat in about two hours. Any type of sealer coat over the filler should be sanded with very fine paper when dry, after which the work is ready for finishing coats of varnish or lacquer.

Applying a wash coat before filling offers the following advantages: (1) it may be used over oil stain as a seal; (2) it promotes better wiping of the filler; (3) it stiffens wood whiskers for sanding after the application of water stain. The wash coat must never be so heavy that it partly blocks the pores—properly applied, a wash coat over stain is invisible.

### Sealer for a varnish, lacquer, or paint base

Shellac has been recognized for years as an excellent undercoater or sealer before using varnish, lacquer, or paint. The shellac for varnish or paint surfaces is applied in the manner described in the section on sealing the filler. Use a 2-pound cut (see Chapter 7 for details on how to cut shellac). When the shellac is dry, it should be sanded with very fine paper.

Two coats of pure white shellac, thinned one-half, may be applied to wood as a base for most lacquers. Both coats should be sanded with very fine sandpaper. This reduces the amount of lacquer required and is economical in time and cost.

Another popular sealer for varnish and lacquer is a special product known as sanding sealer. It is made of a lacquer-shellac base, and it dries ready to recoat in about an hour. It brushes easily, has a good hard surface, and contains a sanding agent that permits clean, powdery sanding without gumming.

Other sealers and undercoaters are described in detail in later chapters.

### Sealing fir and other soft woods

Fir and some other softwoods need a good sealer because of the special character of the grain figure, which is made up of alternate hard summer growth and softer spring growth. If you do not use a sealer, the first coat of paint or stain penetrates unevenly and results in a "wild overconspicuous grain."

To tame or quiet this grain, several special types of resin sealers (see Chapter 13) have been developed. They may be purchased from lumber, paint, or hardware dealers. If the resin sealer is used properly, it allows the stain to soften the darker markings and deepen the lighter surfaces. The finish will be soft and lustrous, with the wild grain figures pleasantly subdued. For application details, follow the manufacturer's directions.

# CHAPTER SIX

# Varnish

**V**arnish makes an excellent transparent finish on wood; it is unequaled for depth or build and possesses good durability and hardness. It is made by mixing tough synthetic resins in oil-derived vehicles, along with driers and other chemicals. When the vehicle and drier evaporate, a durable film of resins remains that is heat-, impact-, abrasion-, alcohol-, chemical-, and water-resistant. Available in glossy, satin, or flat finishes, this film usually is dust-free in 1 to 4 hours, ready for handling in about 8 hours, and dry enough for sanding and recoating in about 24 hours.

In the first edition of this book, over a dozen special varnish mixtures were mentioned. Most of these consisted of natural copal gums and linseed oil mixed with turpentine. But except for some spar and rubbing types, natural-resin varnishes are things of the past. Today, the varnishes contain such man-made resins as alkyd, acrylic, phenolic, polyurethane, and vinyl. These synthetic-resin varnishes generally are easier to apply, last longer, and produce better than the old-time natural-resin types. Of course, when the next edition of this book is published, don't be surprised to read about silicone, epoxy, and water-emulsion varnishes. These materials, along with other synthetic resins, are now being tested and trial-manufactured. The synthetic-varnish-finish field is constantly changing.

### Which type of varnish to use

It is most difficult—for even expert wood finishers—to judge exactly the quality of all the synthetic resin varnishes in advance of their use. Since modern synthetic resin varnishes can be formulated to meet specific conditions by changing or mixing to achieve precise differences in hardness, scuff resistance, clarity, and chemical or water resistance, manufacturers are constantly changing products. For instance, one company recently marketed an excellent varnish by combining alkyd and vinyl resins and the result was a product that contained the good properties of both.

While the synthetic varnishes vary as to their formulations, there are certain characteristics of the resins that will help to predict the finish. For example, the polyurethane, acrylic, and vinyl types of varnish produce the clearest finish and show very little color change in the wood tone. On the other hand, phenolic varnish tends to turn yellow more readily in the same manner that natural-resin varnishes do.

Polyurethane varnish has the highest resistance to abrasion and is most resistant to ordinary chemicals and water. For instance, tests show that polyurethane lasts 25 percent longer than first quality spar varnishes—the old standard for varnish life—in exterior use. It has double the service life of first-grade natural varnishes when used on interior surfaces. While alkyds and phenolics are only slightly less resistant to abrasion and chemicals, they tend to be brittle. For this reason, they will usually scratch "white" and may show a series of fine cracks over a period of time if the wood is subjected to wide variations in humidity.

To be assured of a well-finished surface, purchase the varnish of well-known manufacturers. Never buy a cheap varnish. A small quantity of varnish covers a large area and a cheap grade will never result in a good or lasting finish.

### Rules for successful varnishing

The number one rule of success with synthetic varnishing is to read the container label very carefully, since instructions sometimes run counter to much common practice with regular varnishes. The following rules have been formulated over the years for natural-resin varnishes, and most—if not all—hold good for the new synthetic family.

*Temperature* The ideal room temperature for varnishing is between 65 and 75°F. Many manufacturers recommend that varnish should not be applied in temperatures below 60°F.

While most synthetic varnishes work well at room temperature, some flow better at varnish temperature of between 70 to 90°F. If you wish to experiment, the varnish can be heated by placing the can of varnish in a pail of warm water (about 110°F.) or let it stand near, *not on*, a hot radiator for a day or two. Do not let the varnish get hotter than 90°F., because hot varnish sets quickly and does not allow enough time for cross brushing.

To digress for a moment, it is sometimes necessary, as with varnish, to heat the finishing material for better spreading characteristics. Since most of these substances contain a flammable solvent, extreme care must be taken to keep them from an open flame, sparks, or red-hot heating coils. The best way to assure this is to use either a pot of boiling water, removed from the heat source, or a self-contained electric cooker or frypan.

**Moisture** Most varnishes are made to perform perfectly in normal humidity. However, it is best to keep the windows closed in a room that has been freshly varnished if the weather is excessively hot and humid or cold and misty.

**Ventilation** A room soon becomes filled with fumes given off by varnish, using up the oxygen in the room and slowing down the drying process. Therefore, the more frequently you ventilate the room, the more rapidly the varnish will dry hard. However, do not allow drafts to blow directly upon the fresh varnish because this will cause it to dry flat.

**Dust** Beautiful workmanship is often marred by floating dust settling on the surface. If practical, keep down the dust by sprinkling the floor with water or wet sawdust. If the floor is cement, wipe it with a damp mop. Use clean, fresh paper under your work. Cover your hair with a cap or kerchief, and wear a clean cotton coverall work apron. Do not wear clothing that sheds dust, such as wool or any coarsely woven cloth. Most important, do all sanding and dusting in a separate room—not in the one where you will be varnishing.

Do not pour back into the varnish can any leftover varnish in the cup or container you have been using to apply the varnish. The brush picks up and transfers dust and other impurities that will contaminate all the varnish if this residue is poured back.

**Bubbles**   You can avoid the formation of small bubbles by being careful never to shake the can or stir the varnish. This, of course, applies only to clear varnish. Colored varnishes, or varnish stains, have to be stirred to distribute the coloring material evenly.

Improper pouring can also cause bubbles to form. Pour varnish from the standard-type, rectangular varnish can with the outlet spout up—or the reverse of the way one would naturally pour from a can; that is, with the outlet downward and as close as possible to the container being filled.

**Mixing**   Never mix two different types of varnish, or varnishes made by different manufacturers. Each varnish may be excellent, but they may not blend well and cause trouble. A thinning varnish can be thinned with pure turpentine, mineral spirits, or a high-grade special thinner if recommended by the varnish manufacturer. A first coat of varnish on raw wood requires considerable thinning, but following coats should be thinned very little, if at all, and the final coat should be full strength.

**Straining**   Modern fast-drying varnishes, when left in the varnish cup for any length of time, harden on top and form a skin. You can strain the varnish by pouring it through clean cheesecloth.

Experienced finishers, however, find this unsatisfactory because lint and minute threads can be carried into the varnish. For best results, prepare your filter material in advance by dipping the cheesecloth in thin glue size made with urea-resin or casein glue (4 parts water to 1 part glue).

Spread out the cheesecloth to dry, then cut into pieces convenient for filtering. This may seem like unnecessary trouble, but a really good varnish job requires meticulous care to avoid the surface defects.

### Preparation and equipment

The surface to be varnished should be completely dry—free from moisture, oil, and grease, including film left by fingers and hands. Varnishing over moisture can cause blistering and other annoying defects.

Surfaces treated with wash coat, filler, or stain must be completely dry and hard before the varnish is applied. If the undercoat is not hard-dry, the final coat may craze, flake, and crack.

*Sanding and dusting*    The secret of obtaining smooth, first-class work depends to a great extent on the preparation of the wood (see Chapter 2). For a smooth, level surface use sandpaper. *Then remove all traces of dust.*

Use a brush for all the preliminary dusting, and be sure to clean out all corners.

When you are varnishing pieces of furniture that need refinishing, be sure that there are no traces of wax left on the wood. Work of this nature may be thoroughly cleaned of wax by washing the surface with alcohol.

*Tacking*    The final dusting operation is done with a rag moistened with varnish, and is called tacking. The tack rag picks up the small particles of dust which no amount of brushing ever removes completely.

You can purchase tack rags at your paint store, or make them yourself if you wish. To make a tack rag, take a piece of closely woven cheesecloth or a well-worn white cotton handkerchief, wet it with warm water, and squeeze lightly.

Then wet it in turpentine and shake it out loosely. Now dribble varnish freely over the cloth; fold and twist it into a tight roll to force out the water; then repeat the twisting until the varnish and turpentine are distributed evenly. Use enough varnish to make the cloth quite yellow. It should be sticky enough to pick up dust but not enough to leave moisture on the furniture. The edges of the cloth should always be folded inside to give it a smooth finish. If the rag should dry out while in use, sprinkle a few drops of turpentine and water over it. If it is too moist, shake it in the air for a few minutes.

When not in use, store the tack rag in a covered glass jar to keep it soft and to prevent it from becoming a fire hazard. Never let it dry out. To keep it in condition, periodically unfold the rag, sprinkle it with a few drops of water and turpentine, and wring it out. The rag will last indefinitely and actually improve with age.

**Brushes** For average work use a full-chisel varnish brush about 2 inches wide. You will also want to have on hand two or three brushes of various kinds and sizes in order to handle every job to best advantage. Brushes must be kept clean and properly stored after use. (See Chapter 3 for specific information on brushes.)

Varnish should never be used directly from the can. Pour a small amount into a separate container—a small aluminum saucepan about 4½ inches across by 2½ inches deep is best. The handle of the pan should be shortened and rolled over to form a comfortable loop for the thumb. Stretch a wire (called a strike wire) across the pan, opposite the thumb loop, and use it to wipe your brush on. Do not wipe the brush on the edge of container, as the granules of dried varnish on the rim will fall down into the varnish. Incidentally, varnish cups with a strike wire already attached are available at most paint stores.

### How to apply varnish

First, dip the brush into the varnish, and brush it back and forth on clean, heavy wrapping paper—never newspaper or other paper that gives off lint—to work the varnish evenly through the bristles. Too much varnish on the brush will cause it to drip or run onto the handle. For this reason, never dip the brush into the varnish by more than one-third its length, and always remove any excess from the brush on the strike wire before applying it to the surface.

When brushing varnish, hold the brush much as you do a pencil, using an easy wrist motion. Hold the brush at a low angle so that all the varnish will flow from the bristles. Be careful to use light, even strokes. Too much pressure on the brush can cause bubbles to form.

Brushing will consist of three operations—cutting in, cross-brushing, and tipping off (see illustrations page 128):

In *cutting in*, start from the corners and work toward the center. On some work it may be necessary to use a smaller brush.

Next, *cross-brush* the panel, starting at either side and running halfway across. Lift the brush quickly as the strokes overlap.

Finally, wipe off the brush on the strike wire to remove all excess paint. Now brush lightly with the grain with only the tips of the bristles touching the surface. This operation is called *tipping off*. Always brush from the edge to the center, overlapping in the middle. Clean the brush on the strike wire after each stroke.

Tabletops and similar large flat surfaces should be worked

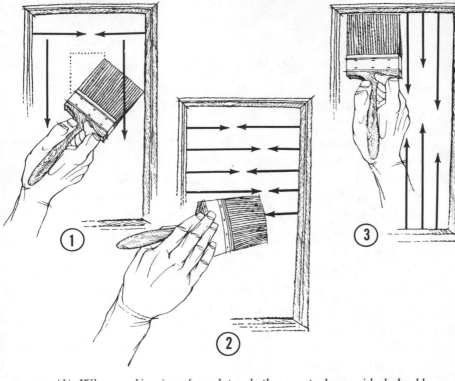

(1) When working in a framed panel, the area to be varnished should first be cut in, using a suitable small brush. (2) Cross-brushing should be done next across the grain, applying a full-bodied coat. (3) Tipping off should then be done with a nearly dry brush, which should just barely touch the varnish coat.

On large surfaces, brush varnish with the grain and from center to ends, never from end to end.

in much the same way, except that cross-brushing may be eliminated. Instead, apply the flow coat with the grain, beginning on the side away from you, and work from the center, brushing to the right and left. Now tip the surface, using a running stroke from one end of the work to the other, with the bristles of the brush barely touching the work. If you don't catch runs, sags, curtains, dry spots, or other potential surface blemishes while tipping off in a given area, forget about them until the surface is hardened. At that time, sand them level as described later in this chapter, and build up with the next coat. Any rebrushing of a partially set area can cause other problems.

Finish the edges with a small brush, working from the center toward each corner. Do not let the brush run over onto the wet varnish coat on the surface.

On vertical surfaces, the procedure should be changed slightly to prevent curtains or sags on the finished work. Employ short, quick strokes, working an area of about 6 inches square, back and forth across the surface, starting from a corner at the top. Then tip off the surface, by brushing down halfway and up halfway, so that the brush is lifted from the surface in the central portion. When varnishing objects that may be easily lifted, turn the item upside down, place on a work bench (boards on saw horses are good) and complete the entire understructure first, and then do the upper part.

Turnings are more difficult to varnish than flat surfaces. The best method is to brush all intricate turnings round and round. Certain parts of the work can then be tipped with lengthwise strokes. Be especially careful not to draw the brush over the sharp edges of the turnings, because the varnish has a tendency to sag at these points.

Despite care, specks of dust and bubbles will show on the finished varnish coat. Dirt specks can be distinguished from bubbles by the highlight that shows on the surface of the bubble. The bubbles will disappear as the varnish sets, but dust specks must be removed. Take a clean sliver of wood and lightly touch the dirt speck. It will cling to the wood and the wet varnish will flow together to produce a smooth surface. This process is called *picking* and should be done as the work progresses. It is useless to pick the surface after the varnish has started to dry.

Many workers prefer to use burnt varnish for picking. *To make it:* Put a quantity of crushed rosin in a small can. Place it in a pan of water, and heat until rosin melts. Add 1 part of varnish to 6 parts of rosin and mix well. This mixture will keep indefinitely. *To use it:* With a stick, pick up a small amount of the mixture, roll it between your moistened fingers, and place this ball on the end of the stick. (Swab sticks, available in all drug stores, are very good for this purpose.) Lightly apply the ball to dust specks, and as each speck is lifted, embed it in the burnt varnish by rolling the ball with your moistened thumb.

If a loose bristle lies on the just completed varnish surface, remove it by jabbing at one end of it gently with the tips of the brush. It will lodge between the bristles and can be picked off the brush with the fingers. The surface can be leveled with a quick brush stroke or, after it has dried, by scuffing with an abrasive paper.

The first varnish coat goes on better if it is slightly thinned. Use 1 part of pure turpentine or thinner to 6 parts of varnish. Do not mix more than you will need for one coat. Stir thoroughly. The thinned varnish must stand overnight before using so that the varnish will completely absorb the turpentine.

When an undercoater such as shellac has been used, apply the varnish as it comes from the can. Unthinned varnish should be used on all following coats. It can be used for the first coat directly on bare wood, but it should be applied thin, that is brushed out instead of being flowed on. It is important to keep in mind that while a shellac undercoater works well under most varnishes, there are some polyurethane-base varnishes that do not adhere well to shellac.

Two coats of varnish should give a good surface if the work has been properly filled, but three and four coats are commonly used on first-class work. Each coat must be thoroughly dry before the next is applied. For the best varnish finish follow the manufacturer's instructions most carefully. Many of the synthetic varnishes have very specific directions. For instance, one popular resin is ready for recoat after 4 hours and up to 8. If it is not recoated in that time period, you must wait the full 48-hour drying time. With this specific varnish, there is a 4-hour period shortly after it is applied when there is a slight softening and bonding action between the two coats. If not recoated during this period, the surface becomes too hard for good adhesion, and it must be left for 48 hours, then scuff-sanded. If a varnish does not have specific instructions by the manufacturer, allow at least 48 hours between varnish applications. Remember that most varnishes become progressively harder, and the harder the surface, the better the sanding and rubbing job that can be accomplished.

Test each coat for hardness by pressing it with your thumbnail. If the varnish does not take an impression of the nail, it is safe to proceed with the next coat. In "educating" your thumbnail for the hardness test, experiment on old varnish to determine the amount of pressure that indicates total hardness.

After the first or any prefinal coat dries—unless specifically directed not to do so by the manufacturer—scuff-sand lightly with very fine or extra fine abrasive paper to remove the gloss and ensure good adhesion. When sanding, be sure to level the "whiskers" of any raised grain as well as dust "nibs." Use only enough pressure to dull the sheen and produce a uniform, level, satiny-smooth finish; but be careful not to sand through the finish, especially at the edges. In fact, when leveling a large surface, such as a tabletop, sand with the grain of the wood toward the ends first and then near the sides, taking extreme care not to rub the finish from the edges or the corners. Then sand the center section with the grain, using long strokes, with an even pressure. Never rub crossgrain or in circles.

When level application defects, such as sags, drips, and curtains occur, keep in mind that it takes longer for these to dry than the surrounding surfaces, because of their thickness. If an attempt to level such defects is made before they are hardened completely, the sanding action will cut through to the bare wood, making it necessary that the job be done over since no later coats would cover a depression of this type. It is also a good idea to cut a thick defect (raised surface) down only part way. Then remove the dust, and let the item dry again for several days. This extra precaution will usually eliminate the necessity of doing the job over. Steel wool (either 3/0 or 4/0 grade) can be used to scarify recesses and depressions that cannot be reached by normal sanding methods.

When the scuffing action is completed, dust the entire surface thoroughly by brush, and follow by wiping with a tack rag before applying the next coat. After the final coat has dried completely, the surface may be rubbed to a satin finish, following directions given in Chapter 9. If a rub finish is not desired, simply leave the final coat alone.

Any type of varnish can be sprayed at can consistency, although a thinning of 3 parts varnish to 1 part thinner is necessary for small compressing units with a suction-feed gun. You can also heat the varnish immediately before spraying to increase the flow. (Spray-gun techniques are found in Chapter 3.)

### Application of varnish stain

Varnish stain generally can be used as it comes from the can. Should it become thick through exposure to the air, reduce with turpentine to easy brushing consistency. Do not shake the can before opening, as this produces bubbles. Stir with a spatula or clean stick.

One or two coats of varnish stain may be required to obtain a finished surface. Before applying the second coat, always remove the luster of the first coat with fine sandpaper or steel wool.

### Varnishing problems and how to remedy them

*Crawling*  The varnish acts like oil that has been applied to a wet surface; it fails to adhere to the surface, but crawls or forms in waves. CAUSES:

Varnish applied to a wet, greasy, or cold surface.
The surface had too high a gloss.

Varnish applied over previous coats that are sweaty or not hard and dry.

Dirty and sweaty finger marks on the surface being varnished.

A film of soap, left after washing the surface without properly rinsing it with clean water.

Oil in the varnish brush.

The condition of the drier, causing the varnish to dry too rapidly. When varnish is manufactured, the correct amount and the right kind of drier has been used. Do not add any drier, as chemical reactions may result.

The mixing together of two or more cans of varnish.

The wrong kind of thinner. If a can of varnish remains open for any length of time, permitting the liquid to become thick, it may be thinned with pure turpentine or the specific thinner recommended by the manufacturer, in small quantities. Never use benzine or linseed oil.

Quick changes in weather conditions—from warm to cold, from dry to damp, or the presence of cold drafts.

Oil in the wood, particularly in cypress. To prevent crawling when this is the cause, give the entire piece a thin coat of oil ($\frac{2}{3}$ linseed oil, $\frac{1}{3}$ turpentine) before varnishing. This will equalize the absorption and cause the varnish to flow evenly. After applying oil, give it 24 to 48 hours to dry. Just before varnishing, wipe the surface clean with a cloth dipped in turpentine. This will remove excess oil that might not have dried thoroughly.

Any temperature below 60°F. Varnish applied under these conditions is too heavy to flow properly and remains in thick and thin spots. Low temperatures cause not only crawling but wrinkling or puckering.

*Running or sagging*   This is another common defect, especially on vertical surfaces. It is sometimes called curtaining. CAUSES:

Most likely to occur near moldings or carvings because they will act as wipers, taking varnish off the brush and depositing it in corners. Do not use a full brush when working near these areas.

Varnish that is too new will run. Like many things, varnish must be aged before it can be used. A reliable manufacturer will not sell varnish that is too new. Slow-drying, elastic, or spar varnishes are subject to sagging because more oil is used in their manufacture. They require considerably more brushing and working than quick-drying, hard varnishes and must be thinly and evenly distributed.

*Wrinkling*   Caused by too thick application. The outer surface then absorbs more oxygen and dries faster than the under surface, causing an airtight film. The under portion of this film contracts as the thinner evaporates, resulting in the wrinkled effect.

*Silking or enameling*   The varnish coat becomes grainy and fibrous in appearance. CAUSES:

Application of varnish in an unheated room. When varnish is cold, it cannot be brushed on properly. Remember that the temperature of the room and varnish should be at least 65°F.

Varnish laid over paint or other varnish that is not thoroughly dry.

Excessive brushing caused by the addition of too much turpentine.

**Sand or gritty texture** Sometimes occurs after the coat has been allowed to dry for about an hour. CAUSES:

Varnish has not been aged, and consequently the various ingredients have not blended together.

Chilled varnish will have small bits of gum resin, oil, or driers that have become congealed by the cold. Exposure of varnish to freezing weather will break down the mixture. The remedy is to heat the varnish by placing the entire can in a pail of hot water (kept at 110°F) for half an hour or more.

Particles left from rubbing down preceding coat. It is common practice to rub down each coat of varnish with fine sandpaper or steel wool before applying the next one. If the abrasive grits or steel-wool particles are not thoroughly removed, the result will be a sandy surface on the following coat.

**Pinholing or pitting** The formation of small holes is a common defect. CAUSES:

Mixing of different brands of varnish

Change in atmospheric conditions such as from dry to damp

Applying varnish in rooms that are very hot or very cold

Brushing varnish over a surface that is not dry

Placing cold varnish on a warm surface or warm varnish on a cold surface

Lack of proper ventilation and uniform temperature

Brushes that have been kept in linseed oil and were not properly cleaned in turpentine (see Chapter 3)

*Sweating*    Varnish that has been rubbed to a dull finish will sometimes change back to a greasy gloss (see Chapter 3) This is called sweating. CAUSES:

> Application of varnish over undercoaters that were not permitted to dry thoroughly
>
> Rubbing down of a varnish coat before it is hard and dry

The best remedy is to allow it to stand as long as possible before applying another coat

*Sinking*    Open-grained wood that has not been filled sufficiently or filler that has not been rubbed in correctly will cause the varnish to sink. If the filler has not been rubbed in properly, the varnish coats will drop or sink into the pores of the wood.

*Tacky, slow-drying surface*    Poor air, lack of proper ventilation, dirt, or grease are some of the causes.

# CHAPTER SEVEN

# Shellac

While shellac's popularity as a top-coat finish has decreased slightly in recent years, it is still favored by many craftsmen because of easy application and quick drying. For many purposes shellac is superior to varnish as a wood finish. It is a very hard gum and withstands a great deal of wear. It has a pleasant luster and brilliance not found in most varnishes, and can be rubbed to a fine finish. It penetrates well into the surface of the wood, filling the pores thoroughly, and it helps to bring out the wood's natural beauty. A thin coat of shellac forms an excellent base for a wax finish; (see page 144), it is probably one of the most beautiful finishes obtainable.

The disadvantages of shellac are that it stains easily,

has poor resistance to water, and none to alcohol. Wet glasses, vases, and similar objects will usually produce white rings on a shellac finish, and hot plates and dishes will cause further damage. For these reasons, shellac should not be used on tabletops, bureaus, bar tops, or other furniture on which wet glasses, alcoholic beverages, or hot objects might be placed or spilled.

### Types of shellac

Shellac is sold in solid granular form or as a liquid when dissolved in alcohol. The liquid shellac is ready for use and is available in three stages of purification: orange, bleached (or white), and dewaxed. *Orange shellac* consists of partially refined shellac flakes dissolved in alcohol. It has a pronounced reddish brown color and is cloudy in appearance. *White or bleached shellac* is a similar solution but is made from bleached resin. *Dewaxed shellac* is usually light in color, but, unlike the other two, it is wax-free and thus perfectly clear.

The three forms are very much alike. However, white (clear) shellac is best for most work and is essential for blond finishes. Orange shellac is used for dark wood or over darkly stained woods. Intermixing white and orange shellac to obtain color effects is not advisable. Should deeper colors be desired to tone a finish where the stain does not seem exactly right, a transparent toner may be used. It can be made by mixing alcohol-soluble powder stain with alcohol and adding it to the shellac as required. The same method can be used to darken lacquer and varnish finishes, using lacquer-soluble and oil-soluble powder, respectively.

One fault of shellac is that in time it goes stale. About a year after it has been made, a chemical change causes the shellac to become so gummy that it will not dry. Some shellac companies date their containers. You can then estimate whether you will be able to use up the contents before the expiration date. Other manufacturers just permit you to guess how long the material may have been on the dealer's shelves. If this might be the case, the shellac should be purchased in small amounts as needed, from a store where there is a good turnover.

When purchasing shellac, always get the best grade. Avoid so-called "shellac substitutes," which are generally composed of cheap resins and contain little or no genuine shellac. These do not dry as hard as genuine shellac, they scratch and mark easily, and they will not stand hard usage.

## Thinning

The concentration of shellac in alcohol is known as its "cut." Most shellac on the market is 3-, 4-, or 5-pound cut; that is, 3, 4, or 5 pounds of granular shellac is dissolved in one gallon of alcohol. The cut is indicated on the label. For almost all purposes, commercial shellac will require thinning with alcohol. Here is a table showing how to convert one cut to another.

| Original cut | | Desired cut | Mixing Ratio | | |
|---|---|---|---|---|---|
| | | | Alcohol | | Shellac |
| 5-lb cut | to | 4-lb cut | 1 part | to | 4 parts |
| 5-lb cut | to | 3-lb cut | 1 part | to | 2 parts |
| 5-lb cut | to | 2-lb cut | 1 part | to | 1 part |
| 5-lb cut | to | 1-lb cut | 2 parts | to | 1 part |
| 5-lb cut | to | ½-lb cut | 7 parts | to | 1 part |
| 4-lb cut | to | 3-lb cut | 1 part | to | 4 parts |
| 4-lb cut | to | 2-lb cut | 3 parts | to | 4 parts |
| 4-lb cut | to | 1-lb cut | 3 parts | to | 1 part |
| 4-lb cut | to | ½-lb cut | 5 parts | to | 1 part |
| 3-lb cut | to | 2-lb cut | 2 parts | to | 5 parts |
| 3-lb cut | to | 1-lb cut | 4 parts | to | 3 parts |
| 3-lb cut | to | ½-lb cut | 4 parts | to | 1 part |

For all ordinary work use:

1 quart    1 pint

To convert a 5-lb cut to a 2-lb cut, use:

1 quart    1 quart

To convert a 4-lb cut to a 3-lb cut, use:

1 quart    ½ pint

To convert a 4-lb cut to a 2-lb cut, use:

1 quart    1½ pints

SHELLAC

Using this table, you will be able to convert any quantity. The word "parts" in the table refers to liquid volume. Any convenient unit, such as quarts, pints, or cupfuls, can be used. For example, if you wished to thin a pint of 5-pound cut to 2-pound cut, you would use 1 pint of alcohol to 1 pint of shellac. When thinning the cut, use only pure denatured ethyl or grain alcohol. Never use acetone, benzol, gasoline, or the antifreeze grade of alcohol.

When shellac is used as a furniture finish, it is often mixed with a nitrocellulose solution called mixing lacquer. The resulting mixture flows better than shellac, dries faster, and sands and rubs more easily. A good mixture is made from 2 parts of 4- to 5-pound cut, 1 part of mixing lacquer, and 3 parts of alcohol.

There are several substances which you can add to shellac to make it dry more slowly and, therefore, brush on more easily. Some finishers use a few drops of almond oil or Venice turpentine, although 1 ounce of pure gum camphor to a gallon of shellac probably works best.

Keep all containers closed, when not in use, to keep out dirt and dust and to reduce evaporation of the alcohol. Store shellac only in glass, wooden, or lead-lined containers—never in an ordinary metal container. Protect it from exposure to sunlight and air until used.

### Application

Shellac may be applied by brushing or spraying. Two rather unique methods—French polishing and the dip-and-rub method—are described later.

Before you use shellac, shake or stir it thoroughly. The first two coats should be thinned to a 1- or 2-pound-cut consistency, while a 3- or 4-pound cut is best for final coat. As stated in Chapter 4, ½-pound cut is ideal for a wash coat before staining, and a ½- or 1-pound cut makes a good sanding sealer.

To apply shellac, use a soft varnish brush. Brush the shellac on with the grain in long running strokes—one stroke to apply, one stroke to tip off. Work quickly, and do not brush back and forth over the surface. If you brush excessively, the shellac will pile up in ridges and show laps. Sags, runs, and brush marks can be smoothed out by lightly stroking the wet surface with the tips of the bristles. If you miss a spot, let it go until the next coat, as it is very difficult to do any touching up without damaging the finish.

Allow 2 to 4 hours for drying between first and second coats and 6 to 8 hours between subsequent coats. To remove specks and dirt between coats, go over with extra fine paper or 3/0 grade steel wool after the shellac has dried. Sandpaper with the grain of the wood. After each sanding, brush the surface, and rub with a cloth dampened with benzine to remove the dust before applying another coat. When sanding, use either cheap flint paper or one of the open-coated papers, because shellac will gum it up rapidly. Of course, the open-coated paper can be washed and brushed out with alcohol, dried, and reused.

In general, take the same precautions when applying shellac as outlined in Chapter 6 for varnish. Shellac is very thirsty; therefore avoid muggy, warm days for your shellac work. Never apply shellac over a damp surface, for the moisture will cause the shellac to cloud. Two thin coats are always better than one thick one; it not only gives a better finish but makes brushing much easier.

When you are applying the shellac with a spray gun, avoid excessive air pressure—30 to 40 pounds pressure is about right. Too much pressure may produce "orange peel"—an undesirable rippled finish.

On rare occasions, shellac may darken oak or fir. This is usually due to a reaction between iron-contaminated shellac (caused by storing in the wrong type of container) and the tannic acid in the wood. It can usually be remedied by applying a solution which is made by dissolving 4 ounces of oxalic acid in a gallon of 2-pound-cut shellac. Brush this over the discolored surface. One coat will usually be sufficient, but two may be required.

Rub with steel wool to give a semidull finish to the shellac. For a flat finish, use pumice stone and oil. See Chapter 9 for instructions on the application of these finishes.

### French polishing

This is one of the most beautiful and lasting of all finishes, and has been used for generations on fine period furniture.

Prepare the surface with painstaking care. Stain with water stain only, and allow to dry thoroughly. Then, thin white shellac with alcohol or commercial shellac solvent to a thin consistency—approximately a 1-pound cut. Apply to the wood with a soft, lintless cloth which is rolled into a ball. Dip the cloth into the shellac and rub onto the wood in rapid, straight strokes, using light pressure. When it is dry, sand the wood and repeat the process. Apply repeated coats, sanding each one smooth, until a light glow begins to appear. The surface can be sprinkled lightly with very fine pumice stone before sanding (see page 171).

After the first few coats, a faint sheen will develop. At this point add several drops of oil to the shallac mixture—boiled linseed oil or pure olive oil—and continue the applications, but changing over to a rotary motion. Add more oil gradually to subsequent coats. The result will be a superb, deeply glowing finish that, with ordinary care, should endure through several lifetimes.

## Dip-and-rub finish

This finish is simpler and easier than French polishing, but results in a finish almost as satisfactory.

If the wood is stained, brush on one thin coat of shellac to set the stain. When this coat is dry, sand with extra fine sandpaper or rub with No. 3/0 or 4/0 steel wool.

Use two saucers—one containing pure turpentine, the other white shellac (4-pound cut). Roll a lintless cloth into a pad and dip first into the turpentine, then into shellac. Rub this onto the wood with a rotary motion until the entire surface is treated. Apply subsequent coats in the same way. Four or five such coats will give a rich, soft gloss. Wet-sand (see page 170) between coats. After this gloss has dried for 18 hours, a still higher polish can be obtained by further rubbing with the cloth dipped in linseed oil only.

# CHAPTER EIGHT

# Lacquers and Synthetics

Lacquers and synthetics produce artistic and very attractive finishes that can be applied with great rapidity, dry with astonishing speed, and can resist water and also alcohol to a considerable extent. Although lacquer and synthetic are entirely different terms, these finishes are grouped together here since they represent the modern developments in finishing materials.

## LACQUERS

The original "lacquer" is an oriental product made by Chinese and Japanese artists from the sap of a plant closely related to our poison ivy. Some of the finer Oriental furniture pieces were finished with over 300 coats of these lacquers and have lasted for centuries.

The principal feature of lacquers is the very rapid drying (fully hardened in 30 minutes to 2 hours), and there is no dust problem when using them. The film is hard, durable, and waterproof, and will not become soft or touchy at high temperatures. Of all the top finishes lacquers also darken wood the least. This is especially true when a lacquer lightener is employed which will leave the wood almost at its sanded color.

### Types of lacquers

*Clear gloss lacquer* A clean lacquer that dries with a glossy finish. It is thinned with lacquer thinner and is applied by spraying. Additional coats can be applied after 1 to 2 hours. They can be rubbed, but a longer drying time should then be allowed.

*Clear flat lacquer* Same as above, except that it dries flat. It can be mixed in any proportion with a similar brand of gloss lacquer.

*Lacquer enamel* Merely a colored lacquer, which can give a flat, satin, or gloss finish.

*Lacquer tinting colors* Colors made with concentrated lacquer which are mixed with clear lacquer to make lacquer enamels.

*Brushing lacquer* Slow-drying lacquer suitable for application with a soft brush. It is available as a clear lacquer and in all colors.

*Water-white lacquer* Exceptionally clear, water-white lacquer which is used on extreme blond finishes, metals, and other products where a protective coating of great transparency is required.

*Buffing lacquer* Very hard lacquer made especially for buffing to a high polish. It comes either clear or in colors.

**Rubbing and polishing lacquer**    Made especially for rubbing and polishing, these are simply the better grades of lacquer or lacquer enamel.

**Vinyl lacquer**    A very hard synthetic lacquer that is available in gloss or flat finishes.

**Metallic lacquer**    Clear or colored lacquer with a metallic luster.

**Bronzing lacquer**    Clear lacquer for mixing with bronze powders to produce metallic effects.

**Shading lacquer**    This transparent lacquer is available in various wood colors and is used for shading and highlighting.

**Novelty lacquers**    These are used for textured effects such as crackle, wrinkle, and Jack Frost.

**Shellac-mixing lacquer**    This is a clear lacquer suitable for mixing with shellac. It can be used "as is" or in combination with shellac.

**Bar-top lacquer**    Proof against mild acids and alcohols. Because it is very durable, it is used for bar and table tops.

**Rubbed-effect lacquer**    Similar to clear flat lacquer, this type is available in various grades of flatting from dead flat to semigloss. It is used to imitate a rubbed surface.

**Automotive lacquer**    These lacquer enamels are made especially for automobile finishing. When several layers of this material are applied to wood, it approximates the old-time Oriental lacquer finish.

**Dipping lacquer**    Made for lacquer finishing by the dipping method. It is available in clear lacquer and in enamels.

**Bleaching lacquer**    A water-white thin lacquer, the kind of finish which is required on extremely light-colored woods.

**Blonding lacquer**    A thin white lacquer used to obtain a blond tone. It can be made by adding 1 part white lacquer to 4 or 5 parts clear lacquer.

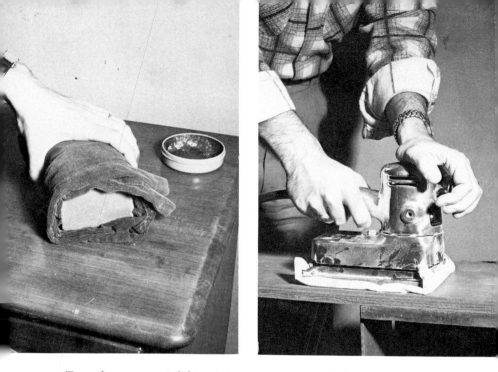

To make your wax-polishing task easier, wrap several thicknesses of soft cloth around a brick. This gives the needed weight to the polishing pad (top left). A sander may also be used as a polisher (top right). On turnings, apply paste wax with a cloth. Then, to polish, wrap a clean soft cloth around the work and pull it back and forth (bottom).

Most soft woods do not require a filler; but it is a good idea to seal the wood with a wash coat of shellac, diluted half-and-half with denatured alcohol. Brush shellac on rapidly. When dry, smooth lightly with No. 3/0 steel wool.

*Then apply the undercoater. Do not overload the brush. Watch for runs and sags, brushing them out before they harden. Allow undercoater to dry at least 24 hours, and then go over the piece with fine sandpaper to remove lapmarks and bumps. Use a light touch; it is easy to cut through the soft undercoat to the bare wood. Dust the surface with a turpentine-soaked rag before applying enamel.*

To paint furniture knobs, push their screws up through a piece of heavy cardboard, and then attach the knobs to the screws as pictured above. When painting furniture legs, you can generally do a smoother job if they are raised slightly off the floor by driving a large tack part way into the bottom of each leg. You can then paint to the very bottom of the leg without difficulty.

*Nonlifting lacquer*   Intended for refinishing over varnish. If thinning is required, a nonlifting (high alcohol) thinner should be used.

### Lacquer thinners

Lacquer thinners are generally classified by their evaporation or drying time—fast, medium, or slow. Fast-drying thinners are the cheapest, although there is quite a difference between a cheap fast drier and a good fast drier. The tendency is to use a fast-drying thinner because of lower cost and to speed the work, but the use of these is the most common cause of blushing, particularly in warm, muggy weather. An extremely fast-drying thinner also contributes to an orange-peel finish, since the coating hardens too quickly for proper leveling. When fast driers are sprayed, they can cause a sandy surface, because the spray is often nothing but a dry dust when it reaches the work. Therefore, use a fast-drying thinner with some discretion.

Always be sure to use the thinner recommended by the manufacturer of the lacquer. In fact, it is a good idea to purchase enough thinner by the same manufacturer to complete the job. Slight differences in lacquer thinner formulations can cause adhesion, blemish, and drying problems.

The thinners used with lacquer are usually blended mixtures and may contain two or more fluids mixable with lacquer. Some of these are true solvents of nitrocellulose, but others become solvents only when in combination with true solvents already in the lacquer itself or as a part of the thinner. The cheaper, nonsolvent materials, such as denatured alcohol, benzol, toluol, and xylol, form the greater part of the thinner, together with lesser amounts of true solvents (ethyl acetate, ethyl lactate, butyl acetate). Thinners with a high percentage of slow-drying solvents are known as re-tarders. They are used to slow the drying time of the lacquer to prevent blushing and to improve flow and leveling qualities.

### Lacquer finishing schedule

The basic lacquer finishing schedule does not differ materially from the basic varnish schedule. It is simply a case of stain, fill, and lacquer, instead of stain, fill, and varnish. In the final analysis, the lacquer finish is dependent upon good spraying or brushing technique. The complete lacquer schedule from bare wood to final finish is treated here.

The best lacquer finishes are made as follows:

1. Sponge all bare surfaces with water to which a small quantity of glue (1 tablespoon to a pint of water) has been added.
2. When the surfaces have dried, sand them with a very fine sandpaper, working with the grain.
3. After making a sample test, brush or spray all surfaces with a water stain of the desired color.
4. Allow time for complete drying, preferably overnight.
5. Apply a very thin coat of lacquer sealer (1 part sealer to 6 parts of lacquer thinner) or a wash coat of shellac (1 part of shellac to 7 parts of alcohol).
6. Sandpaper very lightly lengthwise of the grain, using a very fine dry sandpaper over a soft felt pad. WARNING: Be *careful not to cut through the stain when sanding.*
7. Fill with special fast-drying wood filler made for use under lacquer. Fillers without linseed oil are the most satisfactory. Use a rather heavy paste filler for open-pored woods and a thinner filler on woods with small pores. Nonporous woods require no filler.

8. Apply with a spray gun or brush one coat of "sanding sealer" over the fast-drying filler.

9. Sand smooth with very fine sandpaper, preferably used wet, over a soft felt pad.

10. Apply two coats of gloss finishing lacquer, preferably with a spray gun. If you are working in a small shop or at home you may use brushing lacquer instead. Sanding between coats is unnecessary unless there is some roughness.

11. Gloss lacquers may be rubbed and polished. A coat of velvet or flat lacquer may be substituted for the last coat of gloss lacquer. They will not need rubbing.

### Staining before applying lacquer

Either water or NGR are preferred when the top coat is lacquer. Many spirit and oil stains are not lacquer "compatible." That is, they either dissolve or soften and lift themselves into the lacquer layer. If a pigmented wiping stain is used, allow at least 48 hours for it to completely dry. Otherwise, the lacquer thinner may act in somewhat the same fashion as a paint and varnish remover.

The stain can be brushed or sprayed; a uniform surface is easily obtained by spraying. The work should be sanded with fine paper immediately before staining. Dust from sanding should be loosened with a stiff brush and blown off with the gun, being careful to clean right down to the bottom of the pores. Dust-filled pores make the wood difficult to fill, and may also cause graying of the filler by contributing to slow drying. Allow the stain coat to dry thoroughly before applying filler.

### Applying filler before lacquering

Filler of the silica-base type (see page 113), is still the most popular filler under lacquer despite the introduction of new base materials. Many manufacturers have modified their formulas with silex, producing a filler material which is satisfactory under either varnish or lacquer. (In such fillers, check label to make sure filler contains silica before using with lacquer.) The drying time is about 3 hours. The paste filler should be cut with naphtha or gasoline, using about 3 pounds of paste to a quart of thinner for average work. The filler is brushed on, padded in, and then wiped as soon as it shows flat. Because of the light body of the clear lacquer coat, good filling with perfectly flush pores is important. The filler should be allowed to dry the specified time. Do not rush this stage of the finish—filler not thoroughly dry causes many lacquer failures.

Special fillers that are also made for use under sanding sealers and lacquers are now substituted for standard paste fillers that are commonly used under varnishes. Generally paste fillers contain linseed oil and a thinner such as turpentine or, more commonly, naphtha. You can, however, make your own fast-drying fillers by substituting a little lacquer (see formulas below) in place of linseed oil. The lacquer will also act as a binder (see page 118).

A satisfactory paste lacquer filler containing no linseed oil can be made at home or in the small workshop. It consists of 1 part of powdered silica plus 1 part cornstarch with enough lacquer thinner to make a paste of the proper thickness. Add a small amount of lacquer sealer to act as a binder.

Colored lacquer-type paste fillers can be made by adding spirit-soluble coal-tar dyes to the filler. These dyes are best for the home worker, although they are not absolutely permanent. For a dark paste filler add alcohol stains to special fillers without oil.

The lacquer type of paste filler should be applied with a brush crosswise of the grain. When properly set, it should be wiped off with burlap or other absorbent material, rubbing across the grain. Then clean slightly for finishing by wiping very lightly lengthwise of the grain. If the filler is not too fast-drying, it is preferable to apply it lengthwise of the grain and then finish by rebrushing, crosswise as with a standard filler.

### Sealer coats for lacquer

The natural dyes in several woods, particularly in amaranth, mahogany, and rosewood, dissolve in lacquer solvents causing the surface to "bleed." To prevent this, use a thin shellac washcoat as a sealer, and do *not* sand it. Since the shellac will seal in the dye and keep it from bleeding, you don't want to take the chance of sanding through this safety seal. For most other words, however, a sealer coat over the filler is optional, although shellac or shellac mixing lacquer is frequently used as a base under the lacquer coats. A lacquer sanding sealer is worth two coats of top lacquer, and when straight coats of lacquer are used over the filler at least one and often two extra coats are needed to get the required depth of finish.

Brushing lacquer should never be applied until the sealer coats are absolutely hard. If the sealer is soft, the strong lacquer solvents and the brush action will raise the previously applied coating, and a rough surface will result. When spraying the lacquer, however, this precaution is not necessary.

When the sealer is lifted by additional coatings of lacquer, it is generally caused by the softening of the undercoats that have not been given time enough for thorough drying. The surface of lacquer films dry very quickly, but a considerable amount of time is required before the under part of the coating hardens completely. The drying time of a lacquer coating

To *apply lacquer, use a fine varnish brush and load heavily. Apply with rapid strokes. Lap sides of each stroke as shown above. When finishing a long, flat area, start away from the last stroke and end overlapping as shown below. Work as rapidly as possible, letting lacquer level itself. Do not brush over.*

varies from a few minutes to a few hours, depending upon the kinds of solvents and diluents used by the manufacturers. Fillers and varnishes usually contain linseed oil and should never be used as sealers for lacquers.

## Lacquer application methods

There are several methods of lacquer application. Since home-owners are usually only interested in either brush or spray-gun application, these are the only methods we will discuss in detail. Incidentally, never attempt to brush a lacquer intended for spraying; it will dry behind the brush too quickly for anything but a poor job. It is perfectly all right, however, to use brushing lacquer for spraying.

*Spraying*   The application of lacquer with a spray gun is the best method. Be sure to read Chapter 3 for complete spraying instructions. Lacquer for the finishing coats should be thinned to spraying consistency. Always check the mixture by spraying one or two test patterns first—a little wasted material here is better than sanding it off later. The pattern should be fairly uniform in shape, wet in the center, and blending out to fine dots around the edges. A small wet center, fading in rough blobs of lacquer, indicates poor atomizing or breaking up of the lacquer. A pattern like this will cause an orange-peel finish. It can be corrected by either thinning the lacquer or increasing the air pressure, and, to a lesser extent, by cutting down on the fluid feed. The peanut and heavy-end patterns are caused by dirt in the gun. Rotate the air cap a half turn. If the pattern reverses, the obstruction is in the air cap; if it stays the same, the obstruction is on the fluid tip. A split spray usually results from too much air pressure.

After you obtain a good pattern, proceed with the work. Follow a definite system. If you are lacquering a table, for example, spray the inside of the legs first, then the outside of the legs, followed by the rails and lastly the top. Spray a full wet coat—get enough material on the work so that the lacquer film will have a chance to level itself. Sanding between coats is of no particular value in the lacquer system, although scuffing with very fine paper or 2/0 steel wool is sometimes done to remove nibs of dirt. A second coat of lacquer always cuts the first one slightly and dissolves into it, thus securing it. In the varnish system, this is obtained by sanding all undercoats.

**Brushing**    This is a good method of application, which deserves more use. A practical brushing lacquer is very thin—almost like water—and brushes as easily as shellac.

Select a brush that is not too soft. The brush recommended for lacquering is usually called a "fitch-hair" brush, but only those vulcanized in rubber can be used successfully for lacquer application. A rather wide brush, the 2- or 3-inch size, will hold more lacquer than a small one. This means much more rapid flowing of the lacquer and less danger of laps or uncovered streaks.

New brushes should always be broken in before use. The dry brush should be bent back and forth to remove all loose bristles or hair and dust. Then, wash the brush in lacquer solvent or thinner, shake out the excess of thinner, and place the brush in the lacquer, allowing it to stand for a few minutes or until the lacquer has worked into the brush. Otherwise the first brushful of lacquer will be too thin.

Now fill the brush with lacquer and wipe the tip only enough to prevent dripping. Flow the lacquer onto the surface lengthwise with the grain. Do not attempt to brush it thoroughly as is recommended for varnish. Two or three strokes of the brush are ample if the brush holds enough lacquer. The brush should never be allowed to become too dry, because you may then attempt to spread the lacquer by working back and forth too much. When a full coat is spread quickly, there will be no laps, streaks, or rough places. Those spots that are not properly covered will be coated over the next time and will not show. Never attempt to touch up spots after the lacquer has set, since this will cause roughness. Success in brush lacquering depends upon careful and thorough but rapid work.

The following are helpful suggestions for applying lacquer with a brush:

1. When filling the brush from the container, don't rub off the excess lacquer on the top of the container as you do with paint; if you do, the quick-drying lacquer will become sticky and foul the brush on successive trips to the container. For this reason, it is best to squeeze off any excess against the inner side of the container.

2. Place the articles to be lacquered in a well-lighted area so that the light will be reflected from the freshly finished surfaces and show up any improperly covered areas. The surfaces to which lacquer is being applied should be in a horizontal rather than a vertical position.

3. Finish removable parts separately with the surfaces held horizontally to prevent sags and runs that may occur when a wet coat is applied to a vertical or oblique surface.

4. Avoid brush marks by using a rather large brush of medium soft grade such as a 2- to 3-inch fitch brush.

5. When applying lacquer to uneven surfaces, such as carvings and beadings, make sure that the lacquer does not accumulate in the hollows. Pick up or pull out the excess with the tip of the brush.

6. "Flow" the lacquer by using a rather wet brushful—do not work back and forth as in varnishing. Spread each brushful with the grain of the wood; then turn the brush around, and draw it over the surface in the op-

posite direction. This is enough brushing. Next, dip the brush in lacquer deeply enough to fill it well, and then touch the tip of the bristles to a drip wire over the container to prevent the lacquer from dripping off the brush. If this is done quickly, the next brushful of lacquer may be applied to the edge of the previous brushful without roughness. It is best to coat an entire surface quickly and fully by brushing with the grain whenever possible.

7. Add a small amount of thinner if the lacquer does not spread well. Lacquer causes more "pull" on the brush than varnish does. Use a thinner prepared for the lacquer that you are using.

8. Use bold, rapid strokes when applying lacquer with a brush. Carry each stroke as far as possible without running out the lacquer into separate thin lines. Overlap prior strokes only slightly. If the surface is large, it is best to work from opposite ends, blending the strokes in the center.

9. Any runs or streaks found on surfaces should be removed with lacquer thinner before you apply lacquer.

10. Sanding between coats of lacquer is not necessary unless there is roughness.

11. Undercoats must be fully dry before applying brushing lacquer; otherwise they will be softened or raised and cause roughness.

12. Avoid application of lacquer in damp or rainy weather, because "blushing," a white deposit in the film, may be the result.

## Gloss and flat lacquers

The most popular finish is a satin sheen, which is obtained by using a gloss lacquer and then rubbing down to obtain the required luster. A fairly good imitation of such a rubbed finish is obtained by using a flat lacquer as a final top coat. This dries with a soft, satin luster and is not rubbed. Flat lacquer is simply a gloss lacquer with a small amount of flattening pigment added. The pigment sometimes settles in the can and should be kept in suspension by occasional mixing or turning the container over every now and then.

Gloss and flat lacquers can be mixed in any proportion to secure varying degrees of gloss. Where a flat lacquer is to be used, glossy undercoats will give a better body and also contribute to a clearer finish. Two coats of lacquer over a sealer are generally sufficient. However, in working with small spraying units where a very thin mixture is used to ensure a good spray, four or five coats may be necessary.

The most desirable drying time between coats is approximately 4 hours. Less time may be allowed when necessary, but always remember that atmospheric conditions such as heat, humidity, and cold have their retarding effect upon the drying of any lacquer. Extreme cold will cause the surface to check within a few hours after application as well as retard the flow of a lacquer during application.

### Colored lacquer

An opaque or colored lacquer finish resembles synthetic enamel and is used to color woods. These lacquers are applied in the same way as the transparent type.

For a good colored lacquer finish on new wood, choose a wood of close grain, such as birch, maple, or gum. On these, the use of an oil-base lacquer undercoater is advisable. However, a regular opaque lacquer may be used as a first and second coat. Before starting the refinishing process, test the reaction of the surface by spraying or brushing over a hidden part of the item. If the old finish has an aniline base, this will bleed through the lacquer coat. Let this test area remain for a day. If it has not bled through, proceed with the finishing, using both an undercoater and finish coat of colored lacquer. If there is any sign of bleeding in test area, strip off the old finish completely with paint-and-varnish remover or choose another material for the finish. Be sure to test again before applying it to a visible surface.

### Rubbing and polishing

Lacquered surfaces should be allowed ample drying time before rubbing, usually 18 to 48 hours, depending on the thickness of the film and the time originally allowed for drying of undercoats. The exact rubbing procedure is covered in Chapter 9 (see page 175).

### Refinishing with lacquer

The application of nitrocellulose lacquer directly over an old finish is complicated and the results not always satisfactory. First, determine what the old finish is—shellac, varnish, or lacquer. Sometimes it is impossible to tell, especially when age and wear have destroyed its original identity, and one guess is as good as another. Next, wipe off and remove all wax, grease, and dirt with a solvent such as alcohol, turpentine, or benzine and follow with a thorough sanding. This process will, in most cases, prepare the old finish for recoating. (See Chapter 2 for complete details.)

At this stage other imperfections may show up—spots that require matching up of the stain, exceptionally deep scratches to be "burned in" with lacquer wood cement; loose veneer; and checks, craze, or alligatoring which were not removed by the sanding process. Naturally, any or all of these faults must be corrected before you apply any lacquer coats to the old finish. Fault and damaged cabinetwork should be skillfully remedied (see page 286).

When you have determined the kind of finish that exists on the piece and have made all necessary preparations, you are ready for the final lacquer coat or coats. Lacquer over lacquer will in nearly all cases present no difficulties. Lacquer over old shellac, if well sanded down almost to the wood, will in most instances present little or no difficulty. Lacquer over varnish, however, is always a ticklish proposition. The finisher can often get away with it for the time being if the varnish is of good quality, but premature checking inevitably results.

When a lacquer is applied to any kind of old finish which tends to "lift" and "boil up," the result is fatal, and the best remedy then is to remove the mess to the bare wood and build up an entirely new finish. Shellac-base sealers are excellent protecting coaters and may be used to prevent such ills as premature checking and lifting of the old finish. Specially prepared protecting lacquers, compatible with the varnish underneath, can be applied over an old finish and then followed by one or more coats of regular wood lacquer. Follow the lacquer manufacturer's recommendation as to the specific protecting lacquer to be used with his product.

There is no guarantee against every possible failure when refinishing over old finishes. The lacquer manufacturer may offer his special products for any kind of special work, but the success of its application depends chiefly upon the skill, knowledge, and experience of the finisher and his willingness to follow the manufacturer's instructions.

## Lacquer faults

*Moisture blush*   This is a clouding of the lacquer film through moisture in the film. The moisture may be contained in the ingredients of the lacquer, or may be precipitated from the atmosphere by a fall in temperature, which results in too rapid evaporation of solvents and thinners. Proper application of the lacquer and control of the temperature in the finishing room will usually prevent this type of blush. Sometimes the moisture can be evaporated by ironing the surface with a hot flatiron over two or three thicknesses of absorbent paper (paper toweling or brown wrapping paper).

*Cotton blush*   This is a clouding, or whitish effect of the lacquer film from the precipitation of cellulose and is usually due to an excess of diluents in the formula. This condition often disappears by itself during the drying time; however, when it does not, a light spray coat of thinner will usually "throw back" the cotton to its original transparency. The best guarantee against this difficulty is to use a high-grade, more expensive thinner which is rich in high-boiling solvents and will retard the excessively fast and unbalanced rate of evaporation characteristic of a cheap thinner. A good thinner compensates not only by retarding the "blushing" tendency of a lacquer, but also makes possible a better flowing and level setting film, which means less rubbing to accomplish a smooth surface.

*Orange peel*   This is a roughened appearance of the film caused by too low a proportion of slowly evaporating solvents, such as butyl acetate and butyl alcohol. In this defect, the wet lacquer film "sets up" before it has time to flow out smoothly. Increasing the proportions of butyl acetate and butyl alcohol will remedy this defect.

**Pinholing** This is a pitting of the lacquer film caused by improper formulation, permitting the cellulose to "set" before the solvents and diluents have completely evaporated. The volatile gases of solvents and diluents escape as small bubbles, leaving "pinholes."

**Bleeding** Bleeding is a discoloration of a coating caused by the dye in the underlying surface—usually an organic pigment which is soluble in the solvents of the topcoat. You may prevent this bleeding by applying an undercoating of dewaxed shellac.

## SYNTHETICS

In the first edition of this book we described synthetics as being neither varnish, paint, nor lacquer. Today, most varnishes, paints, and lacquers are synthetics. That is, the vast majority of our wood-finishing products are made from man-made or synthetic resins, rather than from natural products dug out of the ground or obtained from a plant or tree. The word "synthetics" is commonly used in the wood-finishing industry.

Since synthetic varnishes and lacquers are covered in previous chapters, let us look at so-called "special" synthetics.

### Types of special synthetics

**Plywood sealer** This is especially good for equalizing hard and soft areas in fir and pine. It is usually available in a clear type but can also be obtained in white for blond effects. (See Chapter 13 for application details.)

**Penetrating resin finishes** The penetrating resin finishes, often called penetrating wood sealers, are among the more popular clear finishes on the market. They are easy to apply and to maintain. They seal the pores of the wood and give a lustrous finish. That is, penetrating resin finishes sink into the surface of the wood, filling all the pores and other voids with a hard synthetic or plastic material. This creates a surface similar in many respects to the plastic laminates, except that there is no plastic look. The finished surface has all the warmth, texture, and beauty of natural wood.

Some penetrating resin finishes are colored so that staining, sealing, and finishing can be done in one operation. They can be applied either with a lintless cloth or by brush.

**Catalytic finishes**    These are hard, tough finishes that are steam- and alcohol-proof. They are used for tabletops and take 1 to 4 hours to dry. They require a catalyst (hardener) which is mixed with the synthetic before use. Since the introduction of synthetic varnishes and penetrating resin finishes, catalytic finishes have lost some of their popularity. There are, however, several types of catalytic finishes still available.

## Synthetic thinners

Most lacquers and synthetics require thinning for use with a spray gun. In all cases it is best to obtain the thinner recommended by the manufacturer. This is especially important with synthetics, since a thinner for one brand may not work at all with another, even though both are made of the same resin or resins. Where a thinner other than the one suggested by the manufacturer must be used, it should be a coal-tar naphtha (benzol, toluol, xylol), not a petroleum naphtha (benzine, kerosene, turpentine substitutes). Coal-tar naphthas have a greater solvency power than petroleum naphthas and are solvents for a great number of synthetics.

## Application of penetrating resin finishes

Once the surface has been thoroughly sanded, dust it completely using a vacuum or a good dusting brush. Don't worry about dust marks on a penetrating finish, but the wood pores must be entirely clean, or the fine texture of the natural wood will be lost. After cleaning the surface, apply a quick-dry nonsealing alcohol water-base stain with a clean cloth or brush. If the penetrating resin finishes have a wood-tone color, this step is not necessary. It is important to keep in mind that a penetrating resin finish—even natural—will provide a slight darkening effect. This degree of darkening, with most species of wood, enhances the grain and figure of the wood. When a stain is used, there is considerable intensification of the color, a shift in hue toward the reds, and some darkening. Should the wood be lighter in color, a wood bleach may be used. Where there is any question about the finished result, it is best to make test patches on a piece of scrap wood of the same species or on an unseen portion of the project.

When applying the penetrating resin finish, use a cloth pad, brush, or 2/0 steel wool, or on horizontal surfaces pour it on. Whenever possible, turn the work so that the surface that is being worked on is flat. This permits the material to stand on the wood and penetrate as deeply as it can. When using a brush, lay the finish on as thick as possible without runoff. When using a wad of cloth or steel wool, swab the finishing material around on the surface, using only light pressure. This helps to work the finish into the wood.

Keep the surface wet for at least half an hour, often longer, depending on the specific manufacturer's recommendations. If a dull spot appears on the surface, indicating that all the material has soaked in, apply more to keep the surface wet.

After the wood has soaked up all the liquid it will take, use clean rags (preferably old and lint-free) to wipe all the surface resin off. Check the surface for small areas of liquid which are often forced to the surface by air bubbles or heat, and wipe the surface *completely* dry. If any trace of the finish remains on the surface, it will dry to a rather unpleasant sheen. Should this occur, it can usually be corrected by brushing on more resin finish, and then wiping it clean in a few minutes. If the finish resists normal rag wipe-up, moisten a pad of 3/0 steel wool in the liquid resin and gently rub.

It is usually wise to plan two or three applications of penetrating resin finishes, since the material continues to soak in and permeate the pores and spaces in the wood after it is wiped. Remember that the more resin absorbed—with no surface coating—the tougher the finish and the harder the surface will be. The time between coats may vary from 4 to 24 hours, depending on the manufacturer's recommendation. The second and third coat are applied and wiped off in the same manner as the first. While no sanding is required between coats, many expert finishers rub the surface with 4/0 steel wool between coats. This smooths down any places where the grain may be slightly raised and ensures a more satiny finish for the final coat.

After the final coat has been applied and wiped off, allow the item to dry for a day or two. Then rub on a *thin* coat of paste wax for added protection on surfaces subject to wear. Apply the wax sparingly, wipe it smooth, and buff as described in Chapter 10. When using wax on penetrating resin finishes, the pores tend to become clogged, and the finish is robbed of some of its natural textured beauty.

### Application of catalytic finishes

Catalytic finishes are a group of liquid-plastic materials which are cured by means of a catalytic or hardening agent added to the material just before application. Finishes of this type are usually sold under several trade names. The amount of catalyst varies with different products (check manufacturer's instructions before using the finish). They may be sprayed or brushed and are generally dry enough in 1 hour's time for the first coat to be sanded. The second coat requires 24 hours' drying time before rubbing. Since some of the finishes of this type have poor adhesion to undercoats or sealers, they should be applied to bare or stained wood only —do not use any kind of sealer or pigmented stain. Rub with rubbing compound or with extra fine waterproof paper in succession with rubbing oil or water lubricant (see Chapter 9).

Several catalytic finishes require baking for them to cure properly. The baking equipment need not be elaborate, since it can be done quite simply with one or two infrared heat lamps.

# CHAPTER NINE

# Rubbing and Polishing

**M**any articles made of wood, particularly of hardwoods such as mahogany and walnut, can be made more beautiful and the life of their finishes increased by hand-rubbing the surface. Rubbing is the general term applied to the use of sandpaper, steel wool, pumice, and other abrasives in surfacing varnish, shellac, lacquer, etc. On undercoats, rubbing gives the surface a "tooth" for the next coat and also builds up a level surface. On the finishing coat, rubbing eliminates small imperfections, dust specks, and waves, making the surface perfectly smooth and giving it the desired luster.

## Materials used

The important items required for the rubbing operation are:

***Rubbing felt***  One piece of soft, pressed felt, 1 inch thick and approximately 3 × 5 inches, for general rubbing. A few smaller pieces should also be available. Several thicknesses from an old felt hat or several pieces of felt padding sewed together—the kind that is used under rugs and carpets—or a blackboard eraser may be used. Since the felt is to be used for the final smoothing or polishing of a finish, it should be carefully inspected beforehand for glazed spots, grit, bits of steel wool, etc., which might scratch a rubbed surface.

***Abrasive papers***  See Sandpaper Table page 15, for complete information on types and grades. Have several pieces of each type available. The material may be used with a sanding block, if desired.

***Pumice***  Use No. 1 for coarse rubbing, Nos. FF and FFF for fine rubbing. The finer grades should be sifted through a fine cheesecloth into a clean container before using, to remove lumps or foreign matter.

***Rottenstone***  Sold in only one grade and used in fine rubbing.

***Rubbing oil***  Lubricant for rubbing. It may be purchased ready-mixed. Paraffin oil, crude petroleum, or No. 10 motor oil thinned with benzine can also be used.

***Rubbing compound***  Ready-mixed liquid or paste abrasive sold in various grades of fineness.

***White soap***  Used to keep fine abrasive paper from loading. Any good-grade white soap can be used.

***Naphtha***  (Also sold as benzine.)  Used for cleaning up the surface after the rubbing operation is completed.

***Polishing oil***  For obtaining a high polish after rubbing. It is purchased ready-mixed and usually consists of one-half olive oil (sweet oil) and one-half denatured alcohol. A good standard furniture polish can also be used.

*Lacquer rubbing compound*   For rubbing lacquer. Purchased in paste form, ready-mixed.

*Lacquer polish*   For cleaning up compound haze. A large number of ready-mixed products are available.

*Alcohol*   Used to spirit-off polishing oil. It should be denatured (grain) alcohol of the average paint-store grade.

You will also need a 1-inch bristle brush for carvings and turnings, clean cloths, dusting brush, clear water, several pads of No. 3/0 or 4/0 steel wool, and a chamois.

### Rubbing the first coat of finish

The first coat may be rubbed dry or with paper dampened with water on the back only. The finish is very thin at this stage, and the water or other lubricant could easily get under the surface. A very fine finishing sandpaper should be used. The standard sheet, if not used on a sanding block, may be torn into eight pieces for this work. Before using, rub the pieces of new paper together lightly to remove any long teeth. (See Chapter 2 for proper method of using the paper.) Never use water for rubbing shellac.

Rubbing should be done with the grain wherever possible. When cross rubbing is necessary on places hard to get at, it should be done first and the marks then smoothed out by sanding with the grain. Use No. 3/0 or 4/0 steel wool for this, either a regular pad or loose wool made into a pad.

### Rubbing between coats

The second and succeeding coats up to the final coat are cut down with waterproof paper, either garnet or silicon carbide, with an extra fine grit. Water, and plenty of it, should be used as a lubricant. The one exception to this is shellac, which is always rubbed with oil. The paper must be backed with a felt pad or cork sanding block in order to secure a level surface. Water rubbing with coarse pumice (No. 1) can be substituted for wet sanding. In all cases, the work is washed down with water, cleaned with a damp chamois, inspected, and spot-rubbed again where necessary. The surface should be flat and dull, free from all dirt and waves. At least 4 hours should be allowed for drying before the next coat is applied.

On a large surface, such as a tabletop, rub the ends first; then, using a long stroke, rub the in-between area.

### Polish-rubbed finish

Pumice is the time-honored abrasive for rubbing the final coat. Use grade No. FF or FFF with water or oil or both as the lubricant. Water rubbing is faster, cleaner, and leaves a brighter gloss surface, although it requires closer inspection and better judgment during use than with oil rubbing. The surface is then oil-polished as a final operation. Such a rubbed surface needs no further polishing with rottenstone, since the gloss will be high enough if the rubber has been careful not to add fresh pumice stone to the work toward the end of the rubbing operation. Pumice stone grinds finer and finer during use; hence the addition of fresh material will produce an entirely different and much duller sheen on the reworked portion.

It is more difficult to work with an oil lubricant. Oil is hard to remove, even with soap and water, and traces left would tend to slop up, or stop altogether, the drying of any varnish applied over an oil film. For this reason no sanding or rubbing with oil materials should ever be done below the finish top coat.

***Water lubricant***    Sprinkle a small amount of pumice on the work (a sifter-top can is handy), add water (enough to make a paste), and then rub with a felt block, about 3 x 5 inches, and no thinner than ½ inch. Thinner felt can be mounted on a wood block. Rub with the grain, except in such places as panel ends, which can be cross-rubbed first and then smoothed. Keep the abrasive wet by adding water, but do not add more pumice since fresh abrasive will scratch and void the work already done. Inspect the work frequently by rubbing a place clean with the side of the hand. Keep the pad clean—deposits of rubbing slush forming into hard "corns" will cause scratching. When the work is smooth and free from nibs, clean the work with a wet chamois and plenty of water. You will now have a very flat, dull surface, which is ready for the final rubbing operation. Never use water on shellac finishes.

Repeat the rubbing procedure with rottenstone, using oil as a lubricant, and soft felt or a folded piece of heavy cloth as a pad. This brings up a soft, satin finish. Rottenstone does not cut, but will bring up any surface from satin to near-polish by continued rubbing. After you have obtained the desired surface, roughly clean the surface with water and a wet chamois; then clean perfectly with a soft rag and benzine. Place the rag over a sliver of wood to get all the slush out of corners and recesses.

*Oil lubricant*    When the work is to be oil-rubbed, the procedure is almost identical with that of water rubbing. For hand rubbing, mix the pumice with the oil in a shallow dish until the mixture is about as thin as cream, and keep it stirred as it is used. When using a pad, keep the powder and the oil in separate dishes and dip the pad first into the oil and then into the powder pumice. Rub with the grain of the wood, and try to use an even pressure so that some parts will not be duller than others.

When you have achieved a uniform dull luster that has depth and mellowness, polish the surface by rubbing it with rottenstone and oil. This gives a special glow that is well worth the effort. Clean the surface thoroughly so that no oily film remains. Then wipe with a cloth slightly dampened with carbon tetrachloride or naphtha to help remove any remaining trace of oil. Finally, give the piece its last polishing with a soft chamois or polishing cloth.

### Satin-rubbed finish

While the best method to obtain a satin finish is to follow the polish-rubbed technique already described, a suitable satin finish can be obtained quickly on certain wood surfaces by first sanding the final coat very, very lightly with 8/0 to 10/0 finishing paper—lubricated with water. Then rub the surface with 4/0 or finer steel wool, with the grain, until the desired sheen has been reached.

Turnings, moldings, etc., are a bit more difficult to rub than flat surfaces. On turnings, use a 10 x 20-inch strip of cotton flannel. Sprinkle this with the slush being used, and apply in a shoeshining fashion. A stiff 1-inch bristle brush is all that is needed to take the gloss off carved moldings. Any rubbing can be done with pieces of hat felt, special felt blocks cut to shape, or felt glued on piano hammers. Old discarded piano hammers can usually be obtained from any piano tuner or store. They make excellent rubbing tools on such small work.

Many people prefer to finish these small parts or hard places with flat varnish in order to eliminate rubbing.

### High-polish-rubbed finish

To obtain a high polish, proceed as already described, but use water as a lubricant for the rottenstone instead of oil. Use the palm of your hand for final rubbing. Clean the work thoroughly with water and let dry 24 hours. Next, apply polishing oil. Many of the everyday furniture polishes can be used successfully. These polishes slightly soften the top coat of the finish, causing the finish to knit together. If you prefer to make your own polish, use equal parts of olive oil and denatured alcohol, and add a small quantity of sifted rotten-stone if you wish. Apply the polish to a piece of soft cheese-cloth. Rub the work with a circular motion until a high polish appears, and then wipe off with long smooth strokes. Clean the surface with benzine to remove the oil, and finally, to remove every trace of oil, rub with dry cornstarch or bran. The oil can also be removed with alcohol. To do this, moisten a piece of cheesecloth with alcohol. Wring the cloth dry, and further kill the alcohol with a few drops of water, applied with the fingers. Form the cloth into a smooth, wrinkle-free pad. Wipe the cloth over the surface, using a circular motion and very light pressure. Do not permit the cloth to rest on the work—always keep it in motion. Finish with the grain, lifting the pad at the end of each stroke.

An easier method to finish off a high-gloss surface, especially with synthetic finishes, is to smooth with a very light rubbing of 9/0 or 10/0 waterproof abrasive paper, dipped into lukewarm water. The less smooth surfaces may be rubbed very lightly with 4/0 or 5/0 steel wool. If the work is done with a "light hand" and not too much rubbing, the smoothing action should improve the high-gloss effect, rather than dull the surface.

## Use of polishing varnish

When available, polishing varnish can be used as a final coat, and a higher polish can be obtained with it than when employing the conventional varnish. It is applied after the surface has been rubbed with pumice and water in the usual manner. When dry, the polish coat is rubbed down with FF or FFF pumice and water, using a soft felt pad. Then, when the surface is evenly smooth and dull, clean up thoroughly with water. Follow with a rottenstone rub, using water as a lubricant, rubbing with the palm of the hand or with a soft felt cloth. Polish with a dry, soft chamois or a soft cloth.

## Rubbing shellac

Shellac is rubbed in the same way as the other finishes except that oil is always used as the lubricant—never water, since it will damage the shellac. Wipe off the finish with a dry cloth. If a trace of oil still remains on the surface, it can be removed with a cloth dampened with a solution of vinegar or dilute oxalic acid. Never allow this solution to remain on the surface any longer than is absolutely necessary, as it will damage the finish. Dry cornstarch spread on the surface and then brushed up is also a good method of removing oil from a shellacked surface.

## Rubbing lacquer

The pumice and rottenstone rubbing process can be used on any finish, including lacquer, with the exception that rubbing oil instead of water is used as the lubricant when treating shellac. Lacquer, however, is much harder to cut than varnish or shellac and requires a great deal more work. The lacquer schedule generally calls for a rough sanding with very fine dry paper, between coats. The final coat receives a thorough sanding with extra fine paper lubricated with naphtha (benzine). A solution of linseed-oil soap (available at drugstores) with water makes a good lubricant and can be substituted for the naphtha. Extra fine paper gives a satisfactory satin finish, but is usually followed by a rubbing compound, to give increased smoothness and reach any low spots in the finish. Rubbing compounds are to lacquer finish what pumice stone is to varnish finish. The only real difference is in the hardness of the abrasive. Rubbing compounds come in paste form and are thinned with naphtha or water to working consistency. Cleaning up can be done with naphtha or water. The grade of the compound will determine the gloss of the resulting finish—a fine compound will produce a polished surface, while a medium or coarse compound will give a satin finish. To get the highest type of polish, follow the rubbing compound with a lacquer polish such as is sold for polishing automobiles.

### Flat rubbed finishes

Flat varnish or lacquer is often used to avoid the work of hand rubbing and still produce a similar effect. These finishes are improved by lightly rubbing with fine steel wool lubricated with paste or liquid wax.

### Rubbing schedules

**Varnish** (flat)   First coat: Use very fine garnet finishing paper, dry. Second coat: Use No. ½ or 1 pumice powder and water. Third coat: Use No. FFF pumice powder with water or oil.

**Varnish** (satin)   Same as above, but for the third and

final coat use No. FF pumice with water, followed by rotten-stone and oil, or No. 4F pumice and oil.

*Varnish* (polished)   Filler coat: Sand with fine dry garnet finishing paper. First varnish coat: Use very fine dry garnet finishing paper. Second coat: Use extra fine waterproof paper, with water. Third coat: Same as second coat. Final coat should be treated as follows:

1. Rub with No. FF or FFF pumice and water.
2. Rub with rottenstone and water.
3. Clean with benzine; let dry 24 hours.
4. Rub with polishing oil.
5. Spirit-off with denatured alcohol.

*Shellac* (flat, satin, polished)   Same as above but use No. 2/0 or 3/0 steel wool for all undercoats and oil rub for finish.

*Lacquer* (satin)   Scuff all undercoats with very fine paper (8/0 garnet is good). Sand final coat with extra fine water-proof paper with naphtha. When using the paper, rub two sections against each other to remove any large spines; then rub the lacquered surface gently with the paper dipped in naphtha.

*Lacquer* (polished)   Follow same procedure as for varnish (polished) except use lacquer rubbing compound (follow manufacturer's instructions to the letter) in place of pumice and water. Remove compound haze and polish with lacquer polish instead of denatured alcohol. If pumice is used, apply with a rubbing oil and a cloth. Rub with the grain over flat surfaces, testing every now and then with the fingertips to check the smoothness of the surface. As this is done, a slush is worked up which is used on legs of chairs and curved surfaces. Pick up the slush on a length of cloth and "shoeshine" the curved areas.

### Care of rubbing equipment

Good rubbing equipment improves with use if pads and similar items are taken care of properly. Oil pads should be well scrubbed with naphtha or gasoline; water pads with water and brush. Keep them clean and free from any possible dirt and grit by placing in a closed container. Carelessness may necessitate many hours of extra work and material in an effort to correct damage from scratching.

# CHAPTER TEN

# Wax and Oil Finishes

The wax finish, one of the oldest of wood treatments, has a pleasing eggshell gloss and makes a satisfactory finish for furniture as well as floors. Its durability depends on its foundation, and in all cases demands periodic renewal to retain its appearance. Wax finishes will not withstand water or excessive heat, and should not be used where these may be a problem.

## WAXES

Most important of the natural waxes is carnauba or Brazil wax. Because of its brittleness, it is seldom used as a straight wax but is mixed in varying proportions with other waxes such as beeswax, ceresin, and paraffin.

A short description of the natural lump form of each of these waxes follows:

**Beeswax**    Produced by honeybees. Two types—white and yellow. A general-purpose wax of fair hardness. Melting point, 152° F.

**Cadelilla**    Obtained from a Mexican shrub. Practically the same as beeswax for general use.

**Carnauba**    Obtained from a species of palm tree grown in Brazil. Sometimes called Brazil wax. Brittle. Pale yellow. Hardest of all natural waxes, melting at 185° F. Used in varying proportions in practically all commercial waxes.

**Ceresin**    A hydrocarbon wax possessing great flexibility. Melting point about the same as carnauba wax, with which it is often mixed.

**Paraffin**    A translucent white wax obtained from petroleum. Cheap and easily obtained, but a bit too soft. Melting point, 131° F. Excellent as a white pore filler in novelty oak finishes.

Waxes can be purchased in natural lump form and made into paste of liquid wax by the addition of turpentine, the liquid wax requiring more of the solvent than the paste variety.

**Wax formulas**

Homemade waxes are quite satisfactory, but similar waxes purchased ready-mixed are somewhat superior. Typical homemade wax formulas are as follows:

**Hard carnauba wax**    Ingredients: 1 pound carnauba wax; 1 pound ceresin wax; 1 pint turpentine. Shred the waxes into a can. Place can in a pot of boiling water and keep over flame. When wax has melted, add the turpentine, which has been warmed in hot water.

**Beeswax** Use 1 pound white or yellow beeswax with ½ pint turpentine. Mix by heating as above, or shred wax into turpentine and let stand overnight.

**Antique wax** To 1 pint of liquid wax, add about 1 ounce of powdered rottenstone, and dry sienna or Vandyke brown.

**White wax** Shred and melt paraffin wax in a can. Thin as required with a mixture of half turpentine and half naphtha. Color with a little dry zinc oxide (zinc white).

**Colored wax** Furniture finishing often requires a colored wax. This can be made by adding a small amount of color-in-oil to the paste or liquid wax. Oil stains are sometimes added for staining waxes. Powdered rottenstone can be added to wax to give it a "dusty" appearance, making it suitable for antiquing. White and gray waxes can be used to produce novelty finishes on oak and other coarse-grained woods. White wax can be either purchased ready-mixed or made by adding a little dry zinc white to paraffin paste wax. This wax is rubbed into the pores of the wood over a wash coat of shellac and is then topped with two coats of the same wax, clear.

## Applying wax finish

Although wax can be used on bare wood or over stain, best results are obtained if the work is first coated with shellac, varnish, or lacquer. Several coats of wax are necessary on a new surface.

First dust the piece to be worked on. Only paste wax should be used for new work. Place a small amount of wax between several layers of cheesecloth, and apply it with a circular motion. This application through a close-grained cloth prevents lumps of wax from being applied. Never under any circumstances "pile up" the wax by applying too much, for it will be almost impossible to rub it out to a smooth, satin finish.

Allow the wax about 10 minutes' drying time, then rub briskly with a soft cloth, using first a rotary motion, and finish with long strokes with the grain. After drying for at least 1 hour, you can apply a second coat the same way. The heavier the wax, the more effort is required to bring it to a true polish. If you are using a very heavy paste, scrub the surface with a brush, shoeshining fashion, before you start the rag polishing. Hard, vigorous rubbing is always required; a good polish cannot be obtained with an easy, quick rub. If you are working on a flat surface, you can get a good polish by placing a brick inside the cloth.

As a final test, try to make a thumbprint on the polished surface. If it can be seen, rub briskly with the hard cloth until print disappears. Retest in the same manner and continue rubbing until thumbprint test proves negative. Each surface should have an overall luster with no dull spots. It may be brightened from time to time by rubbing first with the soft cloth, then with a hard one, without the addition of new wax.

Very often a thin coat of hard wax can be applied to a varnished surface after it has been rubbed with pumice stone. Apply very little wax at any one time and polish it thoroughly, or else the surface will have a greasy appearance and will show finger marks.

### Repolishing wax surface

Three general types of wax are commonly used for general furniture and woodwork polishing—paste, liquid, and cream.

Paste wax is especially desirable for tabletops and other surfaces exposed to considerable wear and tear. Liquid wax is
similar to the paste in character, but the solvent with which
it has been mixed has cleaning properties; therefore it cleans
the surfaces while, at the same time, leaving a thin film of
wax. The third kind, in the nature of a cream, contains added
neutral soaps and a little water which gives it still greater
cleansing properties. The water and soap will remove sticky,
foreign matter often found on furniture, especially where
there are small children. Most experts, however, recommend
only paste wax for quality wood finishes.

When repolishing an old waxed surface, it is best to remove the dust and dirt together with some of the old wax
with a cloth moistened with turpentine. Some experts prefer
to apply the wax with cheesecloth which has been dipped in
cold water and wrung as dry as possible. Rings or white
marks on table tops can usually be removed by rubbing in a
thin paste of wax and turpentine. When the surface has
dried, polish with a cloth, and then apply a thin coat of wax
in a circular motion.

Polishing is done with a dry cloth—flannel, wool, silk, or
cheesecloth. Old cloths are usually lintless and therefore better than new ones. The best polishing technique—unlike that
of applying wax—is first to rub across the grain with short,
quick strokes and then to polish with the grain, using longer
strokes.

If you want to save time and effort, apply the wax to only
a small area at a time, and polish immediately. Some woodworkers, however, believe that a more brilliant polish can be
obtained by letting the wax dry hard and then rubbing as
long as necessary.

"Self-polishing" floor waxes, which require no rubbing, differ considerably from the waxes just mentioned and are intended only for floors. They should never be used on furniture or other woodwork.

### Typical waxing schedules

Follow this step-by-step procedure for a typical wax finish:

1. Stain the wood and highlight by sanding.
2. Seal with a wash coat of shellac.
3. Apply glazing if desired.
4. Apply a second thin coat of shellac.
5. Follow with four or five coats of wax.

An occasional going over with wax will preserve this finish indefinitely.

When treating walnut, oak, and other coarse-grained woods, prepare the work for the wax polish by staining and filling in the usual manner, then sealing with shellac. You can obtain a natural finish on walnut by staining the wood with a mixture of 3 parts linseed oil and 1 part turpentine. After it has been drying 24 hours, give the work two coats of shellac, each coat being cut back to the bare wood with a medium or fine paper. After the surface is dusted, apply a third coat of shellac and sand lightly with extra fine paper. Follow with several coats of paste wax.

### Care of waxing equipment

Store the polishing cloths, brushes, and liquid wax pads in a clean, covered container. Do not wash them until they become grimy or contain too much wax; then use gasoline. Store the paste wax pad in the container on top of the remaining wax. Keep the lid securely closed.

## OIL FINISH

An oil finish may be satisfactory on hard close-grained woods if you are willing to use a great deal of time and "elbow grease." Many coats are necessary to achieve a fine luster and a surface that does not show heat and watermarks. Warm oil penetrates the wood more quickly than does cold, and brings out a richer color. *Always heat the oil in a double boiler to prevent danger of fire.* A mixture of two-thirds linseed oil and one-third turpentine is generally used.

If you want to add a pleasing reddish tone to brown woods such as walnut and mahogany, you can add a little powdered dark-red oil stain to the oil before applying it.

Thoroughly sand and dust the wood before beginning the oiling. The oil mixture can be applied either warm or cold on plain surfaces, but should be used cold on carved or grooved parts, where there is danger of its setting too quickly.

Apply the oil generously with a soft cloth, and rub it into the wood with your hands until it has absorbed all the oil it can. This takes from 5 to 20 minutes, depending upon the condition of the wood and the temperature of the oil. Wipe off all the oil left, using clean cloths as often as necessary. Get all trace of oil out of the crevices, or it will harden or become sticky and will then have to be removed with alcohol or varnish remover.

Next, rub each part briskly from 10 to 20 minutes with the polishing cloth. Coarse linen makes an excellent polishing cloth, because the friction develops the necessary heat. A woolen cloth wrapped around a brick may also be used, and is easy to handle. Anywhere from four or five to twenty coats of oil are needed to bring out the luster for a soft-finish effect. Each coat must be thoroughly soaked into the wood before another coat is applied. In dry, warm weather, allow at least 2 days between the first and second coats. Between the later coats, an interval of at least a week is needed in dry weather, and several weeks in moist weather. With each coat more time should be allowed for the soaking in. Before applying each coat, test the surface for dryness by placing your hand on the oiled surface for a few minutes. If the surface becomes oily, it is not dry enough for the next coat.

Repeat the process until all dull spots have disappeared and the luster is permanent. The oiling should also be repeated once a month for a year, and once a year thereafter. To prevent warping, oil table leaves on both sides. Use varnish remover to take out the oil that has hardened in the cracks. If the surface remains sticky, it indicates that the oil has not been thoroughly rubbed off.

For a higher sheen, after the final oiling has had time to dry for three or four days, the surface can be rubbed down with FFF pumice and rubbing oil, and if a still higher polish is desired, follow up in a few days with a rottenstone-and-oil rub (see Chapter 9).

If the oiling raises the grain of the wood, rub it smooth with 4/0 or finer steel wool or extra fine sandpaper. Natural filler, if applied to the bare wood before the oiling process, will cut down the wood's absorption qualities and cause the oil applications to build up faster with less work.

### Oil and varnish finish

A luster may be obtained more quickly and the pores filled more easily with a varnish, oil, and turpentine mixture than with the oil alone. Add one-third to one-half waterproof or spar varnish to the oil and turpentine mixture (two-thirds linseed oil and one-third turpentine). This finish must not be confused with the varnish finish given on page 176. It is applied exactly the same as the oil and turpentine mixture. Use as many coats as necessary to give a beautiful even luster to the piece. If the wood is extremely dry, one or two coats of the oil and turpentine mixture may be used first.

Possibly one of the quickest methods of obtaining a so-called "oil" look is to apply a good penetrating resin finish (page 163). After this has dried for a suitable period of time —at least 5 days—coat the surface with warm boiled linseed oil. Then rub in and wipe off the excess oil.

To achieve the linseed oil color, some finishers wipe the oil on the raw wood. After it has dried for 72 hours, a natural penetrating resin sealer is applied. Once this has dried for at least 5 days, a final coat of linseed oil is applied as previously described.

### Modern oil finishes

There are several oil products on the market that can quickly achieve the resemblance of the mellow satin luster of old or antique oil-type finishes. These materials, usually clear, produce a hard finish, soft in appearance, that protects as well as beautifies. They may be used on raw wood or over most stains.

Oil finishes of this type can be applied with a clean cloth, brush, or sponge. Allow one liberal coat to remain on the surface, approximately ½ hour. Buff with clean, lint-free material to produce a uniform finish. Allow curing period of 24 hours before applying over stain finish or when applying additional coats. If a higher luster is desired, more than one coat is recommended. Should the surface become tacky and difficult to buff, apply a light coat immediately, and buff within 15 minutes.

## BUFFING FINISHES

### Wax treatments with a buffing wheel

Buffing gives an attractive finish to bare wood, when used with automobile polishing wax. Buffing of stained surfaces emphasizes the natural grain in the wood. The work is first stained in the usual manner. The buff is then charged with a liberal application of cutting compound. The buffing action cuts the stain off the surface but leaves the grain sharply outlined where it has deeply penetrated the softer portions of the wood. If lacquer is going to be used for the top coats, a wax-free compound must be used for this operation. However, the article can be finished by French polishing if a grease or wax compound is used.

### Lacquer and synthetic buffing

Buffing will give a beautiful high gloss to wood finished in clear or colored lacquer or synthetic. Most lacquers can be buffed successfully, although a few of them are too soft to hold a permanent gloss. Almost any heat- and alcohol-proof lacquer will have the necessary features for a good buffing lacquer. Lacquers especially made for buffing are also available.

Maple is the best wood for buffing. The bare wood should be sanded perfectly smooth, and sharp edges rounded off. Enamel in the usual manner. For best results use only enamel coats—no primers or sealers. Three coats of lacquer will give the required thickness to the finish. The final coat should dry at least 24 hours before starting the buffing operation. Before buffing, wet-sand the surface, using first extra fine and then super fine silicon or aluminum oxide paper. This will cut down any orange peel and eliminate much of the work of the buffing wheel. Then a perfect gloss can be obtained by buffing with an ordinary lime composition—an abrasive bonded into stick form with wax or grease. Remove the remaining traces of compound on the work by sponging with benzine.

A loose muslin buff wheel is most commonly used. It should be built up to a good thickness in order to prevent burning ridges in the work. The wheel can be used solid for preliminary buffing. To soften the action for final buffing the wheel can be packed with either three cardboard disks or smaller cloth disks between two regular cloth disks. Instead of this packing, a softer loose buff, such as flannel, can also be used.

Use a separate buff for each type of abrasive. For good results on colored lacquers and baked synthetics use a surface speed of 4,000 feet per minute (2,500 rpm with a 6-inch wheel). Clear lacquer should be buffed at a slightly lower speed. In all cases, inspect the work for burning and reduce speed as necessary.

Various schedules can be followed. The No. 1 and 2 compounds sold for plastic buffing can be used for buffing lacquer, in addition to any of the softer abrasives such as tin oxide, green rouge, whiting, prepared chalk, etc. The action is usually quite rapid, so that one grade of fine abrasive such as lime is usually sufficient. Some workers, however, prefer a preliminary buff with a coarser abrasive. Even dry buffing will often bring up a considerable polish.

The use of wax-free buffing compounds eliminates final cleaning up with benzine, and many workers prefer this more expensive type of compound for this reason. Successive coats, each coat buffed, can be worked with this type of compound. Instead of using straight color coats, the top coat can be clear buffing lacquer. This has much to recommend it, since any type of enamel can be used for undercoats.

### Lathe treatment of turnings

You can apply regular varnish or lacquer finish to turned work the same way as to any other surface. But if you are using a lathe to produce the turning, use it for the finishing too. It is easy and does a better job. First of all, sand the turning until smooth while revolving between centers on the lathe chuck, using fine sandpaper for the final cleanup. On mahoganies, reverse the lathe rotation, and resand. If you are going to use water stain, first sponge the work with water, adding a small amount of dextrin or glue to the sponging water if desired. After this coat has dried, sand the raised fibers until smooth, and apply the stain. If you are using an oil stain, wipe all end-grain places immediately to prevent darkening. You can also seal the end grain before staining. For oil stains use 1 part linseed oil to 15 parts naphtha; for water stains use a thin glue size (1 part animal or casein glue to 15 parts water). Brush or spray the size on the end grain only. After staining, wash-coat the work with shellac, and sand lightly. Any highlighting and filling can be easily done at this time. The filler should be applied by brush while the work is motionless. After the filler has started to flat, it can be rubbed off with the lathe running at slow speed. When the filler is dry, give it a coat of 2-pound-cut shellac, applying the material a little more heavily on the end grain. Run the lathe at slow speed, or revolve the work by hand, while applying the finishing coats. Rub down with pumice and water, revolving the work between centers.

A wax finish is particularly good on beech, birch, maple, and other hard, close-grained woods. Give the work a thin coat of white shellac. After this has dried, apply the wax by brush or with a cloth. Let it stand about 15 minutes; then polish with a soft cloth while the lathe is revolving. A second coat can be applied 1 hour after the first.

Colored stick shellac or sealing wax can be used as a finishing medium. Hold the stick against the revolving work. It will melt by frictional heat and deposit ridges of shellac on the work. Smooth these out with a cloth pad.

French polishing (Chapter 7) gives turned work a superlative high gloss. Prepare the work for the actual polishing by brushing or spraying with shellac until a suitable smooth surface is built up.

Now polish it with the same kind of pad and the same materials as described in the chapter on patching, moving the pad along the surface of the revolving work. Run the lathe at slow speed. Allow 6 to 8 hours between coats for thorough drying. After the polish is complete, give the work a light rub with a pad charged with denatured alcohol and a pat of water. This smoothes out any slight ridges and leaves the work perfectly polished.

# CHAPTER ELEVEN

# Paint and Enamel Finishes

You can obtain some very artistic color schemes with paints, enamels, and other opaque finishes, and with proper preparation and coating you can successfully obscure cheap wood surfaces. The resulting effects can be very pleasing. In fact, painted furniture has been popular since the early part of the eighteenth century.

Furniture is usually painted for one of three reasons:

1. The basic design of the furniture piece to be finished calls for a painted finish. For instance, many Shaker pieces, Pennsylvania Dutch and Southern types, Windsor and Hitchcock chairs and rockers, and some eighteenth-century French furniture were painted originally and to continue their "authenticity" should be painted.

**192**

2. Because the paint is opaque, it provides the easiest and quickest method of finishing a piece of furniture whose surface has been marred by stain or wear.

3. Many new unfinished furniture pieces are available, but because of the wood from which they are built—pine, gum, poplar, beech, fir—the surface often does not have the beauty of a natural or stained finish. Such pieces are best painted.

## Selecting paint for wood surfaces

Enamels are the most commonly used paints for wood-finishing projects. Although charming color effects can be produced with both paint and enamel, it does not give the same high-grade finish as enamel. Paint coatings as a rule are soft and somewhat spongelike, while enamels are quite hard— similar to varnish when air-dried and almost glasslike when baked on. In fact, enamel is basically a varnish with enough pigment added to give it the necessary opacity and color. Also, like varnish, most modern enamels are synthetic-based alkyd, lacquer, epoxy, polyurethane, etc. The latex- and polyvinyl acetate–based enamels should not be used on wood furniture pieces, since they have a tendency to raise the grain of wood slightly.

When selecting paints for small children's furniture, make sure that it contains no ingredients that would be harmful if chewed or swallowed by them. If an enamel contains even small amounts of antimony, arsenic, cadmium, lead, mercury, selenium, or soluble barium, it is not advised to use it on children's furniture. Have your paint dealer check the label of the paint you are purchasing to assure its suitability for items intended for a child's use.

As with varnish, enamels are available in gloss, semigloss

(satin), and flat finishes. Glossy enamels are the most durable while the flat finish is best for a subdued effect. The latter is often paintlike in its flatness and durability.

## Mixing enamel colors

Modern enamel comes in a complete range of colors. Most paint dealers have a custom-mixed system that offers a color selection ranging from pale off-whites to the deepest brilliant hues. Each color has a factory-prepared formula so that the dealer can mix the color you choose very quickly and can duplicate it any time you wish. Occasionally, however, a special color is essential to complete the color scheme in a room. The use of pure oil colors for tinting purposes then makes possible a much wider range of color.

Successful tinting of enamel requires a good eye for color, patience in gradually adding the colors, and—most important of all—foresight to mix enough enamel at one time to avoid any future matching problems. Use a small enamel sample of the exact color as a guide rather than trying to visualize the color when applying it. Make the sample and not any changes in color when dry.

When mixing your own enamel color, start with white enamel of the gloss finish desired, and plan to buy a little more than is required for the job. You will then not have to worry about rematching the original batch to complete the work. Pour a small proportion of the white enamel into a separate container, add the tinting colors and stir well so that the colors are thoroughly mixed together. The color will, of course, be very much darker than the final shade of the mixed enamel. Now, gradually add this mixture to the white enamel, stirring constantly. After each addition of color, compare the color of the mix with the final color desired.

When approaching the final color, add the tinting mixture a very little bit at a time, being careful not to add too much. You can always add more color, but once it is mixed into the enamel, it cannot be taken out. You may find it necessary to adjust the tinting mixture by adding one or more pure oil colors. For example, if you are matching a green sample and the enamel is too blue, you will have to add a little more yellow to the concentrated tinting mixture. Or should an orange appear too yellow, you will have to add a little more red to the mixture.

Here is a check list of the things to remember when mixing enamel:

1. Add tinting colors little by little until color is right.
2. Stir thoroughly to eliminate any possible streakiness in enamel.
3. Make a final check of your color when dry. Remember that flat enamel usually looks a little lighter when dry, gloss enamel a little deeper, and blue-greens and greens a little bluer.
4. For the deeper "decorator" colors, do not use white as the base. Instead, start with a ready-mixed color similar to the one you want but lighter in tone, and add the oil colors as necessary to deepen and adjust the colors.

### Surface preparation

A smooth, clean surface is a prerequisite to any paint job—big or small. All new wood should be sanded smooth with fine to extra fine abrasive paper. Cracks and nail holes should be filled, using wood dough or putty or a glue powder mixture (mix equal parts of glue powder and dust, then add water). This kind of patching can be done on bare wood.

Never leave dead-sharp edges on wood projects. Sand them

down to a round as big as a pencil lead, and they will still look sharp and hold paint. While paint is usually applied on close-grained wood, do not forget that when painting open-grained wood, you must use paste wood filler to fill the pores. Apply a thin coat of filler on the softwood end grain to kill the natural suction of the wood. On fir and similar woods, give the surface a coat of sealer (see page 209) to control the wild grain. On pine, care must be taken to treat all sapstreaks and knots. Pitchy spots and sapstreaks should be first washed down with several applications of turpentine or mineral spirits to remove any surface deposits. Then coat the immediate area around the sap deposits or knots with a wash coat of 1-pound-cut shellac. The shellac will shield the enamel from the sap. Knots may also require some filling with wood dough or putty.

While unfinished furniture pieces are usually factory-sanded, it is a good idea to sand them lightly before applying the enamel undercoater.

It is a waste of time and effort to apply fresh paint to an old finish in bad condition, since the results will surely be disappointing. Therefore, examine the piece to see if it is:

Scaling—coming off in scales or flakes

Cracking—covered with side splits in the finish

Crazing—covered with a network of fine, hairline cracks

If large areas have scaled or cracked, the old finish should be removed.

There are a number of ways to remove the old finish. You can use a paint scraper, or sand off the old finish with sandpaper. If the usual methods (see Chapter 16 for details on removing old finishes) do not work, then a commercial paint-and-varnish remover can be used. Remember that the paint finish is never any smoother than the surface to which it has been applied.

To obtain a permanent and satisfactory paint job on any material, be sure the surface is dry, free from wax, oil, grease, or other soil when painted. Waxy or dirty surfaces should be washed with a detergent house cleaner; if the work is reasonably clean, wipe with turpentine, alcohol, or any of the special preparations made for cleaning and conditioning old paint.

### Application of undercoater

Before applying gloss or semigloss, you will need to prime new wood with an enamel undercoater. An undercoater is a special formulation which provides an ideal surface for enameling. In many cases an undercoat makes it possible to complete a colored finish in two coats, since you can put more enamel on over an undercoat without the problem of runs or sags. The undercoater is usually white and should be tinted to approach the color of the top coat, or you will never accomplish a one-coat top coat of a darker enamel. Thinned enamel, of course, makes a fairly good undercoater. Use 4 parts of enamel to 1 part of the specific solvent recommended on the container.

To apply the undercoater, use a thoroughly clean 1½- or 2-inch brush. Stir the undercoater thoroughly with a wood paddle. Never shake the can, since this will cause a lot of bubbles. For a smooth, even film two-way brushing is best. Lay the undercoater on across the grain. Then brush lightly with the grain, covering a 6- to 10-inch square area at a time. (See Chapter 3 for brushing techniques.) Always work under a good light, so that the glare on the fresh undercoat will help you to avoid skipped places, runs, and coarse brushing. If the undercoater runs, brush it out with a nearly dry brush; if the runs have had a chance to set, then brush them out with a brush loaded with undercoater. Turn chairs and tables upside down, and paint the underside and legs. Then turn upright, and do the chair seats and tabletops last.

### Applying the enamel

As previously stated, enamel is basically a varnish with pigment; therefore, the brushing techniques for enamel are basically the same as those for varnish. Use a good-quality soft-bristle brush, and try to avoid dipping the brush into the enamel more than one-third its bristle length. Always start on an unpainted area and work toward a painted one when you have just refilled your brush. Flow the enamel onto the surface in long, smooth strokes with the grain. Do not reload; cross-stroke. Then, with your nearly dry brush, go over the surface with the grain, once again using long, smooth strokes. This method provides even coverage and eliminates any excess which might cause runs.

Never let enamel creep up into the heel of the brush. Once the bristles are filled up to the heel, the enamel will run down the handle no matter what you do. Press out the extra material frequently against the side of the paint container. If only the tip of the brush carries the enamel, you can paint overhead easily without dripping. Beware of projections. Nails, uneven surfaces, and the irregularities of some moldings invite trouble. When you draw your brush over such surfaces, the brush will be drained exactly the same as against the edge of the can, and enamel will run from these points. Use less enamel on the brush at such spots. Do not press heavily against the work with your brush. Not only will it drive paint up into the heel of the brush, but also the brush will be deformed and wear unevenly.

Generally, one coat will do for most refinishing work. However, a two-coat system is better when an enamel undercoater is used. For a built-up, mirror-smooth finish, try three or four thin coats. When using two or more coats of enamel, the first coats should be thinned at least 10 percent with thinner of the type recommended by the manufacturer. The final, or top-coat should be full strength. Sand lightly between each coat with extra fine grit abrasive paper. Waterproof abrasive paper and water may be used on enamel surfaces for more rapid smoothing. It is important to bear in mind that although enamels usually dry fairly quickly, allow ample hardening time before applying additional coats. The manufacturer's directions are the best guide to the exact amount of time needed.

If a satin or low-luster finish is desired rather than a high gloss, the surface should be rubbed like a coat of varnish, using pumice stone and water. It can be rubbed with rubbing oil to produce a somewhat more glossy surface. Follow the same methods when rubbing down enamel as when rubbing varnish or lacquer (see page 176). If you are using pumice stone, be careful along the edges not to cut through the surface finish. Allow all surfaces to dry absolutely hard before polishing, or they may roll. If you want a very dull finish, use a very fine waterproof garnet paper for surfacing the finish coat. Fold the paper over a sanding block with rounded edges to prevent cutting through or scratching the surface. Wet the surface to be worked with water, using a sponge. Apply the sanding block with only the lightest pressure, since this material has far greater cutting power than pumice stone and oil. Remember that a rubbed glossy enamel is usually more durable and beautiful than the more convenient low-gloss enamel finish.

Another way to get a semigloss effect is to mix undercoater with enamel: 1 part of undercoater to 3 parts of enamel. The gloss can be lowered even more by increasing the amount of undercoater to this mixture. However, since most undercoaters are made in white only, they will lighten the enamel, and pure oil colors will have to be added to bring the mixture back to the original tint.

Enamels can also be applied by a paint sprayer or aerosol-type spray can. When using a sprayer, the enamel will generally have to be thinned slightly. The amount of thinning will depend on the original consistency of the enamel and on the type of spray equipment employed. But keep in mind that the majority of enamels available in local paint stores are intended for brushing, not spraying. This means that they do not dry as rapidly as those designed for sprayer use. If not applied too heavily or thinned too excessively, brushing enamel will spray almost as well as one made for spraying.

### Quick drying enamels

These quick-drying synthetic enamels are similar to lacquer and are applied as directed in Chapter 8. Although they may be either air-dried or baked, baking increases the gloss, durability, and adhesion by rendering the surface insoluble and infusible. Generally ½ to 1 hour's baking at 200° F. is ample.

These synthetic enamels are usually applied by spraying, and the gun requires a nozzle and tip made for synthetic-enamel spraying. First, coat the piece with only a light spray, and allow it to set about 2 minutes. Then apply a wet coat of just enough material to give a solid cover but no more. When this coat is dry, a second may be applied. However, one coat is usually enough when working with baking enamels. Both baking and air-drying synthetic enamels should be reduced one-fifth in volume (20 percent) with a thinner recommended by the individual manufacturer. Incidentally, many professional finishers prefer colored lacquers (see page 147) to enamels because of their drying characteristics. But when spraying colored lacquers or quick-drying enamels, an external-mix type of spray gun is needed to deliver a steady, nonpulsing stream of air that will atomize the material finely. Many inexpensive spray units cannot be used with either colored lacquers or special quick-drying synthetic enamels.

### Catalytic enamels

In Chapter 8, the catalytic type of clear or natural wood finishes was mentioned. Catalytic coatings are also available in enamels. These coatings are true polyurethanes and epoxies which are composed of a resin and a hardener. But before doing any mixing of two materials, read the manufacturer's directions. Almost all the companies furnish these coatings in kits consisting of two equal-sized containers (2 pints, 2 quarts, 2 gallons, etc.). Use a large mixing pot which will hold more than the combined volume of the two containers you wish to mix (e.g., use a gallon can for mixing 2 quarts). If the manufacturer's instructions say to mix the two ingredients in *equal proportions,* mix the contents of both containers—or measure an equal volume of each component if you do not wish to use the entire kit at one time. Stir the two components vigorously for several minutes—be sure they are thoroughly mixed—just as you would any enamel. Now—this is important—wait for at least ½ hour before starting to apply. This gives the chemical reaction a chance to begin and results in faster drying and a stronger enamel film. Use the mixed enamel in the same way you would a conventional alkyd coating. Brush or spray it, but do not pile on extra heavy coats—you do not want sags, curtains, or drips to form. The catalytic enamel will dry dust-free in 15 to 20 minutes and hard enough to touch in about 1 hour. The enamel will be hard for practical usage after overnight drying but will continue to harden for approximately 1 week at normal room temperatures. (See manufacturer's notes on label.)

When recoating this type of enamel, it is important to follow the manufacturer's instructions carefully. Epoxy enamels of this type contain strong solvents and may *lift* previous coats during certain periods of the drying cycle. Many manufacturers recommend recoating within the first 6 hours of drying or after 72 hours drying. If any thinning is necessary, use only the thinner recommended by the manufacturer. Other thinners may curdle the paint and render it unusable. The potlife of the mixed enamel is limited—generally it is at least 8 hours, and sometimes considerably longer (see manufacturer's notes on label). Since a chemical reaction is involved, the mixed enamel will last longer in a cool place than a warm one.

### Painting outdoor furniture

Your new pieces of garden or porch furniture, playthings, ornaments, arbors, and other projects for outdoor use need a good protective finish against the ravages of the elements. You may also have a number of old pieces that are badly in need of a fresh coat of paint, since the finish on this kind of furniture requires freshening almost every spring. Paint is a vital protection for wood that is exposed outdoors, and a good, durable finish on porch or lawn pieces will save time, money, and effort.

To obtain a smooth, hard finish, proper preparation of the surface (see page 11) is important. First sandpaper the wood and dust it off thoroughly. Before painting, shellac any pitchy spots to prevent the pitch from "bleeding through." Remove grease spots from the wood, if any are present, with green soap or benzine.

Fill large holes in the wood by inserting pieces of wood that match the original, and glue them in place. Fill small holes and cracks with a thick paste made by mixing a little sawdust with waterproof wood glue. Commercial paste filler also may be used for small cracks and holes.

In repainting garden furniture, the condition of the wood as well as that of the old paint must be carefully taken into consideration. If the old paint has weathered down to a soft, dusty appearance, you need only clean and dust the surfaces before applying the first coat of paint. Scrape off paint blisters with a putty knife, and smooth the edges with sandpaper.

Cracking and scaling of the paint film is usually the result of faulty paint mixtures or painting over improperly dried surfaces. It is almost always caused by improper mixing and application of the priming coat, although too many coats of paint applied year after year may also cause cracking and scaling. If most of the old paint is cracked and scaled, you may assume that sooner or later all the rest of the paint will come off. Applying new paint over such surfaces will not check the condition; as long as any of the old paint remains on the surface, fresh paint cannot take a firm hold on the wood. Your only solution is to remove all the old paint right down to the bare wood. In most cases you will have to remove the old paint after every third or fourth painting.

For a transparent coating on outdoor furniture, use spar varnish. This is an exceedingly durable varnish of the type devised for the weather-beaten masts of sailing ships. Hence its name. Several of the synthetic varnishes are also suitable for exterior use. Follow the varnishing directions in Chapter 6.

For colored surfaces, use either exterior oil paint or exterior enamel. Enamel is generally used, since it is easier to keep clean and offers a much brighter surface. For new work, first apply a primer (for oil paint) or an undercoater (for enamel), and follow with one or two coats of finishing paint. For old work, one or two coats are all that are required. The undercoater or primer should be tinted a base color or the same color as the final coat. For instance, a flat buff undercoater can be used under orange, cream, yellow, brown, or red, and a flat gray under green, blue, or gray. After the first coat, work putty into all nail holes and cracks, and when dry apply the final two coats of paint. Each coat of paint, except the last, should be lightly rubbed with fine sandpaper in order to ensure a good, smooth final coat.

To renew wrought iron and other metal furniture, clean thoroughly first. Next, sand away any traces of rust. Prime the spots of bare metal with a quality metal primer such as zinc chromate. Let the primed areas dry, and then apply the enamel. Follow the same procedure for aluminum furniture.

### Painting wicker furniture

When painting or varnishing wicker, reed, or fiber furniture, use a spray gun rather than a brush. If you must use a brush, see the directions on page 42. If the finish is in fairly good condition and the color does not have to be changed, the furniture can be greatly improved by spraying on a thin coat of enamel or lacquer with the type of spray usually used for applying insecticides.

The wicker or reed should be given a thorough scrubbing with a palmetto brush and a solution of ½ cup of washing soda in a pail of hot water, then rinsed with a hose and set in the sun until dry. Fiber furniture can be cleaned with denatured alcohol.

Wicker and reed can be stained after the washing soda treatment with the usual wood water stains (see page 98). The stain should be applied generously with a 4-inch clean wall brush. Begin with the hidden portions, and finish with the back, arms, and front panels. If a second coat is required, do not apply it until the first has dried thoroughly. Use a spray gun if one is available, since it will lay on the stain more evenly and will avoid the wiping which is necessary when a brush is used.

A thin coat of clear spar or exterior synthetic varnish may be used as a sealer over the stain coat without danger of lifting any of the color. Use a spar varnish which has been reduced with 50 percent of pure turpentine (or an exterior synthetic type thinned the same amount with its proper solvent), spray on, and let dry overnight. The next day, spray on a coat of full-bodied spar or exterior synthetic varnish. This should be reduced for spray purposes with 1 ounce (⅓ cup) of pure turpentine per quart of varnish. On new work, two finish coats of varnish are advisable.

Wicker, reed, and fiber furniture can also be enameled and lacquered but do not require the priming coats necessary on ordinary woods. First clean the furniture thoroughly with washing soda, and rinse with clean water. New furniture of these materials should be sealed with a wash coat of shellac or a very thin coat of white lead and oil. A good finish can be obtained by applying two coats of enamel or colored lacquer.

Thin the enamel with an equal amount of turpentine or recommended thinner, and spray it on the furniture in a light, even coat. The amount of thinner required varies with the type of sprayer used. In some cases 1 part turpentine or thinner to 3 parts enamel will be sufficient. Do not use the paint any thinner than you have to.

## PRECAUTIONS

*If at all possible, do your spraying in the open air. In any case, be sure to have good circulation of fresh air to carry away the fumes. The vapor is inflammable.*

It is difficult, but possible, to paint wicker, reed, and fiber with a brush, because the finishing material tends to settle in the wicker intersections in the form of blobs. Use an old clean brush with which you can scrub the paint into the hollows of the woven material. Pour some of the enamel into a shallow pan, dip the end of the brush in the paint, and daub it onto the furniture material, tamping it up and down so that the bristles and paint permeate every section. Never load the brush with enamel and draw it over the surface, because then it only covers the surfaces and does not fill the hollows without puddling.

Frosting is another type of finish that can be applied to wicker, reed, fiber, or willow woven furniture. It also can be used on deep-pored woods. This effect is obtained by applying a contrasting color or a deeper shade of the same color over the ground coat, then wiping off the surface while still wet with a cloth to show the first color in the top surfaces only, with the second color covering the under surfaces.

The ground coat may be paint, enamel, or stain. When these undercoats are hard and dry—or if stain is used, sealed with a coat of shellac—then the second color may be sprayed on. Although oil colors mixed with white lead are easy to wipe off, they are so slow-drying that they may soften the under color. The best material for frosting, therefore, is oil color combined with drier. Since this is faster-drying, apply and wipe off only a section of the frosting at one time. The frosting color may be sprayed or brushed on with an old brush that will work down into the holes. Do not make the paint too thin, or it will spatter and run even after wiping; if too heavy and thick, it will clot the holes.

Another finish is the so-called "drybrush look." To accomplish it, start by covering the rattan furniture with a coat of shellac, brushed on. Then spray or paint on a base color of flat or semigloss enamel. When the base coat is dry, select a bright-colored gloss enamel for the top coat.

Almost any old paintbrush about 2 inches wide will do for applying drybrush paint. Dip the brush in the paint; then brush most of it out on newspapers. With the brush almost dry, stroke the surfaces lightly and rapidly. The bright-colored gloss enamel will build up on the high spots, allowing the base coat to show through elsewhere. No top coat is needed with this finish.

### Refinishing bamboo

Bamboo furniture, when used on an open porch or terrace, loses the natural gloss of the wood. Since this material looks best in its natural color, it should only be treated to a protective coating of spar varnish. Use a small brush for the bamboo poles, and work the varnish well into the corners where one strip joins the other. If the bamboo strips are close together, you may have to use a spray gun. However, when the bamboo forms an open-frame design, the spraying will waste much of the varnish. The furniture piece can also be finished with waterproof varnish in the same manner.

# CHAPTER TWELVE

# Plywood and Composition-board Finishes

In recent years there has been an increased use of plywood and composition board in the home workshop. Most of these materials can be finished in the standard way, but some require special preparation and finishes.

## Plywood

One of the most popular and most economical types of plywood is made of fir. Fir plywood needs a good sealer, because without a sealer the first coat of paint or stain penetrates unevenly, resulting usually in a "wild," over-conspicuous grain.

Several special types of penetrating resin plywood sealers have been developed, which can be purchased from your neighborhood lumber, paint, or hardware dealer. If properly used, the sealer allows the stain to soften the darker markings and deepens the lighter surfaces of the fir wood. The effect is soft and lustrous, with the wild grain figures pleasantly subdued.

To obtain a light natural finish, the wood should first be sanded smooth with fine or very fine sandpaper. It is usually wise to apply a coat of penetrating plywood sealer before doing any sanding. This sanding sealer will help harden the softer wood fibers enough for fine sanding. Be sure to use a sanding block large enough to bridge the largest softwood area. This will help prevent a wavy, dip and hollow effect that frequently occurs when sanding fir surfaces.

After the surface has been thoroughly dusted, apply a thin coat of white shellac reduced to 2-pound cut or another coat of resin plywood sealer. Sandpaper again when dry, and apply either a satin-finish lacquer or a gloss varnish. For a flat finish, substitute a flat or dull varnish. After drying thoroughly, steel-wool and complete with white wax.

Fir plywood can be stained with almost any of the stains mentioned in Chapter 4. Staining on unsealed fir, however, will, as previously mentioned, result in a greatly accentuated grain pattern, with the soft areas taking most of the stain and becoming considerably darker. Because of this, pig-mented wiping stains are ideal on fir plywood because it is possible to hide much of the undesirable wild grain. Wiped varnish stain will have much the same effect. But when using water or NGR stain it is necessary to apply a coat of resin plywood sealer first, and then color with the stain. When the desired degree of penetration is obtained, wipe the stain. Once dry, apply another coat of plywood sealer, and then finish in the same way as for a light natural finish.

For a blond or pickled effect on fir plywood panels use a white penetrating resin plywood sealer or interior white undercoating, thinned as follows: 6 pounds of flat undercoater, 3½ quarts of pure turpentine, and 1 pint of linseed oil. If the white sealer is used, it may be thinned 10 to 15 percent with mineral spirits or turpentine. Paint on the sealer and allow it to set for 3 or 4 minutes. Rub it into the pores, then wipe clean, taking care not to leave a painted effect. Let it dry overnight, and then sand with fine sandpaper. Apply a thin coat of pure white shellac, and sand when dry. Follow with a coat of lacquer or varnish. Steelwool when dry, and wax.

An inexpensive but attractive finish may be had with a single coat of white resin plywood sealer or interior white undercoater. Pigment to the desired tint, and thin sufficiently so that the grain of the wood will show through. A coat of clear shellac or varnish over this will add durability to the finish and give it a deep luster.

If you are going to paint fir plywood, the sealer will provide a smooth, even base, and the enamel may be applied directly over the sealer. For best results, however, sand the surface smooth before applying the enamel.

The textured plywood panels have a brushed surface that gives pleasing texture. They have been popular for years, and one of the reasons is that there is virtually no limit to the effects you can obtain—you can finish them with enamel, stain, varnish, or lacquer; keep them in their attractive "natural" tone; or finish them in bright or dark shades. The four most common methods are described in the chart on page 213.

## Hardwood plywood finishes

You can finish hardwood plywood panels by the same method as any other hardwood. Before applying the finish, smoothly sandpaper all panels with fine sandpaper, and clean the surfaces with a dust brush. Apply two coats of the lacquer or varnish, going over the paneling with steel wool after each coat has dried. When you apply the lacquer or varnish, start at the top of the panel, working downward, and do only one panel at a time. After steel-wooling the second coat, apply white paste wax to give a fine light natural-wood effect. By rubbing the wax soon after applying it you can obtain an attractive soft sheen. If you allow the wax to set longer before rubbing, you can produce a higher sheen. Two coats of wax will produce the best results, and an occasional waxing afterward will keep the wood fresh and new-looking.

For the popular "pickled," or blond, finish use a white penetrating resin sealer or white pigment paint that has been thinned with turpentine or mineral spirits. Brush it on, and allow it to set for 3 or 4 minutes; then rub it into the pores, wipe the surface clean, and let dry overnight. The following day, go over it lightly with fine sandpaper, put on a coat of satin-finish lacquer or varnish, allow to dry, then rub down with steel wool. Now apply white wax, and rub as described above to produce a sheen.

Through popular use, certain finishes have become standard, and a representative group are on pages 216 to 217. These are the most popular finishes, materials, and methods for finishing the commoner types of plywood.

| Finished effect | Method for interior finish | Method for exterior finish | Remarks |
|---|---|---|---|
| Natural | Two coats of satin-finish lacquer or flat varnish steel-wooled between coats and the last coat also lightly steel-wooled | One coat of clear plywood resin sealer and at least one (preferably two) coats of varnish | Satin-finish lacquer is literally water-white. On interior work, it produces the lightest possible natural finish. |
| Contrasted light grooves, "woodsy," effect | 1. Clear plywood resin sealer<br>2. Satin-finish lacquer or flat varnish; filler lightly wiped off leaving some in the grooves<br>3. Dull- or flat-finish varnish | 1. Clear plywood resin sealer<br>2. White plywood resin sealer or glazing filler<br>3. At least one (preferably two) coats of varnish | The clear plywood resin sealer keeps the second coat from showing "painty." White plywood resin sealer produces an attractive "blond" effect, or it may be tinted with colors-in-oil to any desired tone. The varnish protects the work with a matte finish. |
| Contrasted light grooves, with distinctive stained background | 1. Pigmented wiping stain<br>2. Satin-finish lacquer or flat varnish<br>3. White plywood resin sealer or glazing filler<br>4. Dull- or flat-finish varnish | 1. Pigmented wiping stain wiped only across the grooves<br>2. Satin-finish lacquer or flat varnish<br>3. White plywood resin sealer or glazing filler<br>4. One coat of varnish | Satin stains "take" evenly, and the whole procedure produces an unusually distinctive and attractive effect. |
| Painted effect | 1. White plywood resin sealer applied as an undercoater and not wiped off<br>2. One or two coats of flat or eggshell wall finish in the desired tone | 1. White plywood resin sealer applied as an undercoater and not wiped off<br>2. One or two coats of exterior paint in the desired tone | This procedure produces an easily cleaned and attractive solid painted effect. |

## Hardboard finishes

Practically any type of finishing treatment may be used on hardboard—oil paint, enamel, stain, lacquer, shellac, varnish, penetrating resin finishes, or wax synthetics. By following the manufacturer's directions and applying the finishes in the same manner as on a hardwood surface, you will obtain satisfactory results.

See that the surfaces are free of dirt, grease, and other foreign matter before applying the finish. Remove dirt with water and a mild soap; grease with carbon tetrachloride or naphtha. Be sure the board is dry before starting to finish it.

Use a good-quality sealer or primer, and apply it according to the manufacturer's instructions. As a surface-type sealer and primer you may use paint and enamel undercoaters, lacquer sealers, or shellac. Penetrating-type resin finishes are widely used for hardboard floors and other areas where added resistance to abrasion and moisture are necessary.

Paints and other finishing materials may be applied to hardboard by brushing, spraying, wiping, dipping, or rolling. For especially smooth finishes, sand lightly between coats with a fine sandpaper. Hardboard surfaces may be baked at temperatures up to 350° F. for 4 hours with no bad effects on the board.

For most painting or enameling work, three coats are recommended—a good primer or sealer as the first coat and two coats of paint (or an undercoater and a coat of enamel) over the base coat. For interior work, use any good grade of interior paint or enamel. For exterior surfaces, give the hardboard a protective three-coat finish of exterior-grade paint or enamel.

If you apply clear finishes such as varnish, penetrating sealers, or shellac directly to the surface, they will darken the board somewhat. To retain the natural colors, apply two coats of clear sealer reduced 50 percent with benzine. Sand lightly after each coat with fine sandpaper. After the second coat is thoroughly dry and sanded, apply varnish or lacquer. Another less permanent method of keeping the natural appearance is to simply apply a water-white wax and rub to a luster.

Penetrating resin finishes provide an excellent means of finishing and maintaining hardboard work surfaces. They are easily applied, fast-drying, and simple to maintain by cleaning the surface and applying a fresh coat of sealer as necessary.

Three common methods of staining hardboard are (1) with a non-grain-raising stain, (2) with color-in-oil thinned slightly with turpentine, and (3) with a dry pigment or color-in-oil in a clear penetrating sealer. In general, such finishes are brushed on and then wiped with a cloth. The length of time you allow between applying and wiping will determine the intensity of the final color. You may protect the stained surface with a clear varnish or lacquer.

Leather-textured hardboard may be given a clear finish with a sealer, varnish, clear lacquer, or wax, or it may be stained, painted, or lacquered any desired color. A tone-on-tone finish will bring out the natural beauty of textured hardboard and can be applied in any combination of colors.

To obtain a tone-on-tone effect, first apply a suitable undercoater or a lacquer sealer. Over this apply a coat of interior paint, enamel, or lacquer of the ground color. After the ground coat dries, a third coat of a glazing liquid with pigment added is used. This is first applied to the panel and then wiped so that it remains only in the depressions, accenting the leathery effect.

## Common finishes for hardwood plywood panels

| Type of finish | Finishing materials used | Method of finishing |
|---|---|---|
| Light natural | 1. Two coats satin-finish lacquer or flat varnish<br>2. Good-quality paste wax | Apply coat of satin-finish or flat varnish; steel-wool when dry. Apply second coat of lacquer or varnish; steel-wool the second coat and then wax. |
| "Pickled" effect | 1. White plywood resin sealer, or undercoater<br>2. Two coats satin-finish lacquer or varnish<br>3. Good-quality paste wax | The white plywood resin sealer should be thinned 10 to 20 percent with mineral spirits or turpentine. Allow to set 3 to 5 minutes. Rub into the pores and wipe clean, so as not to leave a "painty" effect. Allow to dry 24 hours. Lightly sand with fine sandpaper. Apply one coat lacquer or varnish; when dry, steel-wool. Apply second coat. Steel-wool when dry; then wax. |
| Colonial or Cape Cod effect | 1. Clear plywood (tinted) resin sealer<br>2. Pure-white shellac<br>3. Good-quality paste wax | Thin the clear plywood resin sealer 10 to 20 percent with mineral spirits or turpentine. Thoroughly mix in approximately ½ ounce (by weight) raw umber in oil to the gallon. Brush on and wipe off in 3 to 5 minutes, depending upon the intensity of color desired. Let dry overnight and apply a thin coat of pure white shellac. Sandpaper when dry and wax thoroughly. |
| Blond effect | 1. White plywood resin sealer<br>2. Two coats satin-finish lacquer or varnish<br>3. Good-quality paste wax | The white plywood resin sealer should be thinned 10 to 20 percent with mineral spirits or turpentine. Allow to set 3 to 5 minutes. Rub into the pores and wipe clean, so as not to leave a "painty" effect. Allow to dry 24 hours. Lightly sand with fine sandpaper. Apply one coat lacquer or varnish; when dry, steel-wool. |

| Type of finish | Finishing materials used | Method of finishing |
|---|---|---|
| | | Apply second coat. Steel-wool when dry; then wax. |
| Light Sheraton | 1. Extra-light mahogany filler<br>2. Two coats satin-finish lacquer or varnish<br>3. Good-quality paste wax | Apply extra-light mahogany paste filler, following manufacturer's directions on the can. Let dry overnight. Lightly sandpaper with fine sandpaper. Apply coat of satin lacquer or varnish; steel-wool when dry. Apply second coat of lacquer or varnish, steel-wool when dry, then wax. |
| Modern gray | 1. White plywood resin sealer or tinted undercoater | First tint the white plywood resin sealer with a little lamp black ground in pure linseed oil and a touch of light chrome yellow to equal the shade on the panel. The tinted white plywood sealer should be thinned 10 to 20 percent with turpentine or mineral spirits. Allow to set 3 to 5 minutes. Rub into the pores and wipe clean, so as not to leave a "painty" effect. Allow to dry 24 hours. Sand lightly with fine sandpaper. Apply a coat of lacquer or varnish; steel-wool when dry. Apply a second coat of lacquer or varnish, steel-wool the second coat, and then wax. |
| Sheraton mahogany | 1. NGR stain, medium mahogany color<br>2. Light mahogany paste filler<br>3. Pure white shellac<br>4. Two or three coats good-quality varnish | Apply medium mahogany-color stain evenly. When dry, sand lightly with fine sandpaper. Apply light mahogany paste filler, following manufacturer's directions. Sand lightly. Apply thin coat of pure white shellac. Apply coat of good-quality varnish and sandpaper lightly when dry. Apply second coat of varnish. Sand with extra fine sandpaper. Rub with rubbing compound. |

If you are using a glazing liquid for the third coat, mix it with one-fourth as much turpentine. While stirring the mixture, slowly add color-in-oil. Brush it over the surface of the board, allow it to stand from 1 to 3 minutes, and then wipe with a clean cloth wrapped around a flat sponge or wood block. A final coat of flat or gloss varnish may be applied as protection for the paint. If the first two coats were of lacquer, use a clear lacquer rather than a varnish for this protective coating.

### Particleboard

Particleboard is the newest member of the family of man-made wood-panel products used in furniture and cabinetry. Because it is competitively priced and offers certain woodworking and performance advantages, particleboard is one of the fastest-growing segments of the wood products industry.

When finishing particleboard, just as with all wood products, it is well to know in advance the distinctive characteristics of the material. It is an engineered panel product made by combining wood particles with resins and wax and hot-pressing them into panels of uniform size and thickness. Standard size panels come in 4- and 5-foot widths and up to 20 feet in length, in thickness from ⅛ to 1½ inches. Particleboard has an extremely smooth surface, free of knots, voids, and grain. The basic particleboard surface is somewhat more porous than most finished lumber. Surface characteristics vary from one board to another. Some provide a surface which can be finished without using a filler. Others require a filler to reduce the porosity of the surface. It is a good idea to test scraps to determine the best method for obtaining the desired surface finish.

If a very smooth finish is desired, the particleboard surface should be filled with a paste wood filler or a sanding sealer prior to applying finishes. If the surface is unusually porous, both a filler and sanding sealer should be used. Factory-filled boards, with a surface ready for finishing or painting, are available. Some manufacturers apply a resin-impregnated fibrous sheet to the faces of their particleboards to provide an excellent base for painting.

Particleboard usually contains a small amount of paraffin wax which is added during manufacturing to retard the rate of water absorption. If the paint or finish contains materials which are good solvents for wax, some of the wax will be absorbed in the wet paint film and cause areas with a slower drying rate. The wax can be effectively isolated from interior finishes by applying a thin barrier coat such as shellac, which is not a solvent for wax.

Because of the shapes and color contrasts of the wood particles, interesting decorative effects may be obtained by staining particleboard. A variety of clear finishes and stains can be used to highlight the different colors and shapes of the wood particles. To create these finishes, apply one coat of stain, allow it to set for a few minutes, and then rub and wipe off the excess. The desired color penetration may be determined on some sample material or scraps.

When finishing doors or other free-moving units, it is especially important to finish both sides of the door with an equal number of coats. As with other wood products, particleboard will gain or lose moisture with changes in atmospheric conditions; so unless both sides are finished equally, the less finished side will gain or lose moisture faster than the other side, and the panel will warp. Tops and bottoms of doors should be well sealed with paint to reduce moisture intake.

The edges of particleboard have the same tendency to

absorb a finish as the surface, but usually to a greater extent. When edges are to be exposed to view, they should be filled, before finishing, with paste wood filler or other special filler formulated for the job. Best results on edges are obtained by applying the filler with a putty knife or a coarse cloth applicator. Brush or spray application of filler may be satisfactory on certain boards, such as those having a density above 45 to 50 pounds per cubic foot.

### Insulation board

Insulation board, although generally used as a wall and ceiling material, may also be used as panels in home workshop projects. It may be used in the natural colors applied by the manufacturer or as a base for decorative finishes of various types, including paints, stains and plastic paints.

A single coat of good latex paint will usually give good coverage on insulation board, although two coats are recommended. Some of these paints are available in colors and others can be tinted from the white by the addition of dry colors in accordance with manufacturers' directions.

Stains may be used to modify the natural color of the board without destroying the texture or its sound-absorbing properties. While a variety of stains are available, glue stains usually give the best results on insulation board, and may be made by dissolving ½ pound of flake or ground glue in a gallon of boiling water.

After the glue has been thoroughly dissolved, add the dry color by mixing it with a small amount of water, stirring to a thin paste, and then adding it to the glue solution. Glue stains of this type must be used promptly after preparation. They should, if possible, be applied while they are still warm.

Alcohol stains are not recommended, as they dry too rapidly and leave brush marks.

When oil or synthetic paints are being used on insulation board, it must first be properly sized. Various prepared oil or varnish sizes, ready-mixed and properly proportioned for direct application to insulation board, are on the market. However, a satisfactory glue size may be made by dissolving 1½ pounds of chip or flake glue in a gallon of boiling water. For best results sand the surface lightly after the size coat has dried thoroughly. Apply the paint to this surface, using as many coats as necessary for satisfactory results.

# CHAPTER THIRTEEN

# Novelty and Decorative Finishes

Decorative and novelty finishes discussed in this chapter are both smart and distinctive and are suitable for both brushing or spraying.

## Shading

Shading can be done by spraying the shading material on the finished work, or by coating the work with the shading material and then wiping off to expose the highlights. The effect aimed at is an aged appearance, such as would result from natural wear, although the shaded finish is often used for a novelty effect and in toning various woods to an even color. Other terms applied to this technique include *highlighting, glazing,* and *antiquing,* all of which mean about the same thing.

**Bone-white shaded finish**   Bone white is a typical shaded finish. The color can be purchased ready-mixed or made by adding a little black or brown to white lacquer.

The surface is first coated with bone-white lacquer or enamel and, when dry, is given an overall coat of wiping stain. Raw umber is a good stain for the bone-white finish. It can be brushed or sprayed. Before it reaches a tacky stage, wipe off the stain coat to expose the highlights. The amount of wiping you do will depend on the finish you want. Always leave the color in moldings, carvings, intricate portions of turnings, and other places which would naturally show smudge through long use. (If the satin becomes tacky before you have completed all the wiping, moisten the wiping rag with naphtha.) Allow the surface to dry overnight, and then apply finishing coats of shellac, varnish, or lacquer.

**Shading clear finishes**   Clear finishes may be shaded in any of the following ways:

*Direct stain.* Use any type of permanent stain. Shade directly on the bare wood, using a somewhat heavier application for the darker areas.

*Shading stain.* Spray the stain between coats of finishing material or over filler.

*Wiping stain.* Stain wood in usual manner. Seal. Apply and wipe, wiping stain for highlights. It also can be applied directly to bare wood and then wiped for light areas.

*Sanding.* Use any permanent stain. Allow to dry. Highlight by sanding to bring up light color.

*Oil stain.* When using a penetrating oil stain, highlight by wiping with a cloth while the stain is wet.

On natural wood or wood which has been stained, apply the shaded finish in the same way as already described, except that you use clear varnish or lacquer for the base coat instead of colored enamel. Apply the shading between coats of the finishing material. You can wipe the stain to expose the highlights or spray on the stain to darken the required areas. Spray shading is the most practical for this type of work because it permits a smoother blending of colors. When spraying the stain coat, hold the gun about twice as far as you would hold it for ordinary spraying. Avoid heavy coats—the water-thin stain will puddle if applied too heavy. The shading coat will dry almost as soon as you apply it, and you can work up the darker areas by going over the work twice.

**Direct stain shading** Shading is often done on the bare wood, using water, non-grain-raising, or spirit stains. First mist-spray the work all over to secure a uniform tone. Dilute the stain about half normal strength for this purpose, or control the coating with the spray gun. When this is dry, apply a much stronger solution of the same stain to shade the work.

**Sanding highlights** This technique is the opposite of shading. First stain the work the required color, using any kind of permanent stain except oil. After the stain is dry, pick out the highlights with extra fine sandpaper or steel wool. Numbers 2/0 or 3/0 steel wool are ideal for this purpose, permitting a much smoother blend than sandpaper. You can use steel wool on any wood which does not require a filler. If you are going to use a filler, you will get better results with sandpaper; because the action of the wool cuts away the sharp edges of the pores or grain, leaving a poor anchorage for the filler. However, the steel wool can be used to advantage for blending the edges of the highlight.

**Shading technique** The shading and highlighting technique can best be understood by carefully inspecting factory-finished furniture. As you will see, highlights are applied on the bulbous portions of turnings, in the center of panels and rails, and on raised parts of the carvings. The blend from light to dark is gradual, and the basic color should predominate. In spray shading, you can obtain a perfect blend by drawing the gun back and releasing the trigger at the same time. You can also combine shading with the gun and highlighting with steel wool. Follow the rule of natural wear; that is, highlight all areas which would normally show light through wear, or if the work is being spray-shaded, darken all of the areas which would normally accumulate dirt. There is no fixed rule for tabletops. Darken a very narrow strip all around the edges, widening a little at the corners. Make the blend fairly abrupt, but avoid any suggestions of a regular geometric pattern.

*Uniforming different woods* Shading is also used to blend the various woods used in the construction to a uniform allover tone so that all appear to be the same kind of wood. One method is to spray a light coat of non-grain-raising stain over the entire piece. Then, when dry, certain areas are darkened and highlighted in one operation by the use of a walnut wiping stain. The second method is to control the color at the spray gun, spraying very heavily on the light area and little or none on the darker area. With either of these methods, final toning would be done with shading lacquer between finishing coats. In a brushing schedule, the light area would be brushed with wiping stain and lightly wiped to an even color. The entire piece would then be wash-coated with shellac, after which the darker area would be filled with paste filler and the other treated with a second coat of wiping stain, wiped for highlights.

### Antiqued finish over paint

Antiquing is the application of a glaze coat directly over solid-color backgrounds or over the painted designs and decorations. This glazing is done to mellow and give a soft appearance to freshly painted pieces. Basically, it is accomplished in a three-step process:

1. The surface is painted in a base or background color and allowed to completely dry.
2. A colored glazing liquid is brushed over the surface, one section at a time. It is then partially wiped off with a lint-free cloth, leaving more of it embedded in carvings, grooves, and natural indentations.
3. A coat of flat or satin clear varnish is applied to protect the finish. Some commercial glazes do not require a protective coat over the glaze coat.

Commercial glazing liquids are available at most paint or hardware stores. In recent years, due to the popularity of this finish, many paint companies produce "antiquing kits." These kits include a base coat of a satin-gloss enamel in the color desired, a can of glazing liquid to be applied over it, a piece of cheesecloth (for wiping), and an instruction booklet. Some even supply an inexpensive paintbrush and the necessary abrasive paper.

You may also prepare your own glazing liquid. Mix 3 tablespoonfuls of turpentine, 1 tablespoonful of linseed oil, and 1 tablespoonful of raw umber, raw sienna, burnt umber, burnt sienna, or lamp-black oil color. Of these five pure oil colors, raw umber will make a light gray tone for light-colored paint; raw sienna, a warmer red tone; burnt umber, an interesting brown tone; burnt sienna, a rich reddish brown tone; and the lamp black will make a dull, dirty tone which is best for dark or strong colors. Other oil colors are equally effective, depending upon the base color and the desired effect.

*Applying the glaze* While a glaze coat may be applied over any appropriate finish that is in good condition, the normal procedure, as previously stated, is a coat of semigloss enamel. After the surface has been prepared as described in Chapter 11, the base can be applied. One coat is usually sufficient on previously finished surfaces, but two coats of base should be used on new or unfinished wood. Brush on with crosswise strokes; smooth off with lengthwise strokes working from dry into wet areas. When using a latex-type base coat, apply quickly and liberally, completing a few square feet at a time. Move on to the next section immediately. Latex paint dries very quickly; so wipe up spills and splatters promptly.

After the base coat dries completely—follow manufacturer's directions—apply the thoroughly mixed glazing coat with a paintbrush, applying it to one side of the project at a time. Long, even strokes with the grain of the wood will produce the best results. If the piece has prominent legs, turn it upside down, and paint the legs first, then the top, working downward. Pay special attention to carved trim and crevices, painting them first to allow more absorption of the glaze.

Let the color glaze set from 10 to 55 minutes before beginning to rub or wipe. A touch of the finger and a little experience will tell you when to start the antiquing technique of your choice. Once the glaze has set to the tacky stage, use cheesecloth to wipe it, using a circular motion. Start at the middle and work toward the edges. The center of the panel should be the lightest, with the color gradually darkening toward the edges. Complete this graduated blending by patting with clean cheesecloth, then blending with a dry brush, always working from the center toward the edges. After the final blending is finished, traces of the glaze will still remain in the minute depressions of the surface. Leave them there; they are part of the desired effect. Most commercial glaze liquids are formulated to permit manipulation for up to 45 minutes after application. Most techniques require only a fraction of this time to complete. But if you should have trouble, the entire coat of glaze can be wiped off with a solvent-dampened rag during the 45-minute period, giving you the benefit of a fresh start.

For carved surfaces, such as picture frames, proceed in the same manner as for flat surfaces. If the piece is highly carved, puddles may collect in the depressions. These can easily be picked up with a dry brush. Highlight the raised areas of the carving by wiping off most of the glaze, allowing the background to show through. A little solvent on the cloth will help removal. To slow down the drying time of the glaze (which will give additional time for blending), add a few drops of linseed oil to the mixture. Normally, this should not be necessary except when working on large areas. Glaze that has not dried can be removed almost completely by rubbing with a cloth saturated with the proper thinner, provided, of course, that the background surface was completely dry when the glaze was applied.

There are many other attractive effects that may be obtained by employing the basic glazing techniques. Many of the effects described can be had by more conventional methods which are explained later in this chapter.

**French Provincial**    One of the easiest to handle and most popular antiquing techniques is the so-called "French Provincial" effect, especially appropriate for furniture or other surfaces with paneling, carving, or turning, but equally attractive on simpler construction. Using a soft-textured material, such as a wad of cheesecloth or a piece of carpeting, lightly wipe away most of the glaze coating from the high points of carvings or turnings and from the broad areas of panels and other flat areas. Leave dark accents of glaze in indentations of carvings and turnings and as a narrow, uneven border around flat areas. With a tamping motion, blend the remaining color from light to dark with a clean wad of cheesecloth, carpeting, or a dry brush; this is particularly important on flat surfaces. As a finishing touch, add a very fine spatter of turpentine or glaze. (See directions for spatter, page 249.) Do not overdo it; there should be just enough spatter to add an occasional "pinhole" to the pattern. Complete one section at a time, limiting yourself to an area that can be finished easily within the allotted time span.

**Early American**  Many people find this even easier to accomplish than the French Provincial technique. It can be done very quickly but needs careful planning because overworking will spoil the effect. It is also helpful to apply the glaze a bit more generously than usual. Finished work should have a fine stripe resembling a conventional wood grain. It can be done with a dry, coarse brush or a graining tool. The trick is to stroke firmly through the glaze coating in long, parallel lines, sweeping from one edge to the other with a single continuous motion. A clean, dry tool is essential. After each stroke, wipe brush or graining tool on clean paper toweling or newspaper. When the graining pattern is completed to your satisfaction, add a widely spaced, fine spatter of turpentine or glaze (see discussion of spatter under French Provincial). This technique has more recently been used most effectively on wall paneling where a change in color and general appearance is desired.

*Moiré*   This is worked to resemble the watered, wavy look seen on silk fabrics of the same name. It is done in two steps immediately succeeding one another. Using a coarse steel graining tool, comb lengthwise through the glaze coating to produce relatively straight, parallel lines. The same area is immediately recombed with a fine steel graining tool, this time brought forward in curves and angles instead of straight lines.

*Crumple texture*   This is a method of applying coarse texture with a wad of crumpled material. Use almost anything that will crumple—paper, cheesecloth, burlap, or plastic, to name a few. In fact, the last is best of all because it is nonabsorbent. It will not get soggy and change shape. (Cut up a plastic bag or use sheet plastic.) Crumple the plastic to fit your hand, and press it lightly onto a previously glazed surface. If the surface is thinly glazed or wiped, add more glaze with the crumpled plastic, picking it up from aluminum foil or other shallow surface. Pounce, turning your hand with each motion to assure a random pattern. If the first try does not please you, redistribute the glaze by brushing it in one direction. Start over. For a different effect, give the plastic wad a slight roll or twist each time you touch the surface.

*Marbelizing*   This technique is mainly used to decorate the top surface of an object, and it produces a very dramatic effect. Crumple a piece of plastic wrap to form creases, and lay it over the wet glazed surface. Since the wrinkles form the design, do not stretch the plastic tight nor smooth out the wrinkles. Using a wad of cloth, lightly pat the plastic wrap into the glaze; then lift the plastic straight up from the surface.

*Veining* The classic tool for marble veining is a turkey feather. Drag it across the glaze, to make a straight, thin line; twist and turn the feather a little to vary the width of the line. Occasionally change direction—but at an angle, not with a curve—keeping veining lines straight. String saturated with glaze and dragged across the surface several times at different angles makes a fair imitation of veining.

*Tortoise-shell pattern* This interesting pattern is made by tapping lightly with your fingers over a fairly heavy coating of glaze. For random effect let each tap be from a different angle. For a heavy marble "eye" pattern use rubber gloves. For lighter marble "eye" pattern put your fingers inside a plastic bag.

*Frosting* Beautiful effects, if the work is delicately done, may be secured by glazing with white glaze over furniture enameled in light opaque colors, resulting in a "frosted" effect. Such base colors as pink, azure, or fern, when glazed white will produce a light, delicate look on furniture used in the nursery, bedroom, dressing room, powder room, or even the kitchen. Apply the base coat. When the base coating is dry, brush on glaze coating. White primer or enamel may be used as the glaze mixture. Manipulate the white glaze in the same manner as prescribed for either French Provincial or Early American techniques.

*Distressed wood* This is one of the most popular antiquing effects, and if your piece of furniture is not naturally worn, the effect can be simulated. That is, a distressed wood appearance can be achieved by making random scratches with the point of a nail and dents with pieces of walnut shell or crushed rock pounded into the surface. You can also make the scratches and dents by beating the surface with a heavy tool or a burlap bag filled with chains. Sand the scratches lightly, and then rub raw umber oil color into dents, scratches, and edges. Rub off vigorously, leaving the surfaces around the edges darker.

**Distressed paint** This effect is achieved by applying two layers of contrasting colors to the furniture, allowing each to dry thoroughly. Then take a coarse sandpaper and lightly sand the surface, until the initial color is in evidence. Do this only in the spots where normal wear would occur.

**Striping** For really professional striping, get a long bristled, sign-painter's striping brush available at any paint or art store. Before striping, let your piece dry overnight. This will allow you to guide your brush by resting your hand on the piece and also to repair your stripes by wiping the edges, or to wipe them off completely and try again.

To stripe, dip the brush deep into the glaze, coating the full length of the bristles. Remove excess glaze by drawing each side of the brush against the edge of can. The brush should be loaded but not dripping. To stripe effectively the brush is used with a dragging motion.

For a wide stripe or border, lay brush flat along the stripe line with the full length of the bristles in contact with the surface. Drag the brush in the direction of the stripe. When you run out of glaze, reload and resume your line, overlapping a little.

For a narrow stripe turn your brush to the side of the narrow edge and proceed as for broad stripe. The width of line is a little harder to control in this position.

The easiest kind of striping is where you have a beveled edge or the concave indentation of a molding to act as a guide for your brush. Where there is no such guide, more skill and practice is needed. On the tabletop or border where you want a line to represent a panel on a door or drawer, draw one light guideline with a pencil. Keep the brush to the right of the line (if you are right-handed). Keeping your eye on the line, draw the brush along it with a motion swift enough to keep the line from wavering. Do not go back over it. The grain of the line will give it a finished look.

### Antiquing over stained surfaces

Close-grained woods such as maple, gum, or birch are easy to antique. Since staining alone seldom gives the mellow appearance so essentially a part of this finish, it is necessary to apply a second coat of warm-brown wiping stain, the same as used in the bone-white finish (page 223). Spray or brush on; then wipe off rather cleanly with a dry cloth. Even on areas wiped perfectly clean, enough stain will remain on the wood to give a shaded effect to the finish. Extra-clean highlights can be obtained by wiping the stain with a rag moistened with benzine. After the wiping stain has dried, finish with clear lacquer or varnish.

Open-grained woods such as oak, walnut, or mahogany can also be treated for an antique effect. First, color the piece with a dark tone of stain, then cover with a wash coat of gray paste wood filler, and wipe off on the diagonal rather than at right angles to the grain. Next, protect the filler with two thin coats of shellac or wax, or add a coat of flat lacquer or varnish, and then wax.

You may omit the wood filler when finishing curved surfaces. Use a dull-brown or brownish gray stain. If you are using an oil stain, finish off with shellac; if you are using a water stain, then cover with a thin coat of colorless lacquer.

To give the stained surface an antique effect, make a mixture of a little powdered rottenstone and brown pigments— raw sienna, raw umber, or Vandyke brown—in liquid wax.

The proportions should make a muddy substance, so mix about 4 ounces of pigment and rottenstone together for every quart of liquid wax used. Keep stirring the wax and pigment to keep them from separating. Brush this mixture over the entire piece of furniture, and most particularly in the hollows of the carving. While the coating is still wet, wipe off the surface with a rag moistened in naphtha or turpentine, leaving the mixture in the pores of the wood and in the hollows of the carving and molding. When dry, coat the surface with a coat of shellac, clear varnish, or lacquer; then wax.

To give pine furniture a very antique look, wash it down with 1 part sulfuric acid to 3 parts water solution. The chemical acid eats into all but the hard parts of the wood, causing them to stand out from the rest of the surface. To hasten the process, first sprinkle water on the wood, and then scrub on the acid solution with a wooden-handled wire scratch brush. Be sure to wash all the acid from the wood with a dilute solution of ammonia before staining. After staining, coat the wood with clear lacquer or varnish and wax, or just wax to a dull glow.

## PRECAUTIONS in the use of acid

*When mixing acid and water, remember always to pour the acid into the water; never pour water into acid. Wear heavy rubber gloves and a rubber apron when applying the acid.*

### Leather finish

The glazing technique described for antique can be used to produce an imitation leather finish on wood. The surface should first be given a base coat of white lacquer or enamel, then wet-sanded with fine waterproof paper. Next, brush glaze liberally over the surface, and follow up by lightly wiping off the excess with a clean rag, leaving an even film of glaze on the surface. Then, bunch the rag, letting it wrinkle as much as it will, and with it start patting the glazed surface, starting from one end and working across to the other. Keep this up until the glaze has been mottled into an even, leathery texture. From time to time, the rag can be twisted and reshaped in your hand to work it into a shape that will produce the best effect. When the surface is dry, cover with a coat of clear finish to protect it.

Another method of producing simulated leather is as follows: After the glaze has set for several minutes, blot with a crumpled, dry cloth handled with a slight twisting motion. While the glaze is still wet, brush with a fanning motion, using a dry whisk broom. This makes an interesting finish for tops of tables or chests as well as for feature panels on drawer fronts, cabinets, and doors.

### Wet-gloss look

To achieve the popular "wet" look simply choose and apply any good flat paint or enamel to the surface in the color desired. Then, when dry, apply a coat of high-gloss, water-clear varnish or a coat of special wet gloss clear finish. Incidentally, the wet-gloss clear finish is particularly effective when used over a simulated leather finish.

### Wood graining

Fine wood graining is a skill of the past. However, it is a finishing operation many home craftsmen would like to try. To produce a grained effect, paint the wood a suitable background color. Your choice of color depends on the wood you wish to imitate. For example, to imitate oak, prepare the background paint by mixing 1 pint of white lead with ½ pint of golden ocher pigment, and then add boiled linseed oil and a little drier. For birch, prepare a ground coat of white lead with a little yellow ocher or raw sienna to produce a light buff color. For a maple background, mix a little deep vermilion and lemon chrome with white lead. Walnut is generally best obtained with a sand-colored base coat, while mahogany needs a little more red in the color. Pine and other similar light woods call for a cream- or buff-colored base coat. The glaze color should be similar to the grain color of the wood. For walnut, a dark brown should be used, while for lighter woods a lighter glaze is usually employed. Keep in mind, however, that unless you are matching a specific wood, colors are not overly important.

To accomplish the effect, first wipe the glaze uniformly with 2/0 or 3/0 steel wool, moving it lightly across the surface in order to obtain a streaky effect without removing too much glaze. After wiping the object with the steel wool, follow with a dry brushing, moving the dry tips of the bristles lengthwise along each section to blend the streaks left by the steel wool and to create a more uniform effect. To simulate the wavy effect of a wood grain, twist the brush slightly as it is moved along, or weave it slowly from side to side as you go. Allow the glaze to dry for several days before applying the varnish.

### Gold effects

Several of the finishes described in this chapter require the addition of gold. Here are several of the easiest ways in which this gilding effect may be achieved.

Use gold powder and bronzing liquid (purchase them at

art supply stores). Mix the powder with the liquid only as required. For a gold wipe, apply gold lightly with dry brush. Wipe thoroughly and quickly before gold sets. This distributes the gold in small amounts over the entire area to create gold glints rather than gold spots. The use of bronzing powder will be discussed later in this chapter.

To apply a gold highlighting effect, use the dry brush technique—see page 263. Touch high spots lightly. If too much gold is deposited, wipe lightly before gold sets. Gold can also be applied by the spatter method—see page 249.

Gold in wax is now available. This paste form of gold may be rubbed on with the finger or a cloth, dried, then buffed to a fine sheen that resembles gold leaf. Use very small amounts—a little goes a long way. It is excellent for striping a concave molding line that may be traced with the finger. For flat or textured surfaces, thin with turpentine, and apply gold using dry-brush technique. Thin with turpentine to spatter or for use with striping brush. To repair or remove gold in wax, use turpentine.

### Old World finish

Old World is just a streamlined name for antiquing or shading. The stains that can be bought under this name try to duplicate the natural color that old furniture acquires by aging. However, most of the effect depends on skillful shading, using either wiping stain or shading stain, or a combination of the two. The finish can be filled if desired. For the proper foundation, sand all edges to give the appearance of wear. Artificial nicks and scratches are no longer considered necessary as a part of this finish. After the stain and a sealer coat, the work is ready for shading, which is followed by top coats of lacquer or varnish to complete the finish.

Further aging can be obtained by a wax coat. Use black or dark-brown wax, which leaves a deposit in corners and recesses the same as in the wiping technique. Powdered rottenstone or powdered raw umber mixed with ordinary paste wax can be applied to corners and moldings for a "dusty" effect. The powder can also be mixed with liquid wax and be applied by brush and wiped just like a wiping stain. This technique can be used directly over the permanent stain coat if desired.

**Polychrome finish**

Polychrome finish, which was very popular during the Italian Renaissance, is seldom used now except on surface carvings of small decorative objects. Use a thin coat of shellac as a first coat or sealer. Next, cover the whole object with gold bronze, using either gold leaf laid over the japan gold size or the metallic powder dissolved in bronzing liquid. Apply a coat of white shellac to prevent injury to metal leaf. After the shellac has dried, apply a coat of dull, soft red. While the paint is wet, wipe it from the raised surface to show the rich gleam of the gold beneath. Then apply a coat of a dull olive and wipe in the same manner. If deeper shadows are desired, you can work antique glaze (page 226) on to tone down the whole thing.

**Pickled pine**

Pickled pine is a gray finish which duplicates the effect formerly produced by actually pickling the wood with nitric acid. You may find it necessary to bleach darker wood before applying the gray stain. This stain can be purchased ready-mixed. Apply the stain, let dry, then give the surface two coats of water-white lacquer, and follow with a coat of wax.

Add rottenstone powder to the wax, if desired, for an aged, dusty effect.

The pickled finish is frequently treated with a white glaze. To produce this finish, stain the work as before, and follow with a coat of sanding sealer of 2-pound-cut shellac. Apply the white glaze, and wipe off immediately to expose highlights, leaving the white coloring in corners, recesses, etc. A good glaze for this purpose can be made from soft paste white lead thinned with turpentine and with a little linseed oil and japan drier added. Seal the glaze coat with a coat of white shellac; then wax. Brown wax is sometimes used, leaving dark smudges in the corners. The wax blends into the white glaze, and this in turn blends into the gray body color. The work can also be streak-glazed; that is, the white glaze is wiped off in streaks, wiping in the same direction as the grain of the wood. Some workers prefer to apply glaze on the bare wood or over the stain coat. If this is done, the wood can be sandblasted or eaten by sulfuric acid to give a surface which will retain the white glaze.

Another method of producing a pickled finish on almost any wood is with oxalic acid (page 32). First bleach the wood with the acid, follow with a wash coat of shellac, and then apply a very light amber-colored stain or filler. Follow with a coat of sanding sealer and two coats of flat lacquer. Wash shellac consists of equal parts of 4-pound-cut shellac and alcohol. Make amber stain by mixing ¼ pound raw sienna, 1 ounce yellow ocher, 1 pint linseed oil, ¾ pint turpentine, and ¼ pint japan drier. Sand surface between coats.

### Gesso

Gesso is a heavy-bodied plasterlike opaque paint that can be applied to new wood and over old finishes. It can be textured in many of the ways described for antiquing. It also can be employed to build small decorative "carving" on picture and mirror frames.

While this ancient art was usually done with plaster, water putty such as that described in Chapter 2 may be used, and it is easy to work. Select the desired base color in a flat water- or latex-base flat paint or enamel. Do not mix the material. Pour off the thin liquid on top, and permit the paint to set open until it has turned to a rather thick paste. Then mix the dry-powder water putty with water to make a thick paste, slightly heavier than directed on the container. When the putty is smooth and free from lumps, mix this paste with the paint at a ratio of 2 parts paint to 1 part water putty.

Using an old paintbrush, apply the gesso directly to the surface in a thickness of about $\frac{1}{16}$ inch. Coat only one complete surface at a time. Remember that your brush strokes will remain on the surface. Therefore, brush out the gesso carefully so that the fine lines run parallel to the long dimension of the item being painted. But, since gesso sets up fairly fast, overworking it will result in stuttering brush marks. While this can cause an interesting textured surface, it is not desirable when a smooth, standard gesso finish is desired.

When the first gesso coat has dried—allow about 12 hours —sand it carefully with an abrasive paper in the 6/0 to 8/0 grit range. The sanding is used to level off the gesso and is done in the same direction in which the gesso is brushed on to keep the fine lines parallel. Wipe the surface with tack rag, and apply a second coat. When this is dry, sand with an 8/0 paper only as required to give the desired texture. After the surface has been cleaned, a top coat of clear varnish or lacquer is usually applied. Many gesso finishes are glazed to produce the antique effect so popular with wood finishers.

## Two-tone finish

A two-toned furniture finish is applied in two colors of lacquer enamel or light and dark stain. In the case of enamels, masking tape is used to block off the first color in the required areas. An overall coat of the second color is then sprayed on. A similar effect is obtained with stain. First stain the work overall with a light-colored stain. Then block off certain areas with masking tape, and spray a darker stain on the unprotected parts. You can obtain a similar effect by masking the areas that are to be dark and spraying a bleaching lacquer or clear shellac on the areas which are to remain light. When the lacquer is dry, remove the masking tape, and apply a filler on the bare wood now exposed to slightly darken it. The filler will have no effect on the areas protected by the lacquer coating. Another method for two-toning is to coat with shellac or bleaching lacquer the bare wood of those areas that should remain light. When the work is stained in the usual manner, only the unprotected areas become dark.

## Treatment of wood inlays

A thin coat of shellac or bleaching lacquer will prevent the wood inlay from taking the stain color. Since the inlays are usually hard, close-grained woods, they can also be filled over without darkening. The shellac coat will not, of course, prevent an open-pore inlay from taking filler. However, the light portions of the inlay are invariably close-grained, and take the filler but retain their color. The simplest method of applying the block-off coat is with a small brush and shellac;

when bleaching lacquer is applied by spraying, mask with tape in the usual manner. In preparing inlays for finishing, you may have some difficulty with ebony and rosewood. These woods are very oily, and the dust lifted by sanding usually has enough oil in it to stain light-colored woods. Probably the best remedy for this is to sponge the surface with lacquer thinner before sanding. This removes the surface oil so that any light sanding can be done without discoloration.

### Parchment finish

This finish, very popular for picture frames and small furniture objects, is laid on over a solid opaque color coat. Use a slightly darker color than the ground coat, and thin it with linseed oil and turpentine. Flow this color onto the painted finish quite freely, and then spread it evenly with a rag or cheesecloth. While this is still wet, dapple or stipple the surface with a clean rag. When it dries, spray the surface with a thin coat of flat lacquer, or brush on a thin coat of white shellac.

### Blond sealers

If you wish to eliminate the bleaching process (see Chapter 2 for other bleaching processes), you can still obtain excellent blond finishes by using a blond sealer. This is a very satisfactory method of treating birch, maple, and other naturally light woods. The sealer color can be made by adding white lacquer enamel (1 part) to clear lacquer (4 or 5 parts), or, for amber effect, add tan lacquer (1 part) to the clear (4 parts). Blond sealers of this kind can also be purchased ready-mixed. A uniform, light coat of the sealer will produce a satisfactory blond color without obscuring the natural grain of the wood. This technique is perfect on maple and birch, and can be used to produce an attractive, lighter tone on walnut and mahogany. However, when overdone on dark-colored woods, it gives the wood an unpleasant, painted appearance.

## Novelty oak finishes

Novelty oak finishes feature a contrasting filler, as, for example, white filler in contrast with a gray or green stain. This is generally described as flat frosting and can also be used on chestnut, mahogany, and any other wood with coarse, open pores. Silver or Kaiser oak is typical of these finishes. First apply a gray stain, using a prepared liquid stain or a gray water stain. Seal with bleaching lacquer or thin white shellac, and then apply the white filler, which can be purchased ready-mixed or made by adding white lead or zinc to natural filler. Seal the filler with a thin coat of white shellac, and follow with a clear paste wax. Another method is to use the white wax as a filler. White wax can be purchased or made by coloring ordinary paraffin wax with zinc white, as described on page 181. Complete the finish with ordinary clear paste wax. For a better gray color, the wood can be bleached before staining.

Kitchen furniture is often finished by frosting with lacquer enamel. The bare wood is first coated with ivory, white, or gray-green lacquer, applying the lacquer just heavy enough to give a uniform ground color without filling the pores too much. The pores are then filled with a contrasting color of filler—white on gray, aluminum on gray, white on ivory, gray on ivory, etc. After the filler has been wiped off and allowed to dry, the work is given one or two coats of water-white lacquer or white shellac. White wax can be used instead of white filler if desired, in which case the final finish must also be wax.

### Textured finish

A clean steel wire brush having sharp bristles can be employed to texture wood. Scrub across the grain of softwood and with the grain of hardwood until the softer material is cut away. That is, the harder portions of the grain will stand in shallow relief. Be sure to brush from the center out to the edges, since this prevents splintering and tearing.

Once the desired textured effect is achieved, seal the wood with a wash coat of shellac, and then finish the surface in any of the four ways described for textured plywood—page 213.

### Ebony finish

Any close-grained wood may be given a good imitation ebony finish with a black stain made by pouring 2 quarts of boiling hot water over 1 ounce of powdered logwood extract. After the extract has been dissolved, add to it a solution made by dissolving 1 dram of powdered potassium chromate in a few drops of hot water. Combine these two solutions, and allow to cool before using. If the first coat does not give a sufficiently deep black, apply a second and a third coat. The water stain has a tendency to raise the grain of the wood. It is a good idea, therefore, to sand the surface after each coat has dried. The last coat will usually not cause any noticeable raising of the grain. Protect the ebonized finish by applying a thin coating of shellac after the stain has dried. Rub lightly with extra fine sandpaper to remove gloss of shellac.

## Crackle finish

This finish has actually been developed as a result of a finishing failure. When a quick-drying coat is applied over a slow-drying elastic one, the top coat will invariably crack. Lacquer manufacturers have used this problem to produce a quaint and decorative finish which is known as *crackle*. It is produced with three coats of finishing material—lacquer undercoat, crackle coat, and finish coat. An undercoater, usually lacquer, is essential, since crackle lacquer will not crack over bare wood or metal. Various color combinations can be used. Red crackle over black lacquer produces a Spanish vargueno or Oriental effect. Other good combinations are dark blue over light blue, green over black, green over gold, and brown over ivory.

The surface should be smooth and clean. Apply one or more coats of lacquer enamel, and allow to dry. Then spray on (it cannot be brushed) the crackle coat. This will hold together as a solid coat for about half a minute and will then start to crack, revealing the undercoat in an intricate pattern of irregular lines. A light coat or fast application will produce small cracks; a heavy coat will make a larger pattern. Practice is necessary to get a uniform coating. The work can be touched up with a second coat while the first coat is still wet, but the pattern appears so quickly and dries so rapidly that touch-up work is almost impossible. The only way to get an even pattern is to spray evenly. The crackle coat dries in about half an hour, and a finish coat of clear lacquer, either flat or glossy, can then be applied.

Many pleasing monotone and clear finishes are also possible with crackle lacquer. A "leather finish," a close imitation of pigskin, is typical of these. Any color undercoat and crackle can be used, since a top coat of light-brown lacquer enamel is applied as a finish coat. Thus, all that remains of the crackle finish is the leatherlike texture. The color contrast can be brought out by applying dark-brown japan, and wiping immediately to leave the color only in the cracks. A coat of clear crackle over lacquer or colored lacquer enamel gives a novelty monotone effect.

Crackle finish can also be obtained with a concentrated solution of magnesium sulfate in water. To this add dextrin until the mix is about the consistency of varnish. Add water stain for color. Glue-size surface, and then apply mixture with brush or spray.

### Pearling lacquer

This finishing material is made from fish scales mixed with lacquer and is used for small wood objects. The tiny, pearllike scales remain in suspension in the lacquer and give a unique metallic luster to the finish. Pearling lacquer can be applied in its colorless form tinted with colored lacquer enamel. The usual procedure is to tint the pearling lacquer with the same color used for the ground coats. Any other type of lacquer can be used for the undercoats. Two coats of pearling lacquer should be applied to ensure good coverage. When dry, sand very lightly with super fine abrasive paper. Apply as a final coat a fine spray of lacquer thinner, and then rub and polish the same as any ordinary lacquer. Translucent effects are obtained by using a contrasting ground color, the pearling-lacquer top coat allowing the undercoat to shine through.

### Wrinkle finishes

Wrinkling lacquer is used on a wide variety of products in both wood and metal. It can be obtained in all colors, in a range of patterns from coarse to fine wrinkles, for air drying or baking. It is variously known as *fingerprint, shrivel, ripple,* etc. Because of its rough texture, wrinkle is a one-coat finish since the surface to which it is applied need not be smooth. The material is heavier than ordinary lacquers and can be brushed on quite satisfactorily. If a spray gun is used, it should be applied by pressure feed. Thin slightly with naphtha if required. The heavier the coat, the coarser the wrinkle; very thin coats will not wrinkle at all. Heat is necessary for the wrinkles to form, and even with the air-dry wrinkling lacquer, exposure in front of a gas or electric heater will give a quicker and more uniform pattern. Small objects can easily be baked in an ordinary kitchen oven. Air-dry the piece for about half an hour to permit partial evaporation of the solvent. Then bake at a temperature of about 180° F. for about 1 hour or until the wrinkles are well formed. Increase the heat to 250° F. for about 2 hours to harden the finish coat. No top coat is necessary. However, if a colored finish other than the wrinkle color is required, apply any color of lacquer enamel. The finish coat can be smutted, or a shaded effect can be obtained by spraying a contrasting color enamel with the gun held close to and parallel with the work surface. This deposits the enamel on only one side of the wrinkles and gives a novel two-tone surface.

### Crystal finish

Crystal or crystallizing lacquer produces a finish coat that has a crystalline structure composed of many tiny flakes and is generally used for small wood objects as well as small tabletops. It is another form of baked finish but is also available in an air-dry type. It can be purchased in black and clear. The colored finishes can be worked by spraying clear crystal over a coat of baked synthetic. Like wrinkle, crystal is a one-coat finish, and can be applied by spraying or brushing, thinning with naphtha if required.

To secure the crystal finish, give the bare surface a coat of black crystal lacquer, and allow to air-dry for a period of one-half hour, and then place in an oven with all the dampers and vents closed so that the fumes of combustion will remain in the oven. In about half an hour the crystals will be perfectly formed, after which you may open the vents and finish the baking at a temperature of 200° F. for 2 hours. A crystallized bronze powder finish is very attractive. Apply a coat of clear crystal in the usual manner. After baking, give the work a top coat of any color bronze powder in bronzing lacquer (purchased ready-mixed). This should be applied lightly, since a full wet coat will attack the crystal coat. Or, better still, mix the bronze powder with a clear baking synthetic. After baking, apply a top coat of clear crystal to complete the finish.

### Mottle effect

For a fine mottle texture use a cellulose sponge. Cut it into an irregular shape to avoid a rectangular, bricklike pattern, but retain a flat working surface. For a coarser texture, use a large natural sponge, sliced in half while it is bone dry. In either case, wet the sponge with water, and squeeze out every drop of excess moisture. The objective is to produce a pliable working tool and lessen the absorption of paint.

Brush a single coat of a contrasting color onto a flat·surface. Lightly press the flat side of the sponge into the paint, then onto the surface to be mottled. Repeat until surface is covered with pattern, turning the hand slightly each time a new impression is made. Try not to overlap, but avoid open space between impressions. When more than one color is used, allow a drying time of 2 to 3 hours between the application of each color. Alternate tools for mottling include crumpled newspaper, cloth or plastic wrap, a piece of carpeting cut to fit the hand, or a stippling brush.

### Spatter finishes

Spatter finishes are most attractive and offer a wide range of attractive color combinations. This spatter technique has long been popular for walls and floors, but has only recently been used on wood furniture.

First, paint the ground color and allow it to dry thoroughly. If it is a dark color, then choose light or bright colors for the spatter dots. If it is a light color—white, gray, beige, or any pastel tone—you might use either bright colors or dark colors or a combination of both for the spatter dots. If the ground color is a bright lacquer yellow, green, red, or blue, the spatter dots could be either light- or dark-colored paint or a combination of both.

Mix the colors in a shallow pan. Prepare a practice board (a scrap piece of wood on which the ground coat has been applied) to try out the color combinations and also to practice the distance from the work required for the proper spatter. Place the tip of the brush in the pan of paint, and strike the brush sharply against a stick held in the left hand. This will transfer the paint to the surface under the stick in the form of dots. The size of these dots will depend on your distance from the surface and the amount of paint on the brush.

After you have developed the desired effect, follow it carefully on all the surfaces of the piece being finished. Spatter the first color, stand off at a distance, and inspect the evenness of the application. If any areas need more spots, add them now rather than later. Allow this color to dry thoroughly, and then spatter with the next color. If the spatter dots have been of lacquer or enamel, the finish may be left as it is. If they are only of paint, however, it is more practical to cover the surface with dull-finish varnish or a thin coat of transparent lacquer.

Another way of applying the spatter is to use a very stiff-bristled brush. Dip the tips of the bristles into the paint. Then, holding the brush with the bristles pointed up, draw a palette knife, paint paddle, or your own finger toward you across the bristles, flipping the paint onto the surface to be spattered. Unless you want an extremely coarse spatter, don't try to dip the brush into the can of paint; dip it instead into paint that has been poured, or even brushed, onto a flat surface. A flat-topped toothbrush will naturally produce a much finer spatter than a wallpaper brush, and a slow motion results in a finer texture than a fast motion.

Special spray-gun nozzles are available with which you can obtain many unusual finishes in a spattered, salt-and-pepper effect.

### Hammered finish

This finish, often called *hammertone*, can be achieved in a number of different ways, but all depend on a spatter technique in order to get the indentations which look like hammer marks.

One type of hammered finish is applied in a two-coat system. The special ground coat is sprayed or brushed on clean metal or on a painted surface. After a 2- to 3-minute drying period, the second, or spatter, coat is applied. This second coat looks about like water, and, like water, it must shower down like raindrops. Special spray guns do this perfectly. However, fairly good results can be obtained with a mouth spray or by loading a brush with the liquid and throwing or spattering it on. The whole trick of a good hammered finish is to apply the solvent top coat evenly. If you fail in your first attempt, brush out the combined coat immediately, and try it again.

Hammertone can be applied in one coat with a combined coloring pigment and solvent. This is a spray material which is baked. The object is to have the gun spit, rather than atomize, the fluid. This is easily done if you have a suitable spray outfit, using about 25 pounds air pressure and 15 pounds fluid pressure. You can also obtain fair results with a standard outfit by partly opening the safety valve of the compressor. Air-dry for 15 minutes; then bake for about another 15 minutes at 300° F.

You can easily imitate a hammered texture on wooden bowls and other similar objects made of close-grained hardwood, such as birch or maple. Sand smooth, and then apply a coat of aluminum or other color bronze finish. When dry, indent the surface with either a ball peen hammer or by pounding a roundheaded rivet held with a pair of pliers.

### Metal-lace finish

Metal-lace finish is similar to hammertone except that a small amount of aluminum or other bronze powder is added to the spatter liquid. When the spatter liquid is applied, the aluminum collects around the edge of each drop, forming a lacelike pattern. Both metal-lace and hammertone finishes are fairly transparent and must be applied on clean, uniformly colored undercoating.

## Marble finish

There are several methods of producing imitation marble effects (see page 230). The simplest is the so-called "paper method" which proceeds as follows:

1. After the surface has been properly prepared and a white enamel undercoater has had a chance to dry, brush on an *extra heavy* coat of gloss white enamel. Cover both top and side edges. Allow white enamel to dry about 5 minutes or until tacky.
2. On the white surface, dribble gloss gray enamel. Use a wood applicator. Dribble in a thin marble-vein pattern that is random and irregular.
3. With wood applicator dribble on gloss black enamel. Apply half as much black as you applied of the gray. The black dribbles should roughly follow the gray enamel pattern.
4. Have an ample supply of newspaper before starting. With crumpled newspaper, begin daubing the surface and edges. Follow the pattern of colors.
5. Daub with very light pressure to carry or blend one color into another. Heavy pressure will obliterate the marble pattern you are aiming for. Change newspaper as it soaks up excess paint. When surface is completely patterned, use fresh newspaper to soften hard contrasts where one color blends into another.
6. Now decide if you have achieved the marble effect. If not, continue to add additional amounts of black and gray. *Tip:* Since most genuine marble has strong accents of black, you may wish to add more black enamel. But use it sparingly since the black is for accent.
7. On horizontal surfaces like tabletops, a strong marble-vein

effect may be produced by dribbling additional white in bold, thin meandering lines. Note that the veining is most effective when applied over dark areas to provide contrast. Daub to soften edges where white enamel meets the marble speckled area.

8. Now the marbelizing pattern is complete. Let dry overnight. Allow to dry several days under normal conditions before subjecting to general use. Avoid placing heavy objects on this finish until it has become thoroughly hard.

9. When marbelizing large surfaces, apply gloss white enamel to small areas at a time (3 x 3 feet), and then proceed to complete the finish within that one area. Repeat the process in the adjoining area, overlapping the white base coat into the previously painted area to avoid lap marks. Work quickly to prevent lap edges from becoming too tacky.

Another popular marbelizing method for small woodwork jobs is the float application. To accomplish it, use a container large enough so that the whole object to be finished can be dipped into it. Fill it within ½ to 1 inch of the top. Float the colors on top of the water. Use enamel paints thinned slightly more than for brushwork, for this marbelizing process. Infinite variety can be obtained, ranging from brilliant contrasting colors to the soft black and brown tones of wood grain.

Wood should have a smooth working surface. Apply a primer or sealer, such as lacquer or shellac, and allow to dry before marbelizing.

This finish requires just enough enamel to form a film on the water. Use a small wooden paddle to float the color on the water. Dip the paddle into the enamel; then dip and draw it through the water. Repeat this with all the colors to be added; then gently swirl them until the film has a marbelized effect. As the object is dipped into the water, the design will adhere instantly to the surface. Dip flat work face down. Dip and rotate turned work at the same time, moving it so that it picks up all the paint film. Remove the object immediately, and allow to dry. Experiment with small pieces of scrap before starting on your project.

Each time an article is dipped, paint is removed, so that more enamel must be added. A small board may also be used to concentrate the film in one area for further use. Protect with masking tape those areas on which no color is desired. The tape is easily removed after the finish has dried. You will note the similarity of the water-float method and that of the Easter-egg-dye process.

For the feather marble treatment, first cover the surface you are working on with one good covering coat of paint. Then mix two different colors, either paint or lacquer, for the veining.

Whatever colors you choose, there are two ways you can do the veining—the feather method and the brush method. For the feather method the background color should be completely dry. Dip the feather tip in the pan containing one of the colors, and draw it across the surface in wiggly lines, bearing on more heavily in some areas than others. If a piece of marble or a photograph of marble is available, use it as a guide in making the lines. Add the second color at once, and allow it to blur in with the first color, or, if you prefer, you may add it after the first veining lines have dried.

For the brush method, put one color on with a small camel's hair brush, then add the other color with the narrow side of a stronger bristle brush. You can soften and blend these colors into the ground color by brushing across them here and there with a dry brush. Wipe the dry brush clean on a rag before blending each area. Practice either of these methods on a piece of scrap board and decide which treatment to follow. Find a good combination of lines, and more or less follow this formula on all surfaces, but with enough variety to avoid monotony.

When all the marbelizing is finished, cover with a high-luster varnish or lacquer coat. If the furniture is used out of doors, cover with two coats of spar or exterior synthetic varnish for a weatherproof finish.

### Venetian Gold

Venetian gold is a Mediterranean-style finish that complements every decor, traditional or contemporary. Its brilliant burnished gold richness can highlight occasional tables, chairs, chests, or TV trays that have become worn with use. The Venetian gold finish is accomplished in much the same manner as the paper method of achieving the marble effect. Here is how it is done:

1. After the surface has been properly prepared and base undercoater has had a chance to dry, apply a coat of bright-red enamel directly on the surface being finished. Let dry 24 hours.
2. Stir gold paint thoroughly. Using a wood applicator, dribble gold paint in heavy globs directly on dry red surface. In doing this, form a meandering, random pattern.
3. Crumple a newspaper in a small, loose ball. Then with the newspaper, begin daubing the gold. Follow the gold pat-

tern you have just established. Remember to let the red show through, so that it too becomes a part of the developing pattern.

4. Because the newspaper will soak up excess paint, keep changing to fresh newspaper as you proceed. *Important*: Heavy daubing will obliterate the pattern, so use very little pressure.

5. While the gold is still wet, dribble onto it small globs of a brownish tone antique glaze (see page 226) with a wood applicator. Then daub the glaze with a fresh newspaper using the same method as with the gold. Again, allow the red and gold to show through for the three-dimensional effect. Use the glaze sparingly.

6. Remember, the amount of brown glaze will determine the pattern effect, since it is the final color applied. For dark patterns, continue to add glaze until you have achieved the effect you want.

7. When the pattern is complete, let dry overnight. Before subjecting to use, allow to dry for 48 hours. Surfaces that will be subjected to hard use or wear should be protected with satin or high-gloss varnish.

8. When finishing vertical surfaces, application of all colors may be better accomplished by pouring a small amount of each color into shallow dishes or pans. Lightly touch a balled newspaper into the color, and then transfer the color to the surface by daubing. This method of applying colors will eliminate sagging. Continue to daub color in the same manner as described in steps 1 to 7. When finishing large areas, apply red to entire area and allow to dry. Then apply gold and glaze to small areas at a time (3 x 3 feet). Repeat in adjoining area, and daub into previously finished area to avoid lap marks.

## Mottle finish by dipping

After thoroughly sanding the wood object to be finished, spray or brush a surface or ground color of lacquer or enamel. Allow to dry overnight. Then, dip the object in a container of clear lacquer thinned to half strength or at about spraying consistency. Lift it out quickly, and immediately plunge the object into a container of colored lacquer. If you lift quickly again, the work will take on a smooth color coat. However, if you hold the work stationary for about a second and then lift slowly, the color coat will break, showing some of the ground-coat color. By varying the lifting-process time (one quick and one slow) the mottle effect will appear on the object. Repeat this bonding process as many times as necessary to obtain the effect you desire. Let the work drain a few seconds, and remove bead at bottom with soft cloth or tissue. Hang up to dry in same position as dipped.

## Penetrating finish

Another useful wood finish now available is the penetrating finish (sometimes called the salad-bowl finish). Such finishes are made in one- and two-coat systems. The single-coat finish is a deep penetration of a wax-resin solution. In the two-coat system this film is covered with a special type of lacquer, impregnating the wood and also coating it with a tough, waterproof film. This finish has a waxy feel and is excellent for cigarette boxes and other items touched by hands.

Obviously, salad bowls and serving dishes cannot be finished with anything that has a strong odor such as turpentine, linseed oil, or furniture wax. If a satiny natural finish is desired for bowls, scoops, or plates to be used with cold foods, they may be rubbed with beeswax shaved into mineral oil and melted over hot water. Repeat applications of olive oil during the life of kitchenware to give it a nice patina. However, neither the beeswax nor the olive-oil finishes will prove sufficient protection against grease marks or hot liquids. To successfully withstand either, woodenware must have a tight coat of one of the waterproof spar varnishes or lacquers.

### Charred finish

The charred finish, sometimes called a *sugi* finish, consists of surface charring and hardening with a flame from a blowtorch. The wood appears to be stained from deep brown to pale chocolate. Harder portions of the grain stand in shallow relief. Paste wax seals the surface; repeated waxing builds up a whitish fleck that enhances the whole effect. The item to be finished should be dry, bare of any inflammable material, and in good repair.

The first step is to produce an even, overall char which goes only deep enough to scorch the surface of the wood. As long as the flame stays nearly invisible, the flame of the blowtorch is not burning too deeply. Pass flame back and forth over the work in smooth sweeps. If a circle of yellow flame springs up, the burning is going too deep. Quickly pull the torch away, and avoid that spot in further flaming. Over-scorching produces a surface checking like patches of sun-baked mud. Be especially careful with sharp edges, allowing them less time under the flame. Inside corners also require special care, since the flame cannot get into the deepest portion where cool air insulates the wood. Do not try to burn the light line that forms as dark as the rest of the surface; later brushing will darken the corner to match the surrounding area.

After the charring is completed, use a stiff-bristled brush to remove the soft char, brushing lightly with the grain and blowing the dust away. Use an old toothbrush to get into the corners. Continue the brushing until the finish reaches the desired shade of brown. Puttied holes, which appear light after the scorching, will get darker when brushed. After the scorching and brushing, apply two coats of paste wax, and polish thoroughly.

Any old finish on the wood must be removed before the surface can be charred. Burn off the old finish, scraping it with a piece of glass, putty knife, or cabinet scraper. By the time the old finish is removed, the wood beneath will be charred enough for final brushing and waxing.

### Decoupage

The art of decoupage (pronounced *day-coo-pazh*) was originated by the craftsmen of eighteenth-century Europe in an effort to copy the elaborately engraved and gilded products of Chinese and Japanese lacquer ware. Their discovery, decoupage, involved the arts-and-crafts techniques of applying a cutout print to a desired wood surface and then getting the "picture" to recede into the background by applying many coats of a clear finish. That is, decoupage is the art of mounting printed pictures or designs on previously finished surfaces, then applying coat after coat of an appropriate clear finish until the picture appears to be part of the surface itself. Although black is traditionally the most popular background color, any solid color is appropriate if it looks well with the print you have chosen. Decoupage can also be used on stained and varnished wood and is ideally suited for antiqued surfaces.

*Preparation of surface* The first step in a decoupage application is to have the wood surface completely smooth and clean. Fill cracks and holes with wood plastic or putty and sand smooth with 6/0 or finer abrasive paper. Apply an enamel undercoat or wood stain base coat in the desired color, which should complement the selected decoupage print. When an opaque finish is desired, at least two coats of enamel and perhaps more may be needed to cover the wood grain. Thoroughly wet-sand between coats. After the enameling dries completely, apply a thin coat of the top finish— clear lacquer, varnish, or special decoupage coating.

On surfaces where the wood grain is to appear, apply a thin coat of the top finish over the stain, and then sand lightly with 6/0 or finer abrasive paper to remove any surface irregularities. Use a tack rag to clean up all sanding debris. When selecting the undercoat material, make certain you know the properties of the final clear top coat. If you choose an undercoat material that tends to soften or lift under a specific top coat, you will waste time and effort.

***Preparation of design*** Wrapping papers, stationery, prints, and greeting cards are just a few sources for finding suitable designs. Magazine paper is not usually recommended. Lay your designs on a clean piece of waxed paper. Spray lightly several times with the top coat, and allow to dry after each spraying. Or brush on one coat of the top finish.

To age a piece of paper money, a square picture, etc., burn the edge by repeatedly jabbing it with a cigarette. If you have a very heavy piece of paper, such as a postcard, which you wish to use, you may strip the paper so that it will not be so heavy and so that it may more easily be covered with the top finish. To remove the backing paper from the item, put the picture in pan of lukewarm water and soak. Gently roll off the paper backing a layer at a time, working from center out. If it dries out, put it back in the water. Never strip wedding invitations.

Embossed flowers or raised gold designs may be used most effectively. Make papier-mâché by mixing finely shredded paper tissue with white glue, and pack into back cavity of design. Allow to dry for several days. Black and white etchings may be colored with ordinary colored pencils. Hold the pencil sideways so as not to pierce paper. Color all shadows and line with terra-cotta, coloring in direction of the lines of the drawing. This gives warmth to any color you may put over the terra-cotta. Lightly brush on the top color to set colors.

When cutting paper, use any good cuticle scissors. Learn to turn the paper instead of the scissors. First cut away excess paper. Then cut out inside the cuts. Large, intricate pieces may be handled more easily if first cut into sections. Some craftsmen prefer to tear around the print following the shape of the piece, creating a ragged edge. After tearing a print, sand lightly on the reverse side to smooth out the torn edges. While designs with printing on the reverse side should be avoided if possible, they can frequently be sealed by coating the back with white glue slightly diluted with water and allowing them to dry thoroughly. This usually prevents the printing from showing through on the surface of the design.

**Gluing on the design**  Remember that decoupage designs must never overlap. Place designs on the object, and make small pencil marks to show the correct placement. Now lay the design face down on a clean piece of waxed paper. Squirt on the white glue, and spread evenly with your fingers from center out. Use enough glue so that the edges do not dry out before you are through spreading. On a large solid design, spread the glue with a damp sponge. Carefully remove the design from the waxed paper and place on the object's surface. Using a damp sponge, press the design in place. Then put a clean piece of waxed paper over the design. Use a hard rubber roller, and roll it over the picture in several directions to press out excess glue. Carefully remove the waxed paper, and clean around the edges of the design with a damp sponge. Using a clean piece of waxed paper, roll again and wipe off excess glue. Repeat this until no glue appears when rolled. Glue may leave cloudy spots on the surface, particularly on a dark one. However, the top coats will usually obscure this. Allow design to dry overnight. If any air bubbles appear, slit the bubble with a razor blade. With a toothpick, put glue under the cut edges and roll again. Let dry thoroughly. If your designs extend over the top and down the sides of the object, glue the design on in one piece, and when dry cut along the edge with a razor blade. Sign your work with india ink or paint.

**Building up the finish**    Once the design is glued to the object, the finish building operation can be started. Brush on the first coat of clear lacquer, varnish, or decoupage coating. Allow to dry. If an antique effect is desired, apply the antique glaze, wipe lightly with a soft cloth. Continue to apply the top coating, sanding very lightly with extra fine sandpaper between coats, and wiping with a soft cloth. Always brush from the center out and check the edges for drips. Do not try to keep brush strokes going in the same direction.

It is impossible to give a set rule for the number of coats needed to sink your design, but a minimum of twelve is usually recommended when using lacquer. A few less coats are needed with varnish. But in either case, the final coat should be a rubbed satin finish achieved by using 4/0 or finer steel wool. Rub in a circular motion over the entire surface. Do this with a good light beside you so that you can rub away any shiny spots. When the finish is uniformly dull, apply one or two coats of a good quality paste wax, and polish with a clean, soft cloth.

## Stenciling

Stenciling is the transferring of a design by laying a cutout pattern on a given surface and brushing the cutout pattern with paint or bronze powder. In wood finishing, stenciling is usually associated with Hitchcock chairs, Pennsylvania Dutch pieces, and Early American decoration.

Stencils for wood decorations are available at most art supply stores, or they can be made. Use a stiff stencil paper, architects' drawing linen, or heavy sheet plastic. These materials are available at art stores and at drafting supply houses.

To make stencils, place the stencil material over the tracing of the design. Since most stencil materials are semitransparent, the design will be visible so that you may trace it on with a pencil. Be sure to provide enough stencil material to make a margin of 1 inch around all sides of the motif which is to be cut out. With some complex designs, the placing of ties—connecting links to adjoining parts—is something learned only by observation and experience. The ties should be arranged inconspicuously and logically in the design.

After tracing the pattern, cut it out with a pair of fine-pointed scissors, or lay the stencil material on a piece of glass, and use a sharp craft knife or razor blade. A steel embroidery punch is useful for making small holes. Often the edges of a beginner's stencils are a little rough. These may be filed with the fine side of an emery board. If you make a mistake in cutting a stencil, cover with Scotch tape, and recut that part of your design. Remember, accurate cutting is important as you will use your stencil over and over again.

With the stencil completed, the object to which it is going to be applied must be prepared as described on page 195. For most stencil work a neutral, dark, matte background is best. Black is a favorite for most Early American furniture designs, while brown is popular for Pennsylvania Dutch pieces. Apply the matte background color on the surface to be stenciled; permit it to dry thoroughly.

***Bronze powder stenciling***   Before doing any stenciling, it is well to prepare your bronze powders. The bronze powders most used for Early American decoration are brushed brass, silver, or aluminum; red; gold-leaf powder or gold powder. They are available at most art supply shops. A small tin box makes a satisfactory receptacle for the powders. A piece of upholstering velvet should be cut to fit the box and placed inside. On this, mat your small amounts of each of the colored bronzes that are going to be used. The box actually becomes a small palette and after using may be carefully closed so that the powders are protected.

To begin the stenciling procedure, apply a coat of varnish thinned to 4 parts varnish to 1 part thinner. When the surface reaches the tacky stage—the right moment for stenciling is when the varnish gives a little click as you lift a finger from it—place the stencil in exactly the spot where you wish the design to appear. Wrap around your index finger a piece of fine silk, velvet, or chamois, and pick up a small amount of bronze dust from the velvet palette. Press this finger down along one cutout edge of the stencil, and then release the pressure quickly. As you do this, the bronze powder will splatter out from that particular edge and splash onto the tacky varnish showing through that section of stencil opening. This operation may be repeated wherever you may wish to achieve a graduated-tone effect. You may also use a gentle circular motion to rub your bronze-charged finger over the entire cutout. Always work from the outer edges toward the center, to avoid spilling the powder under the edges of the stencil. It is best not to fill in solidly the larger open areas of the design, but to allow the powder to fade out toward the center of the area—again, for a tonal effect. (A combination of both the above described techniques may be used to good advantage.) Use very little powder at first, in any case, until you are master of the technique. You can always add extra layers of powder to reach the quality of brightness desired. Any extra powder left on the surface of the linen stencil should be picked up with your velvet- or chamois-wrapped finger.

When the bronzing process is completed, remove the stencil with great care, to avoid splattering the excess bronze powder on the damp varnish. If, in spite of care, you do smudge the background, the damage may be repaired after the varnish is dry by touching up the mistakes, using the same paint as that used for the background.

Always wipe the stencil clean with thinner after using. No bronze powder or varnish should be allowed to remain on either the front or back of the stencil. Allow it to dry well, and then place it between the pages of a book until needed again.

Allow bronze powder to dry for at least 2 days. Although it may seem to dry in a few hours, when the next coat of varnish is applied, it is apt to throw the bronze into solution again. Wipe off excess powder with a damp cloth before varnishing. Always apply two thin coats of varnish on the stenciled design before starting to rub down the surface as described in Chapter 9.

*Paint stenciling*   Again, a neutral, dark, matte background is best, but bright colors are usually used for the design. Use a fine brush to bring out the details and to provide visual contrast. Move the brush in a natural direction with the design. When stenciling a leaf, for example, the brush should be moved in the direction of the leaf's ribbing. As with bronze powder stenciling, always work from the stencil to open areas.

When dry, apply a protective coat of clear varnish or lacquer. If the paint used to apply the base coat and the design is a type that will stand up to the requirement demanded in terms of usage, you need not give it a top coat of varnish or lacquer.

## Fabric or wallpaper finishes

Fabric or wallpaper is sometimes used to cover furniture, the inside of drawers, and other surfaces. The fabric or paper should be cut to size with a razor blade or wallpaper knife. Apply wallpaper paste to the area to be covered as well as to the paper or fabric.

The paste should be mixed and applied according to the directions on the package. Always smooth the paste out well, covering all areas so that there will be no loose sections. Smooth the paper firmly in place, working the strip down gradually so that there are no air bubbles left under the surface. Wipe smooth with a clean dry cloth, but use a damp cloth to remove any paste that has smeared over the edges. Remove these spots before they have a chance to dry. After the paper or fabric has dried, it may be treated to a surface coating of special wallpaper wax (wallpaper wax only), or it may be painted or sprayed with a thin coat of clear shellac, lacquer, or varnish.

### Flocking

Flock consists of extremely short lengths of fiber which, when sprayed onto a specially prepared adhesive surface, will stick endwise and form a pile or nap similar to that of velvet. Flocking is available at most art and craft supply stores, and the best way to apply it is with a special spray gun which is similar to those used in applying agricultural insecticide dusts. Unless working on a large project, there is no need to use a power flock sprayer. But do not attempt to apply the flocking by hand sprinkling since the material will mat down rather than stand upright and will fail to form that sought-after velvety nap.

A surface that is to be flocked should be perfectly smooth and the wood pores sealed. Then apply the adhesive—available at the same source as the flocking—to the surface to which the flock particles will adhere. It comes in various colors to match the flock being used and can either be sprayed or brushed on, or the object can be dipped in it. Since most of these adhesives are quick-drying, it is important to apply the flock immediately after the adhesive base has been applied and before any surface set can take place.

Always try to aim the gun at the surface from a direct 90-degree angle and not from an oblique angle. This is to get the particles of flock to hit the adhesive in an upright position and form a uniform nap. Allow the surface to dry 12 to 24 hours. Shake and brush to remove any excess flocking. These fibers can be reused.

### How to paint tole pieces

While tole pieces are not made of wood, their finishing is somewhat similar to some of the wood finishing techniques described in this chapter. Actually, *tole* is the name given to certain types of decorative trays, coffee urns, dishes, lamps, etc. The articles are usually made of tin which has been finished in various colors, such as black with gilt designs. Pleasing effects can also be created through the use of various combinations of bright reds, yellows, browns, and oranges.

Before starting your project, practice making several strokes on a flat smooth surface to get the "feel" of painting tinware. Practice any curlicues or thin lines on cardboard first before decorating your item. If the article to be decorated is already painted, apply paint remover. Then wash with water and a strong detergent, and let dry. If the article is unfinished, merely wipe clean. To eliminate any surface slipperiness, wash with turpentine or mineral spirits before painting.

The first step is to apply an undercoat of flat brown oil paint, using a soft camel's hair brush with a width of 1 inch. Brush lengthwise in both directions and let dry for 24 hours. Sand lightly before applying a coat of flat paint in the color you have chosen for the background. This paint should be thinned with turpentine to the approximate consistency of cream. Use two or three thin coats—allowing 24 hours' drying time and sanding between coats. Use the same type of brush as you used to apply the undercoat, working crosswise in both directions, then lengthwise. To eliminate any ridges, sweep the tip of the brush over the surface.

When the last coat is dry, apply a coat of clear varnish to permit erasures and corrections in the designs. Allow the varnish to dry for 48 hours, and sand lightly. Designs may be copied or traced from other tole items, obtained from magazines, or drawn freehand. They usually consist of floral or fruit patterns with bold splashes of two or three colors and with thin, curly lines representing stems, vines, and leaf endings. Often the edges or sides of tole pieces are bordered with a thin stripe painted in a contrasting color—such as yellow on a red or green background. Swirls, teardrop strokes, and polliwog (wide flat strokes that taper to a fine point) strokes can all be used to create interesting effects. If you do not have a printed pattern to follow, it is best to examine other tole items and get ideas about various designs you may wish to use.

Make a pencil tracing of your design on this white paper. Turn this pencil outline over, and rub the reverse side with white lithopone tracing powder. Cut around the edges of the paper so that it will fit onto the object you are decorating. Tape the tracing in place with the powdered side down. As you go over the outline with a pencil, the design will be transferred onto the surface of the metal.

For the brush strokes of the design it is best to use a French quill brush, series 4 or 5, size 2. Before filling in the design, mix oil colors (in handy tube form) with a palette knife until you reach the shade desired. Dip the point of the brush in clear varnish, and then stroke it through the paint, working back and forth on a palette pad to load the brush. Practice your strokes first, and then apply paint to fill in various sections and make shaped strokes. Fill in the larger areas of your design first, but don't paint two adjoining areas of different colors on the same day. Let stand overnight before filling in the rest of the design. Wait another day before painting any finishing overstrokes.

For fine stripes and curlicues only, add a tiny touch of turpentine with the varnish so that the paint will flow faster. Use a No. 1 quill brush for these thin lines and curlicues.

Wispy swirls and polliwog strokes can be made with a wider brush, but be sure to practice a bit first to get them *just* right.

Allow at least 24 hours' drying time, and then varnish to protect the paint. If an antique effect is desired, add a small amount of raw or burnt umber in oil to the next-to-last coat of clear varnish. A week later mix fine pumice with No. 20 automobile oil. Rub this mixture gently and evenly over the surface to remove the shine and make a smooth finish.

# CHAPTER FOURTEEN

# Reviving
# Old Finishes

**A**lthough your old furniture may need refinishing, remember that part of the charm of old furniture is in the signs of age and use. Therefore, in refinishing old furniture, do not try to have the pieces look new. Unless they disfigure the piece, leave some signs of age, such as traces of paint, the marks of the cabinetmaker, and signs of wear. The proof that a piece is an antique, and hence its commercial value, often rests on these marks. Many old pieces of furniture need only to be cleaned, and this should be the first step if a finish is still on the wood.

A good solution for washing varnished furniture at housecleaning time, and for cleaning old furniture that has been neglected, is made by combining 1 quart of

hot water, 1 tablespoonful of turpentine, and 3 tablespoonfuls of boiled linseed oil. The turpentine helps to cut the
dirt, and the oil lubricates, feeds, and polishes the wood.
Keep this mixture hot in a double boiler while using. First
rub the wood with a soft cloth dipped in this solution, and
then polish it with a dry cloth. Clean only one section of the
piece at a time. You may use furniture polish or wax after
this cleaning.

### Cleaning old finished surfaces

Some pieces may need additional treatment to remove all the
old dirt "adhering" to the white spots. Some form of friction
agent—either very fine steel wool or pumice powder—must
then be used with oil (linseed oil, mineral oil, or machine
oil). Keep the wool or powder wet with the oil as you rub it
over the surface. Use a cloth, felt pad, or the pads of your
hand. On carvings, use an old toothbrush or nail brush to remove the dirt from deep crevices. After all the dirt has been
removed in this way, thoroughly remove all traces of the oil,
pumice, or steel particles with a soft dry cloth until no finger
marks show.

Remove the dirt and wax with a cloth dampened with turpentine, then rewax. If the wood is dark, use colored wax
(see Chapter 10).

You can also obtain an excellent finish by rubbing down
the antique with a final coat of lemon oil mixed with powdered pumice. Never use linseed oil. Remove all traces of the
final polishing with a clean soft rag. This will give a gleaming
polish that brings out the true beauty of the wood.

If a duller finish is desired, use pumice and water for the
final rubdown. Work the final finish only in good weather, to
avoid a surface bloom or cloudy look. If the furniture has be-

come cloudy, use the lemon-oil-and-pumice rubdown to remove the bloom.

### How to identify the old finish

Before you can do anything with an old finish, you must know what type of finish it is. To find out, test a small area in an inconspicuous spot with different solvents. The solvent that affects the finish surface will determine the type of finish. If the finish softens or rubs off with pure turpentine, you know that it is a varnish or paint finish. A shellac finish will soften when rubbed with denatured alcohol. Lacquer thinner affects only lacquer. But before making the test, remove any wax with a soft cloth moistened with turpentine. Actually, old wax should always be removed before anything is attempted with the old finish.

### Repairing old surface finishes

*Scratches on the surface* Shallow scratches or hairline cracks can be removed by softening the finish so that it runs together. Flow on turpentine (for varnish surfaces) or denatured alcohol (for shellac surfaces) with a small artist's brush. Let dry 48 hours; then rub smooth with fine pumice or rottenstone. Clean and wax.

Repair a lacquer scratch the same way, using lacquer thinner as the softening solvent. If the mar is very small, drip in the solvent with a toothpick. When the surface is dry, rub with rottenstone and water; then wax.

A scratch that does not dig into the finish can often be hidden by rubbing it with oil from a Brazil nut, black walnut, or butternut. Break the nut meat in half and rub well into blemish. Rubbing the mark with linseed oil may also help, but do not use crude oil—this could soften the finish on the wood. Also try coloring the minor scratch or blemish with a brown crayon. Or use wax sticks—these are made especially for furniture in wood tones. They are softer than an ordinary crayon and easier to work with. Fill the scratch with wax and rub in well with your finger. Wipe with a soft, dry cloth.

To conceal scratches on red mahogany, use new iodine; for brown or cherry mahogany, use iodine that has turned dark brown with age. For maple, dilute iodine about 50 percent with denatured alcohol.

Paste shoe polish can be used to hide minor scratches and blemishes. Use polish in the brown shade for walnut, the cordovan shade for mahogany, and the tan shade for light finishes. Apply with a cotton-tipped toothpick, rubbing carefully on the blemish; then buff dry. If the color is darker than the wood tone, erase with naphtha. Black paste shoe polish can be used to touch up scratches on black lacquered wood. Remember that the polish will provide a shine when it is buffed, so that the repaired area could be noticeable if the furniture has a dull finish. A scratch that does not penetrate the wood also can be hidden by coloring with stain polish of the right shade, then filling with two coats of good automobile wax.

The best way to repair an enamel scratch is with some of the original enamel, dipped in with a toothpick. After the enamel dries, rub it down with rottenstone. A simpler treatment is to fill the mar with a wax crayon matching the enamel color, followed by wax polish. An enamel scratch can sometimes be flowed together with turpentine.

**Scars and gashes** When damage is too conspicuous to be hidden by simple remedies, try this more professional method. First clean the area with naphtha to remove all wax or oil.

**1.** *Stain.* An oil stain of the proper color is ideal for this job. Do not use a spirit stain; this could soften the finish on the wood. For light wood dilute ¼ teaspoonful of stain with a few drops of naphtha or turpentine—mix in the cover of the stain can. Apply with a small brush or cotton-tipped toothpick, wiping with a cloth and reapplying until the stain matches the original finish. Let dry at least 12 hours.

**2.** *Seal.* Fill the scratch with white or orange shellac to seal in the stain, using a toothpick or fine watercolor brush. (On some maple, the orange shellac will match the shade of the wood, and the stain can be eliminated.) Let dry at least 4 hours. Repeat until the scratch is filled, allowing the 4-hour drying time.

**3.** *Sand.* To even off the surface, sand with a very fine sandpaper (8/0) or the fine side of an emery board. Bend the board about an inch from the end. Rub lightly with the grain of the wood until the scratch is even with the finish.

**4.** *Rub Down.* Finish by rubbing with rottenstone and oil, as described in Chapter 9. Use a paste wax for a final polish and subsequent protection. Mars that really go through the finish and into the wood—deep scratches or bad cigarette burns—call for special care. First scrape the mar clean with a knife, especially if the wood is burned. After scraping, rub lightly over the mar with a strip of extra fine sandpaper to complete smoothing and cleaning. For a shallow mar, sanding without scraping may be sufficient.

If the mar is deep, fill with wood plastic almost level with the surface. In both cases finish the mar by filling with stick shellac of the appropriate color to match the finish of the surface. The stick shellac is softened by means of a soldering iron so that it drops into the mar. Do not heat the stick shellac too much or it will char. Use just enough heat to flow it without bubbling. When the mar is filled, level the patch with a heated spatula.

You will have better success if you mask the crack with masking tape or cellulose tape. You can then pack the crack full of shellac without any danger of burning the surrounding surface. After you remove the masking tape, scrape the ridge of shellac with a razor blade until it is as level as you can make it. Then take a small piece of extra fine finishing paper, and dip the paper in alcohol first, then in rubbing oil or water. Rub the patch quickly and firmly, using five or six strokes. This will roll off any excess shellac around the crack. Repeat if necessary, but beware of rubbing through the finish around the crack. Dull the patch by rubbing lightly with 3/0 steel wool—and the job is done.

If the finish around the crack is made thin by rubbing, it can be brought back by spraying a coat of clear lacquer or ether varnish on the spot, feathering the edges. It will then be necessary to rub down the whole surface with pumice and oil. It should be noted here that if the patch is to be sprayed, water, not rubbing oil, should be used in rubbing off the excess shellac.

Despite care in selecting the stick shellac color, the cracks may be a bit off color. In this case, mix a little spirit-soluble stain, and apply it to the crack with a small pencil brush. In selecting the shellac color for repair, choose a slightly lighter color rather than a darker one. The light shellac can always be stained dark, but the dark shellac cannot be made lighter.

If there are scratches or mars on table or chair legs, rub

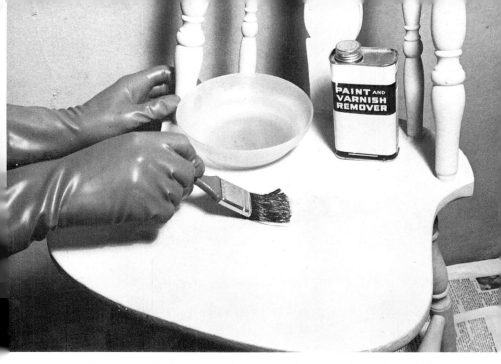

To remove old finish, apply heavy coat of remover with a clean old brush. Allow time to work down to the wood; then scrape off with putty knife.

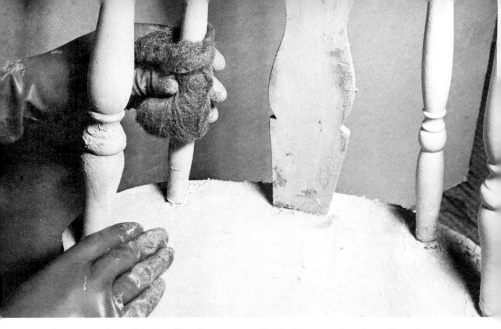

Coarse steel wool is handier than a putty knife for removing the softened finish from curves or corners. To neutralize the remover before applying the new finish, saturate a cloth with denatured alcohol, and wash the surface clean. Be sure to clean recessed edges.

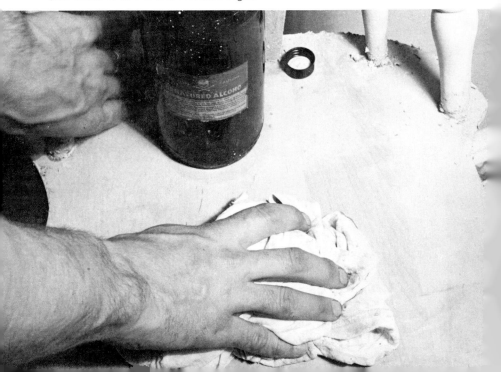

To remove shallow scratches, flow on turpentine (for varnish) or denatured alcohol (for shellac). Let dry 48 hours; then wax. To repair a larger scratch (below), melt a little stick shellac in it with a soldering iron. Rub spot with pumice; then wax.

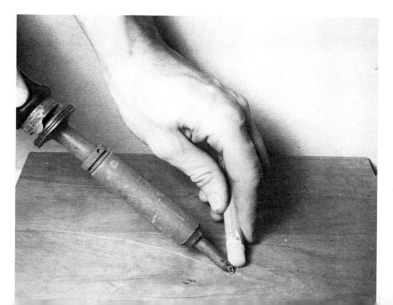

Shallow scratches in mahogany surfaces can often be hidden by painting them with iodine. On other wood finishes such scratches can be hidden by using shoe polish of the same color. Rub it on evenly with a soft cloth. In either case, two coats of wax complete the job.

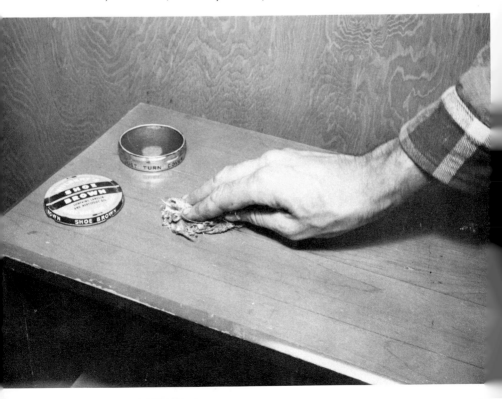

them down, using a coarse cloth and rottenstone. If the leg is turned, use a cloth about 2 feet long, dipping it in boiled linseed oil, and then scattering on the rottenstone. Loop the cloth around the turning, and work back and forth until the scratch is sanded as smooth as possible. If the mar or gouge is too deep for this, fill with stick shellac or wood plastic tinted to a darker shade, and then polish off with the wrapped rag as above.

When working on carvings, build up the surfaces as nearly as possible like the original shape with colored wood plastic slightly darker than the surrounding wood. Either mix the color into the paste, or apply it afterward.

**Removing dents**   Some dents may be raised without removing the finish. Place several thicknesses of damp cloth over the dent, and then place a bottle cap on top. Rest a warm iron lightly on the cap to swell the wood fibers. The bottle cap localizes the heat right on the dent. Do not hold the iron down for long, but lift it frequently to check. If the dent does not raise after several applications, use stick shellac instead. If necessary, refinish the area by rubbing with rottenstone; then wax.

**Checks, cracks, and holes**   Checks in the wood are unsightly but do not seriously weaken the wood. First fill them with fresh wood putty or sawdust mixed with casein glue to slightly below the finish level. When dry, apply stick shellac to match the finish. If the surface is not highly polished, the cracks and knotholes can best be filled with a nonshrinking paste crack filler applied with a spatula. Finish by rubbing with rottenstone and then polishing with wax.

The holes left in the wood when an ornament or drawer pull is removed can generally be hidden. First drill the hole a bit larger to expose fresh wood. Fill the hole with wood plastic, then with stick shellac, finally rubbing with rotten-stone and wax.

**Cracked finish** Sometimes a varnished finish takes on a cracked appearance, with tiny cracks crisscrossing the surface. If they are not deep, they may sometimes be eliminated without going to the trouble of refinishing the entire piece. Prepare a mixture of clear varnish, boiled linseed oil, and turpentine in about the proportions of 3 parts varnish, 4 parts linseed oil, and 2 parts turpentine. Rub the surface with this until the mixture starts to dry, and then wipe off the excess with a clean cloth. This will fill the cracks and blend their edges together. It may be necessary to repeat this procedure several times to eliminate the cracks completely.

To remove cracks as well as superficial scratches, it is also possible to use a liquid called *amalgamator*, which can be obtained at some well-stocked painting-supply house. (Amalgamator is not a trade name.) When applied to the surface, this liquid softens the old varnish, causing it to flow and level itself, after which it hardens again.

**Removing stains** There are various solutions and compounds that remove marks on varnished surfaces caused by water, alcohol, perfume, and rings made by hot cups, plates, or glasses. Most of these stains can be removed with a paste made of finely powdered pumice (FFF) and just enough linseed oil to make it medium thick. Apply it with a soft clean cloth, rubbing gently with a circular motion. During the operation, wipe off the paste frequently with a cloth dampened with turpentine to see if the spot has been removed.

Ordinary cigar ash or table salt mixed with either mineral oil or machine oil will sometimes be effective where the paste is not. First moisten the tip of the index finger in the oil, and then dip into the cigar ash or salt. Rub the spot gently and inspect it frequently. After the spot has disappeared, wax the area.

If surfaces have been turned white by wetting, use the French polishing method to restore the surface (described on page 144). French polishing also may be used to remove surface scratches.

White blemishes caused by heat are usually very difficult to remove without complete refinishing. If the damage has not penetrated too deeply into the finish, stroke the spot lightly with a cloth moistened with camphorated oil. Do not use a linty cloth, as fuzz may stick to the wood. Wipe immediately with a clean cloth. If rough, rub with 3/0 steel wool dipped in paste wax or lubricating oil. For a varnish or shellac surface (do not use on lacquer), it is worth trying to remove the blemish by using a dampened cloth with spirits of camphor or essence of peppermint. Daub on the spot; do not wipe. Let dry undisturbed for at least 30 minutes. Then rub down with rottenstone and oil.

**Other surface treatments** If you don't want to go through the above scraping and refinishing, there are a number of other treatments that you can use. Often they will be satisfactory and, in any case, are worth trying before scraping off the finish. When old varnish has fine cracks and has lost its life, it can be greatly improved by brushing over with a strong solvent called *crack remover*. This liquid consists of a mixture of amyl acetate, acetone, ether, and other solvents. First, wash all dirt and wax from the surface with turpentine. Then apply the solvent. It will melt the old varnish finish and allow it to spread evenly on the wood. When the varnish has dried, sand smooth and apply a fresh coat of varnish.

If the varnish is not cracked but is very dirty, it can be

cleaned by washing with 1 part muriatic acid to 10 parts water. The cleaning can also be done by applying a coat of kerosene oil and letting it remain on the surface for a while before wiping off with a cloth. If there are ink spots or other stains on the finish, they can be removed by using a little nitric acid.

White spots and rings can usually be removed by the following treatment: Rub the spot lightly with a little alcohol on a cloth, being careful not to remove the varnish by rubbing too long at a time. Follow the alcohol rub with linseed oil. Another effective method consists of rubbing the spot with olive oil mixed with a little spirits of camphor. This oil rubbing is much more effective if the varnished surface is first moderately heated by holding an electric iron about 6 inches above the spot. The moderate heat helps the gums in the varnish to fuse together and, at the same time, drives out whatever moisture is present. The finish can then be rubbed with fine pumice stone and oil and polished with furniture polish. If a very high finish is wanted, the article can be rubbed with rottenstone.

If a highly polished surface grows foggy, rub it with a cloth dipped in vinegar solution (1 tablespoonful of vinegar to 1 quart of water). Rub with the grain until the surface is thoroughly dry.

If paper sticks to a wood surface, saturate it with a lightweight oil. Let stand, and then rub lightly with 3/0 steel wool. Then wipe the surface clean with a dry cloth. The process may have to be repeated several times.

If the varnish is not very dirty, it will be necessary only to rub the surface with a reviver. A good reviver may be made as follows: Combine 2 ounces of raw linseed oil, 2 ounces of rottenstone, and 4 ounces of turpentine. Mix thoroughly; then add 2 ounces of saturated solution oxalic acid, and 1 ounce of alcohol. Apply the reviver to the surface, and rub in circular motion with a felt pad. This mixture will clean and polish at the same time.

Another reviver can be made by mixing equal parts of turpentine, raw oil, and vinegar. This is easy to use, as it is not likely to damage the finish. In a great many cases a varnish finish can be made to look like new by rubbing with fine pumice stone and oil, and then with rottenstone and oil. When using pumice stone on old varnish, rub only very lightly to avoid cutting through the finish coat.

Although a wax finish is easily stained and damaged by water, it can just as easily be restored. First clean all the dirt from the surface by going over it with a cloth saturated with turpentine. The amount of wax which should be removed will depend on the condition of the furniture. Any stains should be bleached out, and if there are any rings and white spots that have not been completely removed by the turpentine, try rubbing the spot with a little alcohol and then with a little raw linseed oil. Then the surface can be waxed and polished. A good wax polish for old furniture can be made by mixing beeswax and turpentine to form a thin paste. A little of this can be applied from time to time to keep the furniture in good condition.

If the surface is not very dirty, the finish can be cleaned and revived by polishing with a liquid made as follows: Mix together 4 ounces of beeswax and 4 ounces of raw linseed oil to form a paste; then add 1 quart of turpentine and mix thoroughly. This polish is rubbed on with a cloth and then allowed to dry. The furniture can then be brought up to a nice polish with a soft cloth. This treatment is recommended for antiques, as it cleans the surface and at the same time protects the patina and luster of the old wood.

An oil finish can also be revived with the above polish if the surface is in good condition. However, the best way to clean an oiled surface of all dirt is with warm water and soap, then repolishing with hot raw linseed oil, using a pad and plenty of rubbing.

Wax should not be used on a surface that has been French-polished, as it gives a cloudy appearance to the finish. A good reviver should be used instead. The safest method of reviving a French polish is to rub with rottenstone and oil. If the finish is in bad condition, it can be rubbed down with pumice stone and oil, and when the oil has been thoroughly removed, the surface can be French-polished in the usual manner.

Another reviver can be made by mixing 1 part vinegar with 1 part turpentine and adding 1 part alcohol. Mix these ingredients thoroughly, and then add 1 part raw oil. This mixture is applied with a cloth and will clean and revive the finish. Another reviver for French-polished or shellacked surfaces is made of 8 parts olive oil, 1 part spirit of camphor, and 2 parts alcohol. Care should be taken in applying these mixtures because of the alcohol; however, they are good revivers and should remove rings and water marks.

### Refinishing

If the surface is in bad condition or cannot be repaired, the only solution is refinishing. There are no shortcuts to a good refinishing job—it takes time, and each step must be done well before beginning the next. Failure to do this always ends in difficulties that take more time and patience to correct than if more careful work had been done from the beginning.

The main steps in refinishing are the removal of the old finish, the preparation for the new finish, and the application of the new finish. Directions for removal of the old finish are given here, while the preparation for the new finish is explained in Chapter 2, and the application of the new finish is given in Chapters 3 to 10.

Before you start work, remove the handles, knobs, and hinges of table leaves and doors to make the finishing of parts easier. Find out what finish is on the piece. Remove any wax with a moistened cloth, and make the test as described on page 273.

For the majority of pieces, paint-and-varnish remover will cut the old finish. There are certain other liquids which can also be used to remove paint and varnish—benzole, trisodium phosphate, caustic soda, ammonia, etc.—but as a general rule it is better to use the commercial paint-and-varnish removers. These removers come in liquid, semifluid, or paste form. Generally the liquid form is used for flat surfaces, and the paste on vertical surfaces because it will remain without running. Different removers will require different methods of cleaning the surface afterward to stop the action of the remover. Manufacturer's directions appear on the container and should be followed carefully. Some require the use of alcohol, some of naphtha, some of turpentine, and a few, of water. Use only the recommended neutralizer, otherwise any new finish applied may refuse to dry, peel from the surface, crack in fine lines, or check.

Pour some of the paint remover into a saucer, and dip an

old brush into it. Spread newspapers on floor under piece to be refinished. Wear gloves to protect the hands. Dust the surface of table. Flow on the paint-and-varnish remover liberally with the grain. Be careful not to spill it on the skin or any fabric. Do not brush it back and forth or work it in. Paint remover works best when applied in a thick, even coat. Most paint removers have a wax base that forms a skin over the chemical, retarding evaporation. Brushing back over remover may break this skin, and full effectiveness would not be obtained. Never cover the entire surface in one operation. Do about 1½ to 2 square feet at a time. Wait until varnish bubbles up, blisters, and crumbles. If, after 10 or 15 minutes, the remover has not softened the old paint, apply another coat on top of the first.

Remove the crumbled varnish with a broad-bladed putty knife, holding it away from the body and pushing firmly with grain. Do not apply too much pressure, or the knife may gouge the wood. Dispose of loosened varnish at once, as it is inflammable. Apply remover and scrape at least twice, until the wood surface is clean of old varnish or paint. Use the scraper for flat surfaces only. To clean carvings use an old toothbrush, a sharpened lollipop stick, an orange stick, or a meat skewer. On turnings and curved surfaces, use a piece of burlap or crumpled paper to remove the first layer, and steel wool to remove the last. A burlap thread or a piece of twisted steel wool is helpful in removing the finish from the fine grooves. Use No. 1 steel wool to remove the softened finish from curves or corners.

Take great care to see that varnish remover does not run onto parts that are not yet cleaned or onto those that have already been cleaned. Careful watching can prevent such staining of the wood; a run should be wiped off immediately with a cloth dampened with denatured alcohol, a solvent for varnish remover.

When using a wax-free remover, the final cleanup can be done with steel wool dipped in the remover. However, if the remover has a wax base, the residue must be washed away completely, so that it will not interfere with the adhesion of the new finish. For this washing use lacquer thinner, turpentine, naphtha, or denatured alcohol as directed by the manufacturer of the remover. Just saturate a cloth with the neutralizer, and wash the surface clean. Be sure to clean recessed corners. If there are any shiny spots or places from which a light powder can be scraped, it means that the old finish is still present. All remains of old finish and remover *must* be cleaned off, or the new finish will not dry.

On many old pieces, usually on those made of pine, the wood has been covered with a penetrating dull paint—usually red, green, or black—which was made by mixing pigment with skim milk or buttermilk. This so-called "refractory" paint was at one time considered desirable because it thoroughly covered all knots and imperfections and gave an effect somewhat like that of the richer woods of mahogany and cherry. Varnish remover will not remove this paint. To remove it, the surface must be kept moist with denatured alcohol or full-strength ammonia solution and rubbed with sandpaper or steel wool. If the paint has penetrated deeply into soft wood, try bleaching (see page 32) or sanding with an electric sander. Slight indication of the original color is generally desirable, since an antique collector would find this a sign of age. In addition, such traces add interest by giving a variation in color.

The standard varnish removers do not work too well on some of the catalytic coatings. In such cases, the only way the finish can be removed is by mechanical sanding or with an electric-element remover. The latter softens and blisters the old finish so that a putty knife can lift it off easily. There are several types of electric-heating-element removers on the market.

### Removing old shellac, lacquer, and wax

To remove shellac from wood surfaces, brush on denatured or wood alcohol, and scrape up the soft residue as rapidly as possible. Then wash over the whole surface with the alcohol as a final cleanup. Repeated application of the alcohol may be necessary to remove all of the shellac. Paint-and-varnish remover generally will remove shellac, but it is more expensive than alcohol. Turpentine does not dissolve shellac.

To remove lacquer from old wood surfaces, brush or spray on a lacquer thinner, and scrape up as fast as possible, since lacquer thinner dries very fast. Do a small piece of work at a time. Repeat the application of lacquer thinners until the surface is clean. Paint-and-varnish remover may also work.

Before revarnishing, painting or any refinishing operation, the old wax surface must be removed; otherwise the new coats will not dry. All the wax must be removed, including what has lodged in the seams, cracks, and pores of the wood. Waxes usually can be removed with benzine, turpentine, and denatured alcohol. If you want to remove the wax without injuring the varnish or shellac under it, do not use alcohol. Apply the liquid with a soft cloth, and rub until all wax has been removed.

*Sanding*    The same procedure is used for refinishing old work as for new work (Chapter 2). After removing the old finish to the bare wood, begin with the coarse abrasive to re-

move discoloration and surface irregularities, and then follow
with the finer grits in the same sequence as on new wood.

On old work where you merely want to smooth the old
finish preparatory to varnishing or enameling, use a fine waterproof sandpaper, applying water or rubbing oil as a lubricant and also to prevent the paper from clogging with
loosened particles of the old finish. When preparing enameled surfaces for refinishing, use open-coat abrasive papers.
These papers have widely spaced abrasive particles to prevent
clogging. The abrasive also cuts faster on rough work, where
scratches will later be removed with the use of finer abrasive
paper.

After the old finish is removed and the surface sanded, almost any finishing schedule (Chapter 16) can be used, depending of course, on the wood of the old piece. However,
before refinishing the old piece go over it carefully to be sure
that the surface is in perfect condition. The beauty of the
final finish depends upon the condition of the wood under
it. It is important to spend plenty of time on repair of any
defects.

### To remove dark spots

Dark spots usually may be removed by bleaching them with
a saturated solution of oxalic acid or a combination of oxalic
and tartaric acid. To make a saturated solution of oxalic acid,
mix 1 ounce of powdered oxalic acid (or 2 ounces of crystals
of oxalic acid) to 1 pint of hot water. Some woods, particularly maple, may need a saturated solution of one-half oxalic
acid and one-half tartaric acid. Apply the solution with a
brush or cloth, and allow it to dry. Repeat the application if
required. To assure a finished effect, use the acid over the
entire surface and not only on the dark spot. Wash off the

acid with a weak ammonia solution (1 tablespoonful to a quart of water) followed by clear water, and allow the surface to dry for 24 hours. Other bleaching techniques can be found in Chapter 2.

When the wood has a gray, faded appearance, you can freshen the color by washing the entire piece with this mild bleaching solution. *Wear a mask when sanding after this process.*

If you cannot remove the bad spots by bleaching, you can sand or scrape the wood slightly. However, too much sanding, planing, or scraping reduces the "patina"—the mellowness, richness of color, and texture of the surface, which is the result of age and usage. Also, the new wood that shows through will not be the same color as the rest of the piece which has not been scraped. Therefore it is better to let an experienced person do this, with a warning against removing any more surface than is necessary.

**Regluing loose joints**

If joints need regluing, be sure to scrape away all traces of the former glue, as fresh glue does not stick well to old glue. Clamp the joint together until the glue is thoroughly dry. Very loose joints must be rebuilt with wood or cloth shims. If joints are loose but cannot be tightened completely, glue may be injected by a hypodermic-like glue injector (available at craftsmen's supply dealers) or by rocking the joint and forcing the glue into it. For certain type of joints, it may be wise to use one of the so-called "wood-swelling" compounds, available at hardware stores. When using one of these materials, be sure to wash away any that gets on the surface— this holds for the glue, too—since it may cause trouble when the final finish is being applied.

### Regluing loose veneer

When refinishing antique furniture or any furniture made before the introduction of modern glues and gluing methods, it pays to inspect the surfaces carefully for any spots where the veneer is loose. Tap the area with your finger. A slightly different, snapping sound means that the veneer has come loose from the cross-banding.

Frequently the veneer is slightly loose but not loose enough to permit glue to be inserted underneath. Do not let such places remain unrepaired, however, because they are likely to show under the new finish and may get worse in time. Instead, loosen the veneer further by laying a piece of wet felt over the spot and applying a hot laundry iron. The moisture and steam will soften the veneer and glue so that the veneer can be lifted far enough to insert new glue.

If necessary, you can split the veneer with a razor blade along the grain. Prop up one side of the slit with a couple of safety-razor blades while you force the glue underneath. Treat the other side of the cut in the same way. Then lay a piece of wax paper or tin over the area, and apply clamps.

When veneer has to be reglued on a curved surface, use a cloth bag filled with sand or salt to distribute pressure of the clamps evenly.

If you are using the fast-setting polyvinyl resin glue, you can omit the clamping process and merely press down the veneer with a moderately warm iron. The heat will cause the glue to flow thinly and uniformly under the loose veneer, where it will set quickly.

After the veneer has been reglued and new veneer patched in to replace any missing portions, the old finish can be removed and the work refinished. Do not strip off the old finish, however, until all gluing has been completed.

To replace broken or damaged veneer, remove all old glue on both parts, and apply the new glue to the base only. Veneer can usually be obtained from a cabinetmaker. The new piece should, if possible, match both the grain and the color of the part next to the patch. Trim off irregularities in shape, and cut the new piece exactly to fit. Then put the piece of veneer in place, and clamp it until the glue is dry.

### Repairing blistered veneer

With a sharp knife, slit the veneer near the side of the blister where the glue still holds. Soften the old glue underneath so that the new glue can be absorbed by the pores of the wood, by pouring vinegar into the blister. Allow it to stand for about 8 hours. Make certain that the wood is thoroughly dry before you insert the glue. Place a pad of paper and a block of soft wood between the wood and the clamps to ensure even pressure and protect the wood against damage. Over a patch on a curve, use a sandbag as a weight.

### Repairing large surface areas

If the damaged section has a natural finish and is so large that it cannot easily be filled by stick shellac, insert a piece of old wood that exactly matches the wood of the furniture. Cabinetmakers and finishers of old furniture collect old pieces of wood for this purpose. On some furniture a small piece of wood may be cut from the under part. To make the joining less noticeable, cut these pieces diagonally so that no edge will be at a right angle to the grain of the wood.

### Care of wood finishes

Natural-finished wood, whether covered with wax, varnish, lacquer, or shellac, should have periodic waxing or applications of good furniture polish. Rub the surfaces frequently with a soft clean cloth to keep the protective wax or polish coating in good condition. When the finish becomes so dirty that wax or polish will not clean it, then wash it. Never flood the wood with water, since this may damage the finish and cause the glued joints to loosen. If the wood is veneered, any moisture may cause the veneer to peel off. To properly wash wood, use a cloth dampened with mild soap water or a solution made as described on page 271, and then wipe it with a clean cloth dampened with clean water. Remove all moisture before applying wax or polish. For waxing techniques, see Chapter 10.

For painted, enameled, or colored lacquered surfaces you need only remove accumulated film by periodically dusting and wiping with a clean cloth dampened in mild soap water. Then wipe with a clean cloth dampened with clear water. Be careful not to get the surface too wet.

# CHAPTER FIFTEEN

# Finishing and Refinishing Wood Floors

**A** wood floor is usually the largest project faced by the average wood finisher. In most cases, however, the procedure is about the same as for furniture pieces.

### Types of woods

The most commonly used hardwood in residential flooring is oak. This is available in a number of species, of both red and white. For the purpose of this chapter no distinction will be made among them, since the same treatment applies to the various species of both red and white oak. Hard maple is commonly used for flooring where heavy wear is expected, such as for bowling alleys, workshops, theaters, and assembly halls. Other flooring hardwoods are beech, birch, and pecan.

While softwoods are not used too frequently at present, fir and pine flooring are available. Actually, the species of wood does not influence the applied finish except in special cases.

### Preparing the surface

New flooring must be sanded after installation to obtain the smooth unblemished surface so important to successful finishing. This is usually done with power sanding equipment, which can be rented. You will need a small drum-type sanding machine for the main floor area, and an edging machine to sand all exposed floor up to the molding. If you are not familiar with the use of power sanding equipment, be sure to follow directions carefully. Great care should be taken not to gouge the floor.

### *New floors—sanding grits*

| Species of wood | Operation | Grade of abrasive paper |
|---|---|---|
| Hardwood: Oak, maple, beech, birch, pecan | First cut | Medium coarse 2 (36) |
| | Second cut | Fine 1 (50) |
| | Final sanding | Extra fine 2/0 (100) |
| Softwood: Pine, fir | First cut | Medium fine 1½ (40) |
| | Second cut | Fine 1 (50) |
| | Final standing | Extra fine 2/0 (100) |

Three sandings with successively finer grades of abrasive paper are generally needed to obtain a perfectly smooth surface. The first cut may be across or at a 45-degree angle to the grain, but successive cuts should be taken with the grain of the wood. When sanding, start at one wall and move to the opposite. Then pass the sander back along the same path. This return pass enables the machine to pick up the dust created by the first pass. Each complete pass (from wall to wall and return) should overlap the previous pass by 2 or 3 inches. Be sure to follow this procedure throughout the entire sanding schedule. Remember—never stop the forward motion of the sanding machine while the sanding drum is in contact with the floor. This is particularly important when sanding soft woods such as pine with coarse open-coat paper in the sanding machine. If the machine is allowed to rest heavily in one spot, deep cuts, scratches, or gouges in the wood will result. If severe, such indentations are impossible to level with the remaining floor area in the subsequent sanding operations.

On parquet and other block-type floors, where it is impossible to sand with the grain, special care must be taken and somewhat finer grades of sandpaper are advisable. When the final sanding has been completed to your satisfaction, all dust must be removed from the floor and other parts of the room such as window sills and baseboards. This can be done best with a vacuum cleaner followed with a dry, absorbent dust mop. A freshly sanded and dusted floor must be protected from disfigurement or dirt. Moisture vapor will cause grain lifting, and dirt or stain is difficult to remove. Therefore, it is imperative to apply the first coat of finish immediately. It is good practice for the finish applicator to work in his stocking feet to avoid marring the floor.

### Staining the floor

The first step in finishing a floor is staining. Stain is used, of course, to change the color of the wood and to accentuate its grain. If the color of the wood in the floor is already satisfactory, this step is omitted.

A clear finish will darken the floor slightly, and so this must be considered when deciding on the use of a stain. Pigmented wiping stains, colored penetrating sealers, NGR stains, or water stains are the most common products used in staining floors. As described in Chapter 4, a brush or rag is used to apply the stain evenly. With a dark-colored stain, the surplus remaining on the floor after about 5 minutes should be wiped off with rags. Wiping also helps distribute the color. If the stain becomes gummy and hard to wipe, a rag wet with a little fresh stain or mineral spirits will remove it. Light-colored stain should not be wiped. It must be brushed evenly in a very thin coat and left alone. All stains should dry overnight before the next finishing operation is started.

### Filling

As in furniture finishing, some flooring hardwoods (see Chapter 5) require filling. Either a paste or liquid filler may be used. A paste will bear the proper directions for thinning on the label. Either type is applied with a brush, and in application the first brushing is across the grain. This is followed by brushing with the grain. Let the filler dry a few minutes. The surplus must be removed immediately after the gloss disappears, so that the area covered at any one time should be only that which can be wiped off quickly. The wiping is done with burlap—first across the grain and then gently with the grain, changing to clean burlap frequently. The floor will be completely smooth when the filler has been properly applied. The filler should be allowed to dry thoroughly in accordance with manufacturer's directions, before applying the finish coats. Fillers are available in a number of colors to accent the grain of the wood, but so-called "natural" fillers are most popular. Such products are readily available at paint stores.

## Top finishes for floors

The top finishes for floors are basically the same as those applied to other wood surfaces—penetrating resin finishes, varnish, synthetic coatings, shellac, and wax. They are usually formulated especially for floors, and they are sometimes applied in a slightly different manner than are furniture-type finishes. Be sure to read the manufacturer's instructions before applying.

*Floor sealers*    Penetrating resin floor finishes or sealers are becoming the most widely used material. They penetrate the fibers of the wood and form a wear-resistant surface which does not extend above the surface of the wood.

Touch-up is easier with sealer than with varnish. Floor sealer is applied in a liberal coat, usually with long-handled lamb's wool or nylon applicators. First move across the grain of the wood and then with the grain to ensure complete coverage. If the manufacturer's directions so indicate, the surplus should be wiped up with rags. (Rags soaked in sealer are liable to ignite spontaneously, and so they must be picked up at the end of a day's work and stored where they will not cause a fire—or, better, destroy them by burning. Another safe method is to put them in a bucket of water.)

After the drying time specified by the manufacturer has elapsed, the surface should be buffed with steel wool. An electric buffer requires less work than hand buffing. Any steel wool particles or dust left on the floor should be picked up with a vacuum cleaner, after which a second coat of sealer is applied. This coat should be thin and applied only with the grain. After the second coat has dried, the floor is ready for use. If a greater gloss is desired, the sealed floor makes an excellent base for varnish, or a wax coat can be applied over the sealer.

**Varnish**  A good floor varnish presents a pleasing appearance and ensures long wear to a floor. Floor varnishes are available in several degrees of gloss. They can dry with a high gloss, a medium gloss, or a low gloss. The selection is a matter of preference, but the high-gloss varnishes are more wear-resistant. The kind of service expected of the floor also determines the type of varnish. There are varnishes especially designed for schools, gymnasiums, and other public buildings, and they should be selected for the intended use.

Adequate drying time for the stain must be permitted—at least overnight, but preferably for 24 hours. If a sealer is not used, at least two varnish coats will be required to obtain a uniform appearance. In applying a varnish, it is important to use a dust-free brush and to work on a dust-free floor. Many varnishes require several hours to dry. The directions on the label will tell you how many. Some are much faster-drying than others, but in any event it is important that dust be prevented from falling on the wet varnish. Air bubbles sometimes form in varnish films. These are created by the bristles of the brush and can be minimized by avoiding excessive brushing. When they do appear, they can be removed by brushing back into the area with light feathering strokes before the varnish begins to set.

Gymnasium floors are usually constructed with hard maple flooring. They are usually finished with special phenolic varnishes. These varnishes are durable, nonslippery, and do not show rubber burns. They provide an ideal surface for sports or gymnastics.

**Synthetic clear coatings**  Where extremely high abrasion resistance is required, the newer polyurethane finishes will give excellent results. There are three general types of these finishes: polyurethane oils, which look and act like conventional varnishes but have somewhat better abrasion resistance; moisture-cured polyurethanes, which dry by reaction with moisture in the air; and two-component, or catalytic, polyurethanes, which must be mixed just before use and which have a limited potlife. The abrasion resistance increases in this order, and so does the strength and odor of the solvent.

As is true with most relatively new materials, it is especially important to read and follow the manufacturer's instructions. Each product may differ slightly from others of the same type, and the exact procedures are often required to get maximum performance.

**Shellac**    Shellac is very light-colored, and it dries rapidly. It is not equal to a high-quality varnish in resistance to wear, and water readily spots it. However, a well-waxed shellac finish will last for a long time. Shellac is more easily repaired than varnish if small areas are damaged. A dry shellac film may appear rough, and so it is wise to sand lightly between coats and, if necessary, after the final coat. Old shellac films should be removed completely before refinishing with varnish, as some varnishes may not give satisfactory service over shellac.

Two or three coats (2-pound cut) are required for most floor work. Allow at least a 3-hour drying time between coats.

**Wax**    The finish on a floor can be protected by keeping it waxed. Wax should not be applied to unfinished wood, because it penetrates the wood and is difficult to remove. Wax by itself is not a durable finish. The wax takes wear, and as long as it is intact, the finish is protected. A newly finished floor should have at least two coats of wax—and if a liquid wax is used, additional coats may be necessary to get an adequate film. Liquid wax contains solvent, and the film formed is therefore thinner than that obtained with a paste wax. If the wax coating is kept intact, the floor's finish will retain its beauty indefinitely. At times, wax will react with shellac—and so shellacked floors should be waxed with caution. If waxing is desired, a small area should be tested first to determine if the particular wax and shellac are compatible.

Waxes are not recommended for use on maple floors. The heavy wear, for which maple flooring is most frequently employed, destroys the wax finish.

### Renewing the old finish

The surface of a floor that is properly maintained can be renewed several times without complete refinishing. A well-finished, waxed floor should be satisfactory for many years before the old finish needs to be completely removed. The surface, however, should be renewed periodically. First, the wax is removed with mineral spirits. Good ventilation is necessary. It is important to wipe up all solvent before it can dry and to redeposit the wax. Steel wool can be used to loosen thick spots of wax. If the finish is in good condition, a new coat of wax will satisfactorily renew the floor. When the finish becomes worn in spots, it will be necessary to revarnish or refinish with some other coating material. Before applying the varnish or shellac, the floor should be cleaned to remove dirt and stains. Then it should be sanded using fine to medium sandpaper—moving with the grain to remove rough spots and glossy areas on the old finish.

Small worn spots may be successfully retouched. If this can be done without leaving lap marks, it saves complete removal of the finish. Sometimes the wood is roughened from wear after the finish has worn away. When this has occurred, a penetrating sealer should be applied to the spot before varnishing. Otherwise the color in the varnish will make the spot darker than the balance of the floor.

### Replacing an old finish

Floors in poor condition, that is, cracked, chipped, badly discolored, and worn down to the bare wood in many places, need complete refinishing. The old finish should be removed with power sanding equipment, following the technique previously described for new floors. Two or three sandings with successively finer grades of sandpaper are generally needed to obtain a perfectly smooth surface. The corners may have to be done by hand—possibly with the help of paint and varnish remover.

### *Old floors—sanding grits*

| Floor | Operation | Grade of abrasive paper |
|---|---|---|
| Covered with varnish, shellac, paint, etc. | First cut | Coarse—3⅓ (20) |
| | Second cut | Medium fine—1½ (40) |
| | Final cut | Extra fine—2/0 (100) |

After the old finish has been removed and before any refinishing, the floor should be examined for badly scratched or broken boards. Repairs should be made before the final cleaning of the floor. If a scratch is deep, it is sometimes possible to fill it with one of the plastic-sawdust compounds on the market, although where possible the scratch should be sanded out. The plastic materials must dry thoroughly before they can be sanded, and they must be sanded if the finished floor is to be smooth. When strips of flooring are replaced, care must be exercised to be certain that a different color is not introduced. For instance, red and white oak react to finishes differently, and so the same species should be used as in the original floor.

If the same species is not available, it may be possible to use a light oak stain carefully so as to match the old floor.

The final operation before applying the finish is cleaning. It is just as important to have a clean floor when refinishing as it is when applying finish to a new floor. Any dust not collected by the sander can best be removed with a vacuum cleaner. To complete the task, a mop dampened with mineral spirits will be satisfactory if care is taken not to wet the floor to any degree. Oil mops are not satisfactory. They will darken the wood, and oil left on the floor will interfere with the drying of finishes.

After cleaning, the finishing operations are the same as for new floors. If the filler is still intact, the first step should be application of a sealer, with subsequent operations as previously described in this chapter.

**Painting floors**

Generally, hardwood floors are finished with clear coatings that enhance the beauty of the grain. There is a growing interest, however—especially among interior decorators—in finishing floors with colored enamels. Application of decorative designs to match draperies or wallpaper or to blend with furniture coverings, is also becoming popular. Since floor enamels come in such a wide range of colors, there is no limit to the variety of pleasing decorative schemes that can be achieved by the imaginative.

Floor and deck enamels are playing a most important role in the restoration of original flooring in older houses. They add a touch of authenticity—especially when houses of the

Colonial era are being restored—since many of the floors of the better Early American homes were painted.

Pigmented polyurethane materials may be used, particularly where excellent abrasion resistance is required. Their properties, which were discussed previously, do not change much with the addition of pigment.

Sanding and filling operations, previously described, are a must when finishing floors. After the filler is dry, use three coats of self-sealing floor enamel for best results. The first coat may be thinned with about 10 percent of mineral spirits or turpentine, unless the manufacturer's label calls for a special thinner. Allow each coat to dry thoroughly before adding the next coat. When the floor is thoroughly dry, a coat of wax will help protect the enamel and give additional luster to the floor.

## Seamless flooring systems

The so-called "seamless flooring systems" are colorful, decorative, and extremely durable. Most seamless systems consist of liquid base coats, colored chips or other decorative materials, and liquid sealer or wear coats. All coats are applied in a continuous flow without seams, which is ideal for counter- and tabletops as well as floors. The type of seamless system used will determine the exact application techniques required. However, the usual steps are:

1. Fill the seams and cracks with wood plastic and sand level. Apply a seal or prime coat, if recommended.
2. Apply base coat and chips or other decorative materials. The latter add the color, excitement, and texture that makes seamless floor coverings individually yours. Excess decorative materials and chips can be easily removed,

after the base coat has dried, with a clean broom or vacuum. Sand high areas where chips have overlapped and are not firmly bonded. Vacuum thoroughly. Allow base or chip-receiving coat to dry thoroughly before applying glaze coat. Some dry in 4 to 6 hours—others recommend overnight drying time. If the base coat is not the chip-receiving coat, apply and let dry thoroughly. Then apply the manufacturer's recommended chip-receiving coat, and apply decorative materials as above.

3. Apply the glaze, seal, or wear coat. Some final coats can be applied as soon as the chip-receiving coat is hard enough to use—others require a longer, more thorough drying of the chip-receiving coat. Apply generously—if only one coat is recommended. Where more than one coat is recommended, apply glaze or wear coat, allow to dry according to manufacturer's directions, sand if recommended, and apply second coat. Often extra coats are recommended if less texture is desired or to create a high-build, tougher surface.

Seamless floor coverings require little maintenance to retain their beauty and sparkle. They are tougher and more durable than most counter- and tabletop materials. Clean with a damp cloth when dirty.

# CHAPTER SIXTEEN

# Finishing Schedules and Specifications

The standard schedule for all uniform color finishes in coarse-grained woods is quite simple—stain the wood, fill with wood paste filler, and then apply top coats of varnish or lacquer. Close-grained woods do not require filling, making the basic schedule simply one of staining and varnishing. There is no change in the basic schedule for red mahogany, brown mahogany, or wheat mahogany other than a change in the color. Once the finisher has mastered the technique of various operations in the basic schedule, he can apply the schedule to a wide variety of woods to obtain a considerable number of different finishes. Study the basic schedules in this chapter. Refer to previous chapters for instructions on any specific step of the schedule, such as staining, filling, or sealer coats. You are then ready to go ahead with any specific wood finish.

## BASIC SCHEDULES

### (1) Basic lacquer schedule

A high-grade finish for walnut, mahogany, oak, or other open-grained woods.

1. Sponge work with warm water. Add 2 ounces of dextrin per gallon of water if desired. Allow to dry 1 hour before continuing.
2. Sand with fine paper. Dust.
3. Stain with water stain of desired color. Dry 12 hours.
4. Shellac wash coat (7 parts alcohol to 1 part shellac). Dry 30 minutes.
5. Sand with fine paper. Dust.
6. Fill with paste wood filler stain. Wipe clean. Dry 4, 24, or 48 hours, depending on type of filler. Follow manufacturer's recommendations.
7. Spray one coat clear gloss lacquer. Dry 2 to 4 hours.
8. Scuff with very fine paper or 3/0 steel wool.
9. Spray second coat of clear gloss lacquer. Dry 4 hours.
10. Scuff with very fine paper or 4/0 steel wool.
11. Spray third coat of clear gloss lacquer. Dry overnight.
12. Rub to satin finish.

### (2) Basic varnish schedule

1–6. Follow Schedule 1 to operation 6.
7. Brush or spray 2-pound-cut shellac (white for light finishes; orange for dark; half-and-half for medium tones). The addition of 25 to 50 percent shellac mixing lacquer is recommended.

8. Optional. Sand back to bare wood, using previous coat simply as filler.
9. Brush or spray first coat of cabinet rubbing and polishing varnish. This should be thinned 1 part turpentine to 7 parts varnish or used at can consistency but brushed out to a thin coat. Dry 24 hours.
10. Sand with very fine paper.
11. Brush or spray second coat of same varnish at can consistency. Dry 48 hours.
12. Sand with extra fine waterproof paper with water or No. 1/2 pumice with water. Dry 12 hours.
13. Third coat of same varnish. Dry 3 to 4 days.
14. Rub to satin finish.
    NOTE: Operation 7 can be eliminated if desired.

### (3) Basic lacquer schedule

A fast-spraying schedule for walnut, mahogany, oak, or other open-grained woods.

1. Spray quick-drying, NGR stain. Dry 1 hour.
2. Fill with quick-dry paste wood filler. Dry 4 hours.
3. Spray one coat sanding sealer. Dry 1 hour.
4. Sand with very fine paper.
5. Spray one coat clear gloss lacquer. Dry 1½ hours.
6. Scuff with very fine paper.
7. Spray one coat clear flat lacquer.

### (4) Basic varnish schedule

A fast-brushing or fast-spraying schedule for open-grained woods.

1. Brush or spray non-grain-raising stain. This should be a 3-hour-dry type for satisfactory brushing.

2. Wash coat of shellac. Dry 30 minutes.
3. Sand with very fine paper.
4. Fill with quick-dry paste wood filler. Dry 4 hours.
5. Brush 2-pound-cut shellac (orange or white as required). Dry 2 hours.
6. Sand with very fine paper.
7. Brush or spray thin coat of rubbing varnish. Dry 4 to 6 hours.
8. Sand with extra fine paper.
9. Second coat of rubbing varnish. Dry overnight.
10. Rub to satin finish. Rubbing can be eliminated by final coat of flat varnish if desired.

### (5) Close-grained woods

Lacquer system for birch, beech, maple, etc.

1. Stain with non-grain-raising stain. Dry 3 hours.
2. Spray or brush sanding sealer. Dry 1 hour.
3. Sand with very fine paper.
4. One to three coats of clear gloss lacquer.
5. Rub.

    NOTE: Operations 1 and 2 can be omitted for natural finish. Add extra coat of lacquer.

### (6) Close-grained woods

Varnish system for birch, beech, maple, etc.

1–5. Follow Schedule 1 to operation 5.
6. Two or three coats of rubbing varnish. (See schedules 2 and 4.)

### (7) Close-grained woods

Spray only, double-stain system.

1. Spray pigment wiping stain. Wipe clean with rag. Dry 1 hour.
2. Thin same stain 1 part to 3 parts naphtha. Spray-shade the work. Do not wipe. Dry 1 hour.
3. Spray sanding sealer. Dry 1 hour.
4. Sand with extra fine paper, dry. Dust.
5. Two coats of lacquer.
6. Rub.

   NOTE: For quality work, more coats of top material can be used to get a thicker film for thorough rubbing.

### (8) Close-grained woods

Brush or spray, double stain.

1. Brush or spray pigment wiping stain of desired color. Let dry until it starts to flat; then wipe with rag. Dry 1 hour.
2. Brush or spray sanding sealer. Dry 1 hour.
3. Sand with extra fine garnet, dry. Dust.
4. Second coat of sealer.
5. Pigment wiping stain, same as in operation 1.
6. Varnish or lacquer top coats as desired.

### (9) Uniforming schedule

For finishing open- and close-grained wood in same piece.

1. Spray or brush stain of desired color. Drying time according to type used.
2. Apply paste wood filler to all open-grained wood and to

*Aside from the vacuum, which is optional equipment, here are the rental tools necessary to do a first class job of refinishing your old and worn floors.*

Floors in poor condition, that is, cracked, chipped, badly discolored, or worn down to the bare wood in spots, need complete refinishing. For large areas, use a drum-type sanding machine such as shown above, and make two or three sandings with successively finer grits of paper. You will need an edge sanding machine to sand all exposed wood up to the molding (right, above). The corners may have to be done by hand with a scraper— possibly with the help of paint and varnish remover (bottom).

When using varnish as a final finish, oak and other open-grained woods should be given a coat of paste wood filler (top). When a penetrating type of finish is used, filling is usually omitted. This finish may be applied with a floor applicator as shown here (below).

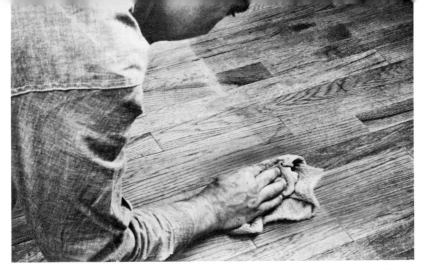

To keep the floor in top shape, apply a coat of good paste or semi-paste wax (top) and buff with a power buffer (bottom). When properly maintained, cleaned with wax and polished, a floor should last a lifetme without refinishing.

end grain only of the close-grained wood. Wipe and let dry.

**3.** Brush or spray pigment wiping stain of matching color on close-grained wood only. Dry 30 minutes.

**4.** Brush or spray sanding sealer. Dry 1 hour.

**5.** Sand with extra fine paper.

**6.** Repeat operations 4 and 5.

**7a.** Spray or brush pigment wiping stain over the entire piece, wiping and blending with rag as needed for color value. Dry 30 minutes.

**7b.** *Alternate*. Spray shading stain or diluted wiping stain to uniform the wood. Do not wipe. Dry 1 hour.

**8.** Top coats of varnish or lacquer.

## (10) Uniforming schedule

For finishing wood with wide grain variation.

**1.** Apply non-grain-raising stain to light sapwood. Wipe with cloth dampened with alcohol to get color match. Dry 10 to 20 minutes.

**2.** Spray non-grain-raising stain. Spray lightly on dark wood, heavy on light wood. Dry 1 hour.

**3.** Spray lacquer wash coat over all.

**4.** Sand lightly with extra fine paper. Dust.

**5.** Fill all open-grained wood with paste wood filler.

**6.** Reduce same filler, 1 part filler to 2 parts naphtha. Apply to close-grained wood. Wipe off and let dry.

**7.** Spray wet-coat sanding sealer. Dry 1 hour.

**8.** *Optional*. If further color toning or shading is required, spray shading stain or thin pigment wiping stain.

**9.** Top coats.

### (11) Uniforming schedule

A fast-spraying schedule for uniforming birch and gum in combination with walnut or mahogany.

1. Spray quick-drying, NGR stain. Apply heavy on birch and gum; very light on walnut or mahogany. Dry 1 hour.
2. Fill all wood with quick-drying paste filler, matching color to walnut or mahogany. Wipe off. Dry 3 hours.
3. Spray coat of sanding sealer. Dry 1 hour.
4. Even up the color with shading lacquer. Dries immediately on application.
5. Apply top coats of clear lacquer.
   NOTE: This schedule is equally satisfactory but slower with water stain.

### (12) Straight shellac

1. Brush or spray 1-pound-cut white shellac. Dry 1 hour and scuff-sand with extra fine paper.
2. Second shellac coat, 2-pound cut. Dry 2 to 3 hours and sand with extra fine paper.
3. Final shellac coat, 2- or 3-pound cut. Dry 4 hours.

### (13) Shellac and wax

1. Apply one or two coats of shellac according to Schedule 12.
2. Place a small quantity of paste wax inside double thickness of soft cloth. Apply even coat. Dry 10 to 20 minutes.
3. Rub briskly with clean soft cloth pad. Use rotary motion; finish with long strokes. Dry 1 hour or more.
4. Repeat operations 2 and 3.
   NOTE: For a dull finish, wipe final wax with damp rag.

## (14) Synthetic catalytic finish

An extremely hard and durable finish for tabletops and bar tops.

1. Stain if color is desired. Do not use pigmented stain, as the adhesion is not good on undercoaters of any kind.
2. Mix synthetic with required amount of catalyst (check manufacturer's instruction), and apply with brush or spray. Mixed solution must be used within 4 hours. Surface dries in 1 hour.
3. Sand with extra fine paper. Dust.
4. Second coat of synthetic. Dry overnight.
5. Rub and polish.
   NOTE: Some synthetic finishes require baking.

## (15) Penetrating resin finish

The penetrating resin finishes are among the most popular of all clear finishes.

1. Stain, if color is desired. Use a nonsealing alcohol- or water-base stain, and apply with clean cloth or brush. Dry about 1 hour.
2. Pour on liberal amounts of the penetrating resin finish. Swab the finishing material around on the surface with a wad of 3/0 steel wool, using only light pressure. Keep the surface wet for 15 minutes or longer, adding more finish if required.
3. When penetration stops, wipe the surface completely dry, using soft absorbent cloth.
4. If second coat of resin finish is desired, apply it in 3 to 4 hours, following operations 2 and 3.
5. For more luster, let dry 4 hours, then wet sand lightly

with extra fine paper with a small amount of resin finish. After wet-sanding, dry wood thoroughly with a clean cloth; then polish briskly with another cloth.

## BLOND OR LIGHT FINISHES

(*See Chapters 2 and 12 for details*)

### (16) Pigment coloring system

Spray system for select white woods.

1. Spray uniform coat of blond lacquer.
2. Spray two coats of water-white lacquer.
   NOTE: This can be used for other colors—gray, cream, green, yellow, etc. A gray or tan may be used on dark woods.

### (17) Pigment coloring system

Brush system for maple or birch.

1. Brush light-color pigment wiping stain (blond, platinum, toast, wheat, etc.). Allow to dry until tacky, and then wipe clean with soft cloth. Dry 1 to 4 hours as required.
2a. Top coats of varnish.
2b. *Alternate.* One coat of 2-pound-cut white shellac, followed by coat of paste wax.
   NOTE: After the wood is colored, any top finish can be used. Water-white top coats are preferable, since they retain pure tone of stain.

## (18) Stain system

Attractive light tones can be obtained on select white wood
by stain. However, the wood cannot be made any lighter
than its natural color.

1. Spray or brush diluted stain solution of desired color.
   Yellow, orange, pink, and green tones are practical. Drying time depends on type used.
2. Finish according to Schedules 1, 2, 3, 4, 5, 6, or 7 on
   pages 305 to 308.

## (19) Bleach system for open-
### grained wood

A two-solution commercial bleach gives positive light tones
on most woods and provides the proper surface color for
attractive blond finishes. Color in this system is obtained
entirely from the filler.

1. Mix one part of No. 1 bleach with two parts No. 2. Apply with rubber sponge. Bleaching is complete in 1 hour,
   but work should dry 12 hours.
2. Sand lightly with extra fine paper. Dust.
3. Apply paste wood filler. Wipe and dry.
4. Finish with sealer; sand; apply top coats; rub (see Schedule 1).
   NOTE: Use natural filler for lightest finish; tint natural
   filler with oil color or oil stain for other colors.

## (20) Bleach system for open-
### grained wood

Color in this system is obtained from the stain.

1. Bleach the wood. (Use two-solutions commercial bleach
   for best results as per operation 1, Schedule 19.)

2. Brush or spray diluted non-grain-raising stain. This can be yellow, orange, pink, light green, etc.
3. Wash coat of shellac. Dry 1 hour.
4. Apply filler. Use natural or tint with oil color to approximate color of stain.
5. Top coats.

### (21) Bleach system for close-grained wood

Ideal for maple, beech, birch, etc.

1. Bleach the wood. (Follow operation 1; Schedule 19.) Let dry.
2. Sand lightly with extra fine paper. Dust.
3. Brush or spray desired color wiping stain, such as platinum, champagne, toast, wheat, or suntan. Let stand until stain begins to flat, then wipe clean with soft rag.
4. Brush or spray sanding sealer, preferably water-white. Dry 1 hour.
5. Sand with extra fine paper, dry. Dust.
6. Spray two coats water-white lacquer or brush one coat clear synthetic.
7. Rub.

    NOTE: After bleaching the wood, it can be finished by following any schedule for close-grained wood.

## SPECIFIC WOOD FINISHES

### (22) Colonial maple

1. Stain with antique maple stain of the water or non-grain-raising type. If water stain is used, follow Schedule 1 to operation 3 (page 305).

2. Wash coat of shellac. Dry 1 hour.
3. Sand with very fine paper.
4. Brush or spray second shellac coat, 2-pound cut. Alternate treatment—sanding sealer. Dry 2 hours.
5. Sand close with very fine paper.
6. Uniform color with shading stain for maple, shading at same time if desired. Alternate treatment: Brush or spray maple wiping stain, wiping for even color and shade.
7. Two coats of clear lacquer or varnish.
8. Sand with extra fine waterproof paper with rubbing oil or water as lubricant.
9. Clean up and wax with brown paste wax.

   NOTE: Operation 1—There is no fixed color for colonial maple. Three or four different shades in brown, red-brown and orange-brown are available. The finisher can make his own by shading any medium-brown stain with a touch of orange.

## (23) Colonial maple—wax finish

Also suitable for birch, beech, cherry, and other hard close-grained woods.

1. Sponge work with warm water. Two ounces of dextrin per gallon of water can be added if desired. Dry 1 hour.
2. Sand with very fine paper. Dust.
3. Stain with water stain of desired color. Dry 12 hours.
4. Shellac wash coat (7 parts alcohol to 1 part shellac). Dry 1 hour.
5. Sand with very fine paper, highlighting at same time. Number 2/0 steel wool can be used for blending.
6. Brush or spray 2-pound-cut shellac. Dry 2 hours.

7. Brush or spray maple wiping stain. Wipe clean, leaving dark smudges only in recesses, corners, etc.
8. Brush or spray 2-pound-cut shellac. Dry 4 hours.
9. Apply 4 or 5 coats of furniture paste wax.

## (24) Colonial maple

An inexpensive system for brushing or spraying.

1. Brush or spray maple wiping stain on bare wood. Wipe to desired color and for highlights. Dry 3 hours to overnight, depending on type of stain.
2. Use 2-pound shellac or lacquer, tinted to stain color.
3. Sand with very fine paper.
4. Two coats of lacquer or varnish.
5. Rub with 4/0 steel wool dipped in liquid wax.

## (25) Lauan wood (Philippine mahogany)

A high-grade system for brushing or spraying.

1. Sponge with warm water. Dry 1 hour.
2. Sand smooth with very fine paper.
3. Stain red or brown as desired with water stain. Dry 12 hours.
4. Brush or spray wash coat of shellac, lacquer, or sanding sealer. Dry 1 hour.
5. Sand with very fine paper.
6. Apply filler. Pad this well into the wood. Dry 4 hours.
7. Apply second coat of filler. Dry 48 hours.
8. Seal with 2-pound shellac or sanding sealer. Dry 2 hours.
9. Brush or spray mahogany wiping stain. Wipe off, blending highlights with a soft brush. Dry 3 hours to over-

night, depending on type of stain, whether fast- or slow-drying.

10. Spray two coats of clear lacquer or brush two coats of varnish.

11. Rub to satin finish.

### (26) Lauan wood (Philippine mahogany)

An inexpensive spraying schedule.

1. Fill the bare wood with an orange-brown filler. Dry 24 hours.

2. Spray sealer coat. This should be tinted with orange-brown lacquer enamel and the coating controlled for depth of color. Dry 1 hour.

3. Sand with very fine paper.

4. Spray first coat of clear lacquer. Dry 2 hours.

5. Spray and wipe mahogany wiping stain or shade with shading stain.

6. Spray second coat of clear lacquer.

   NOTE: This is a surface-staining technique with slight obscuration of the grain, but quite pleasing in light colors.

### (27) Harvest wheat mahogany

A bleached finish. Suitable for all light mahogany tones.

1. Bleach the wood. Use any good commercial bleach. Dry overnight.

2. Sand with very fine paper.

3. Stain with non-grain-raising stain. This should be harvest wheat color (a creamy orange).

**4.** Wash coat of shellac or bleaching lacquer. Dry 1 hour.

**5.** Apply filler. Use natural or tint with raw sienna and orange to desired color. Dark pores should be avoided.

**6.** Finish with two or more coats of water-white lacquer.

> NOTE: Operation 3 can be omitted if a tinted filler is used. Operation 6—Unless the tone is very light, ordinary clear lacquer can be used.

### (28) Honey-tone maple

A bleaching schedule, also suitable for other light-colored woods.

**1.** Bleach the wood. Commercial two-solution system best.

**2.** Sand with very fine paper.

**3.** Stain with honey-tone maple stain (light amber). Can be mixed with 5 parts orange to 1 part blue and 2 parts yellow. Any light stain is satisfactory.

**4.** Wash coat of water-white lacquer or bleaching lacquer.

**5.** Blend color with a tinted lacquer if required.

**6.** Two coats of water-white lacquer.

> NOTE: Operation 1 can be omitted on selected white wood. Operation 3 can be omitted if bleached tone is even and satisfactory color. Operation 6—Water-white lacquer is essential for very light tones.

### (29) Honey-tone maple

A surface coloring method. This is the system most used on selected white wood. Also used for lighter-than-natural effect on any other wood.

**1.** Spray uniform coat of blond maple sealer. This can be purchased or made by tinting clear lacquer with white lacquer enamel. The material should be well diluted and sprayed thin.

**2.** Spray two coats of water-white lacquer.

### (30) Old World

A brushing or spraying system for walnut or mahogany.

**1.** Spray NGR stain. Dry 1 hour.
**2.** Spray one coat of clear gloss lacquer. Dry 2 hours.
**3.** Scuff with 2/0 steel wool.
**4.** Brush and wipe pigment wiping stain for highlights and smudges. Dry 3 hours to overnight, depending on type.
**5.** Spray second coat of clear gloss lacquer. Dry 2 hours.
**6.** Spray third coat of clear gloss lacquer. Dry 4 hours.
**7.** Rub with 4/0 steel wool.
**8.** Apply dark-brown or black wax, leaving a fairly heavy coat in recesses. Powdered rottenstone or powdered raw umber can be mixed with clear wax for a dusty finish.
  NOTE: This finish is correct with open pores. However, a filler may be used if desired.

### (31) Old World

Another Old World finish for open-pored wood such as walnut, mahogany, or oak. Feature of this schedule is that all shading and color is obtained by a single coat of pigment stain.

**1.** Stain the wood medium to dark brown using pigment oil stain. Let stain dry 5 minutes, and then dry brush, wiping brush occasionally on cheesecloth to remove excess stain. Then, with clean cheesecloth pad, wipe centers of panels clean, blending stain to darken at edges. Let dry overnight. Do not sand.

2. Brush or spray sanding sealer. Dry 1 hour.
3. Scuff-sand with extra fine paper.
4. Top coat of lacquer or varnish.
5. Rub with 4/0 steel wool.
6. Apply dark brown or black wax and polish.

> NOTE: A wash coat of clear plywood sealer or shellac can be used as a primer if desired and will facilitate smooth blending of stain coat.

### (32) Stained fir

A subdued-grain finish for Douglas fir, white or yellow pine, and similar soft woods.

1. Brush or spray clear plywood sealer. Dry 4 hours.
2. Scuff sand with extra fine paper.
3. Brush coat of stain, pigmented type. Let stain dry 5 to 10 minutes. Wipe clean with cheesecloth. Dry overnight.
4. Top coats of varnish or lacquer.

> NOTE: Both the sealer and pigmented stain help to subdue the grain. After coat of plywood sealer, the wood can be finished with any schedule for close-grained woods. If NGR stain is to be used, reduce the priming sealer coat with 25 percent turpentine.

### (33) Aromatic red cedar

1. Spray 2-pound-cut pure white shellac. Dry 2 hours.
2. Rub down with 2/0 steel wool.
3. Second coat of shellac, 3-pound cut. Dry 2 hours.
4. Sand extra fine paper or 3/0 steel wool.
5a. Top coat of clear gloss varnish.
5b. Alternate: Top coat of 3-pound-cut shellac. Rub with 4/0 steel wool and then apply furniture wax.

NOTE: Schedule 12, page 310, can also be used. Shellac is essential as a first coat to seal the oil in cedar. When used for closets, box interiors, etc., it should not be finished.

## (34) Pickled pine

A gray finish on white pine.

1. Bleach the wood. Dry overnight.
2. Apply non-grain-raising gray stain. Dry 3 hours.
3. Spray two coats of water-white lacquer. Rub down.
4. Wax. Rottenstone can be added to wax if desired.

## (35) Pickled pine

Optional color ground with glaze coat.

1. Stain the wood any desired shade of gray or brown. Bleaching is required for very light tones.
2. Brush or spray lacquer sealer or 2-pound-cut shellac. Dry 1 hour.
3. Brush overall coat of white glaze. Use concentrated white wiping stain, or make a glaze from soft paste white lead thinned with turpentine and with a little linseed oil and drier added.
4. Wipe glaze while wet to expose highlights as desired. Use a soft brush to blend the highlights. Dry overnight.
5. Brush or spray coat of white shellac.
6. Apply wax. The wax can be tinted with burnt umber in japan if desired.

## (36) Limed oak

A popular novelty finish for oak, chestnut, and other open-grained woods showing white pores on a gray ground.

**1a.** Bleach the wood and stain with non-grain-raising silver-gray stain. On select white oak, bleaching can be omitted.

**1b.** *Alternate.* Spray a coat of thin gray lacquer on the wood. This is an easier method than bleaching and equally good.

**2.** Wash coat of shellac or lacquer. This is required only if the wood has been stained; lacquer toner provides its own seal. Dry 2 hours.

**3.** Fill with white paste wood filler. White wiping stain can also be used, although it does not have the pore-leveling effect of filler. Dry 12 hours.

**4.** Finish with top coats of white shellac, water-white lacquer, or water-white synthetic.

**5.** Wax.

### (37) Ebonized oak

This is the same as limed oak but with different ground color; numerous color combinations are possible. It is suitable for open-grained woods.

**1.** Spray diluted black lacquer on bare wood, just enough to get desired color.

**2.** Fill pores with white filler or white pigment wiping stain.

**3.** Top coats.

### (38) Ebony on close-grained woods

A finish for birch, maple, beech, etc.

**1.** Stain with hot, concentrated black non-grain-raising stain. Let dry and repeat.

**2.** Scuff-sand with extra fine paper.

**3a.** One or two top coats of any clear finishing material.

**3b.** *Alternate.* Finish with black polishing wax.

## (39) Flat frosting for open-grained woods

A novelty finish with contrasting pores such as oak or chestnut.

**1.** Stain with gray oak non-grain-raising stain or water stain.

**2.** Wash coat of shellac. Dry 2 hours.

**3.** Fill with white wood paste filler. Wipe off clean, leaving white pores.

**4.** Water-white lacquer or 2-pound-cut white shellac.

**5.** Wax with clear wax.

## (40) Platinum blond maple

A novelty finish for close-grained woods.

**1.** Sand smooth with very fine paper. Dust.

**2.** Bleach the wood with an efficient two-coat bleach.

**3.** Sand lightly with extra fine paper. Dust.

**4.** Apply a coat of bleaching lacquer.

**5.** Without sanding the lacquer coating, brush or spray two or three coats of very pale white shellac, and sandpaper each coat with fine, dry sandpaper over a soft felt pad.

**6.** Apply a coat of a very dull lacquer.

**7.** Rub and polish.

NOTE: Varnishes should not be used in place of lacquer in the platinum-blond maple finish, because they give an amber or yellow tinge and become more strongly yellow with age.

### (41) Cayuga sand

For fir and other soft woods.

1. Sand with very fine paper.
2. Mix 1 part ivory or cream-eggshell wall enamel with 1 part clear plywood sealer. Brush or spray on a light, even coat so that wood grain is subdued but not covered. If brushed, use a dry, wide wall brush to blend the coating gently in continuous straight lines the entire length of the panel. Wipe bristles quickly at end of each stroke to keep them dry and clean. Work with tips of bristles only, and use no pressure. Dry 24 hours.
3. Use 3/0 steel-wool pads to secure the final even tone.
4. Wax. Dry 15 minutes. Polish.

   NOTE: If color is desired, use glazing colors as for Quaker gray (see Schedule 43) or autumn green (see Schedule 42) or use walnut or mahogany and blend out soft and evenly. First try out a sample panel on an area that doesn't show. Keep a record, and check the results. A glazing liquid for colors over Cayuga sand is mixed as follows: 4 ounces flat varnish, 2 ounces boiled linseed oil, and 1 ounce pure turpentine.

### (42) Autumn green

For fir, pine, and other soft woods.

1. Sand with very fine paper.
2. Mix: 1 pint soft-brown 4-hour enamel, 1½ pints natural wood filler, and 1½ pints turpentine. Also mix 1 pint jade-green enamel, 1½ pints natural wood filler, and 1½ pints turpentine.
3. Brush on each color in various areas about the size of

your hand, leaving many open portions between to show natural wood. Blend each color with rags to give cloud effects devoid of sharp margins. The color values should grade from heavy at the bottom to quite light at the top in order to give color balance in the room itself.

4. As soon as colors are wiped off, coat in the entire panel with clear wood preservative; then use rags and 3/0 steel-wool pads to secure desired blend and weight of colors. Keep best panel as a master panel against which to check all subsequent matching and blending. Dry 45 minutes.

5. Steel-wool clean and bright. Dry 24 hours.

6. Recoat lightly with wood preservative. Dry 15 minutes. Wipe off clean.

7. Dry 12 hours.

8. Wax. Dry 10 minutes. Polish.

NOTE: By following the same specifications, but using gray, tan, green, and the natural wood, a four-color blend called "forest" or "chromewald" can be obtained. Keep the colors soft and subdued, in clouds rather than in heavy areas, which would give a spotty effect.

## (43) Quaker gray

For fir, pine, and other soft woods.

1. Sand with very fine paper.

2. Mix: 1 quart gray 4-hour enamel, 3 pints natural wood filler, and 3 pints turpentine.

3. Brush on entire panel. Wipe off quickly.

4. Apply wood preservative coat immediately and blend color with rags for even tone or cloudy effect, as desired.

5. Dry 45 minutes. Use 3/0 steel-wool to achieve clean and bright finish.
6. Dry 24 hours after blending and using steel wool.
7. Recoat with wood preservative. Dry 15 minutes. Wipe clean and bright.
8. Dry 12 hours.
9. Wax. Dry 10 minutes. Polish.

### (44)  White finish on open-grained woods

This finish is suitable for oak, walnut, etc.

1. Sand with very fine paper.
2. Brush or spray coat of white enamel undercoater.
3. Sand with extra fine paper and dust with a cloth dampened in turpentine.
4. Make and apply glaze of raw umber and linseed oil thinned with turpentine to a wash consistency.
5. After brushing, immediately wipe off with a rag.
6. When dry, apply a coat of white shellac.
7. Polish with wax.

   NOTE: Because of the open grain of oak and walnut the glaze that drops down into the pores will remain there when the surface glaze is wiped off.

## ENAMEL FINISHES

### (45)  Lacquer or synthetic enamel

1. Spray mist-coat lacquer enamel.
2. Sand back to bare wood with extra fine paper.
3. Apply two or more coats of enamel, sanding between the coats with extra fine paper.

## (46) Enamel with undercoat

This schedule applies generally to oil, lacquer, and synthetic enamel.

**1a.** Wash coat of shellac. Dry 1 hour.

**1b.** *Alternate.* Brush or spray plywood sealer thinned 1 part turpentine to 3 parts sealer. Dry 1 hour.

**2.** Sand with extra fine paper. Dust.

**3.** Brush or spray undercoater. Spray lightly or brush out well. Dry as required.

**4.** Apply full wet coat of undercoater.

**5.** Patch. Use water putty, lacquer putty, thickened undercoater, or other suitable patching material.

**6.** Brush or spray first enamel coat. Scuff-sand with extra fine paper when dry.

**7.** Second enamel coat.

**8.** *Optional.* Spray a finish coat of water-white clear lacquer, or regular clear with a small amount of enamel added.

**9.** *Optional.* Rub down with extra fine waterproof paper with water, followed by rubbing compound for high-gloss finish.

> NOTE: Undercoater in operation 4 may be tinted with the enamel color if desired, using 25 to 50 percent enamel.

## (47) Ebony black

A combined stain and enamel schedule for a permanent gloss black.

**1.** Stain with black non-grain-raising stain.

**2.** Fill pores with black paste wood filler. Dry 12 hours.

**3.** Two coats of black lacquer.

4. Two coats of water-white lacquer.
5. Rub and polish to high gloss.

   NOTE: On close-grained wood, the filling operation is not required.

### (48) Antiquing or glazing technique

The following is the basic method of applying an antique or glazed finish. For the many variations of this basic method, see Chapter 13.

1. Apply a full coat of base color for a prime coat. Allow to dry thoroughly, usually for 1 hour. Sand lightly with fine sandpaper to remove any nap from the wood.
2. Dust thoroughly and apply a second coat of base color. While one coat is usually sufficient on previously finished surfaces, two coats should be used on new or unfinished wood.
3. Allow 2 to 4 hours before applying the antique glaze over the basecoat. The glaze should be permitted to "set" for 10 to 45 minutes. Then the glaze can be wiped to produce the desired effects—see pages 226 to 233.
4. One coat of clear lacquer or varnish.

### (49) Charcoal effect

A good finish for softwoods such as fir or pine.

1. Texture the surface with a steel brush as described on page 244.
2. Color with a flat black latex enamel or paint. When surface is dry, brush in a thin coat of white glaze. Let dry for about 30 minutes; then rub with clean cloth to obtain the precise charcoal shade desired.
3. Two coats of clear lacquer or varnish.

**(50) Feudal oak**

1. Texture the grain with a steel brush.
2. Stain with burnt umber.
3. Apply a deep brown glaze made from black and pure red colors in oil. Wipe glaze, following antiquing Schedule 48.
4. Two coats of clear lacquer or varnish.

**(51) Oriental lacquer finish**

To duplicate the lustrous Oriental finish that is so popular, apply a tinted varnish transparency over a base coat of a brilliant solid color.

1–7. Follow Schedule 46 to operation 7.
8. Apply a coat of varnish tinted to the base coat.
9. Rub and polish with super fine paper, using water as a lubricant. Finish with pumice stone and a rubbing oil made of 1 part boiled linseed oil and 5 parts paint thinner.

**(52) Flat frosting-lacquer enamel**

1. Spray thin coat of lacquer enamel, any color, just enough to color the wood.
2. Fill with white paste wood filler.
3. Two coats of water-white or clear lacquer.
   NOTE: Operations 1 and 2 can be reversed for a softer effect, the white pores showing through the thin coat of lacquer enamel.

**(53) Shellac for unpainted furniture**

1. Sand surface, always with the grain. Wipe thoroughly.
2. Mix 1 part pure white shellac (4-pound cut) and 3 parts

denatured alcohol. Apply this thin mixture with the grain. Allow at least 1 hour to dry. Sand lightly with extra fine paper and dust.

3. If a stain of any particular color is desired, apply water stain, carefully following the manufacturer's instructions. For a pickled finish, substitute a light coat of zinc white for water stain. For a natural finish, eliminate stain or zinc white.

4. Mix shellac and alcohol—1 part shellac, 1 part alcohol. Brush on freely with wood grain and allow at least 3 hours to dry. Sand lightly and dust with dry brush.

5. Apply another coat of shellac, same mixture as last. Allow 3 hours to dry.

6. If desired, apply coat of good paste wax and buff.

## RUBBING SCHEDULES

### (54) Rubbing schedule (satin) for steel wool

1. Rub with 4/0 steel wool. Alternate treatment—3/0 steel wool with oil or wax.

2. Polish with soft cloth.

### (55) Rubbing schedule (satin) for pumice

1. Rub with FF pumice and water. Flush with water. (Use oil in place of water for shellac.)

2. Rub with rottenstone and water, or rottenstone and rubbing oil for shellac.

3. Wax or furniture polish, if desired.

**(56) Rubbing schedule (satin)**
**for paper**

1. Sand with extra fine or super fine waterproof paper. Use water or naphtha lubricant. Soap can be added to water if desired. (Naphtha lubricant must be used for shellac.)
2. Rub with rubbing compound, using water or naphtha lubricant (this will depend on type of compound used).
3. Clean up. Various cleanup liquids are available.

**(57) Rubbing schedule**
**(satin-to-polish)**

1. Rub with ready-mixed rubbing compound. Use burlap pad.
2. Clean up and wax.
   NOTE: This produces a satin-to-polish finish, depending on the grade of rubbing compound used. This is as fast as a steel-wool rub and has more gloss. About 10 strokes bring up a satiny polish.

**(58) Rubbing schedule (high polish)**

1. Follow any satin schedule. Dry 12 to 24 hours.
2. Rub with polishing oil.
3. Spirit off with denatured alcohol and heighten polish with any lacquer polish.

**(59) French polish (high gloss)**

1. Apply any finish with lacquer, shellac, enamel, or varnish.
2. Sand with extra fine paper. Dust.
3. Dilute ready-mixed French polish with about 25 percent of proper solvent recommended by the manufacturer.

Apply mixture to cloth pad and flatten pad on palm of hand. Pad the work with circular strokes, and then finish with the grain.

NOTE: Use only improved French polish which requires no lubricant. For other methods of applying French polish, see page 144.

## REFINISHING SCHEDULES

### (60) Refinishing schedule

Where the old finish is to be removed.

1. Brush on even coat of varnish remover, brushing as little as possible.
2. Let stand 3 to 5 minutes to soften coating.
3. Remove old finish with putty knife.
4. Apply second coat of varnish remover where necessary.
5. Scrub with alcohol and No. 1 steel wool. An alcohol wash is important to remove wax residue. This operation is not required with a wax-free varnish remover.
6. Sand with very fine paper. Make necessary repairs. Finish same as new wood.

### (61) Refinishing schedule

Where the old finish is to be recoated.

1. Sand with very fine paper to as smooth a surface as possible without cutting through to stain coat.
2. Apply one coat varnish.
   NOTE: Any top-coat schedule can be followed. If the old finish is varnished, do not apply regular lacquer. If a lacquer finish is desired, use a nonlifting lacquer.

## Covering-capacity specifications*

| Material | Sq ft per gal |
|---|---|
| Bleaching solutions | 250–300 |
| Lacquer | 200–300 |
| Lacquer sealer | 250–300 |
| Paste wood filler | 36–50  (*per lb*) |
| Liquid filler | 250–400 |

* General average—will vary considerably, depending on thickness of coat, application to porous or nonporous surface, etc.

| Material | Sq ft per gal | Material | Sq ft per gal |
|---|---|---|---|
| Water stain | 350–400 | Spirit stain | 250–300 |
| Oil stain | 300–350 | Shellac | 300–350 |
| Pigment oil stain | 350–400 | Rubbing varnish | 450–500 |
| Non-grain-raising | | Flat varnish | 300–350 |
| stain | 275–325 | Paste wax | 125–175 |
| Paint | 650–750 | Liquid wax | 600–700 |

## Drying-time specifications*

| Material | Touch | Recoat | Rub |
|---|---|---|---|
| Lacquer | 1–10 min | 1½–3 hr | 16–24 hr |
| Lacquer sealer | 1–10 min | 30–45 min | 1 hr sand |
| Paste wood filler | | 24–48 hr | |
| Paste wood filler (*quick-dry*) | | 3–4 hr | |
| Water stain | 1 hr | 12 hr | |
| Oil stain | 1 hr | 24 hr | |
| Spirit stain | zero | 10 min | |
| Shading stain | zero | zero | |
| NGR stain | 2 min | 15 min | |
| Penetrating resin finishes | 15–45 min | 3–4 hr | 4 hr |
| Pigment oil stain | 1 hr | 12 hr | |
| Pigment oil stain (*quick-dry*) | 1 hr | 3 hr | |
| Shellac | 15 min | 2 hr | 12–18 hr |
| Shellac (*wash coat*) | 2 min | 30 min | |
| Varnish | 1½ hr | 18–24 hr | 24–48 hr |
| Varnish (*synthetic*) | ½ hr | 4 hr | 12–48 hr |

* Average time. Different products will vary.

## SOLVENTS FOR FINISHING MATERIALS

*Bronze powders* are not soluble, but are held in suspension by lacquer, varnish, shellac, etc. Best results are obtained by using a special bronzing liquid which can be bought in either a varnish or lacquer formula.

*Filler—paste wood filler* can be mixed with turpentine, naphtha (benzine), or a half-and-half mixture of turpentine and gasoline.

*Filler—quick-dry*   Same as above. Naphtha usually recommended.

*Filler stain*   Same as above. The addition of 20 percent benzol or toluol will ensure better penetration of the stain.

*Lacquer*   Usually a blended mixture which can be purchased in fast-, medium-, or slow-drying type, and sold under the general name of lacquer thinner. A standard formula for clear lacquers is butyl acetate 23 percent, ethyl acetate 8 percent, toluol 69 percent. A standard formula for pigmented lacquers is butyl acetate 28 percent, ethyl acetate 29 percent, butyl alcohol 26 percent, toluol 17 percent.

*Lacquer sealer*   Lacquer thinner.

*Rubbing compound*   Can be lubricated with water, soapy water, naphtha, low-test gasoline, or kerosene. It is advisable to follow the manufacturer's recommendations.

*Stain—non-grain-raising stain*   Special.* Many brands can be reduced with denatured alcohol. Some types reduce with butyl alcohol (butanol).

*Stain—penetrating oil stain*   Naphtha, turpentine, benzol, toluol.

---

* "Special" indicates that a special blended solvent is provided by the manufacturer and should be used for best results.

*Stain—pigment oil stain*   Naphtha, turpentine.

*Stain—spirit stain*   Denatured alcohol.

*Shellac . . .*   Denatured alcohol. Wood alcohol. Butanol. Denatured alcohol is probably the best, in view of price and workability. It should be no less than 190 proof.

*Synthetics*   Special.* Toluol can be used for most products.

*Varnish—oil varnish*   Turpentine.

*Varnish—synthetic varnish*   Some synthetic varnishes require special reducers. Many can be thinned with turpentine; others with toluol and other materials.


## MAIL-ORDER HOUSES

While most of the materials mentioned in this book are available at your local paint or hardware stores, a few mail-order houses carry all the furniture-finishing specialties. They are:

H. Behlen & Brothers, Inc.
10 Christopher Street
New York, New York 10014

Craftsman Wood Service
2729 South Mary Street
Chicago, Illinois 60608

Albert Constantine and Son, Inc.
2050 Eastchester Road
Bronx, New York 10461

Minnesota Woodworkers
Supply Company
925 Winnetka Avenue, North
Minneapolis, Minnesota 55427

---

* "Special" indicates that a special blended solvent is provided by the manufacturer and should be used for best results.

# Glossary of Wood-finishing Terms and Materials

ABRASIVE: Coated papers or cloth, or pumice stone, used for cutting down finish surfaces.

ABSORPTION: The act of taking up, or assimilation, of one substance by another. Do not confuse absorption with adsorption, which is a surface phenomenon.

ACETATES: Solvents for nitrocellulose. Various alcohols combined with acetic acid.

ACID DYE: Aniline color of an acid reaction, or used in an acid bath. Wood stains which need no acid, as such.

ACID STAIN: Stains of an acid nature. Soluble in water. Water stains are often called acid stains.

ADHESION: Mechanical affinity of any finish coat for the one directly under it.

ADSORPTION: (Do not confuse this term with absorption.) A type of adhesion which occurs at the surface of either a solid or liquid which is in contact with another medium.

ADULTERATION: Any mixture of materials of lower grade than the accepted standard.

AGING: A time-blending process applied to varnishes and oils in storage.

ALKYD: A synthetic resin developed from various oils, used in enamels and varnishes as the film-forming material.

ALLIGATORING: A form of paint failure in which cracks form on the surface layer only. It is caused by the application of thick films in which the underlying surface remains relatively soft. Another common cause is applying fast-drying paint over slow-drying paint (or sometimes interior paint over exterior paint). It is also caused by application of paint over unseasoned wood, and by the use of thinners which evaporate too rapidly. As the name implies, an alligatored surface is one that resembles the hide of an alligator in that it appears to be cracked into large segments.

AMALGAMATION: The act of combining separate parts into a uniform whole—as amalgamating crazed shellac.

ANHYDROUS: Free from moisture.

ANILINE: A coal-tar derivative. The basis of most modern stains.

ANILINE DYE: Soluble color made from an aniline oil base.

ANTIQUE FINISH: A finish usually applied to furniture to give the appearance of age by making certain parts of the furniture appear to have had greater wear.

ASPHALTUM: A natural bitumen or asphalt. Gilsonite is a very high-grade asphalt.

BAKING ENAMEL: One which requires a heat range of 2 hours at 150° F. or 20 minutes at 350° F.

BANANA OIL: Amyl acetate. Also bronzing liquids containing cellulose, gums, and amyl acetate in solution.

BASE: A heavy-bodied paste or liquid, ready for thinning.

BASE COAT: The first coat of the final finish. Also, the basic color coat used under a glaze.

BENZINE: A light-gravity petroleum distillate. Varnish makers' and painters' naphtha (V.M.&P. Naphtha).

BENZOL: A coal-tar naphtha. A more powerful solvent than

benzine. It is toxic and should be used with proper ventilation.

BINDER: The residue left after the evaporation of the thinner or solvent from a paint, varnish, enamel, or lacquer film.

BLEACH: Any chemical solution used to lighten the color of wood.

BLEACHING LACQUER: A sealing lacquer applied to light wood to prevent it from being darkened by filler. Has no bleaching action.

BLEEDING: Occurs when an undercoat which is soluble in the finishing material applied over it works into and blends with the top coat. Oil and spirit stains bleed.

BLOOM: Bluish cast on a lacquered surface. Usually caused by rubbing too soon; also from greasy residue in the rubbing oil.

BLUSH: White to gray cast on lacquered surfaces. Usually caused by water (due to humidity and moisture in the air) trapped under the lacquer coat. Quite common in summer. Corrected by using a slower-drying thinner.

BODY: When used to describe paint, it refers to consistency and opacity. When describing clear coatings, it refers to viscosity only.

BOILED OIL: A process used to improve drying ability of linseed oil.

BRIDGING: Ability of a finish to film over minute pores and cracks in wood or a previous finish.

BRONZE: Metallic flakes used in a binding liquid to produce a coating simulating various metals. Also, the phenomenon by which oil-soluble stains become iridescent after drying on wood.

BRUSH CLEANER: A varnish-remover solvent. Also, water solution of one or more phosphates in which the brush is soaked. Remover is by far the safest method for cleaning bristles.

BRUSH KEEPER: A container used as a storage container for paint and varnish brushes, in which a medium keeps them soft, clean, and ready for use.

BRUSHING LACQUER: A lacquer solution, clear or colored, for brush application.

BUFFING COMPOUND: A soft abrasive bonded in stick form with wax.

BURNING IN: The process of patching with heated shellac and a knife.

BURNISH: The act of producing a lustrous, shiny surface by rubbing with a firm smooth tool.

CARNAUBA WAX: A yellow wax. Sometimes called Brazil wax. Hardest of all waxes, melting at 185° F.

CATALYST: A substance which usually accelerates or changes the speed of a chemical reaction by taking part in the reaction, but which is formed again as a reaction product. Driers, for instance, act as a catalyst in the oxidation of vegetable and marine animal oils.

CATALYTIC FINISH: A hard, tough finish which is steam-, alcohol-, and waterproof. Used for tabletops and bar tops. Requires catalyst which is mixed with synthetic before use.

CHECKING: Shallow cracks which are the result of a finishing failure. Generally caused by a hard surface coat over a softer undercoat.

CHINAWOOD OIL: Oil obtained from the nut of the tung tree. Used in making varnish. Also called tung oil.

CLEAR FLAT: A clear finish which dries with a flat finish.

CLEAR GLOSS: A clear finish which dries with a glossy finish.

CLOSE-GRAINED WOOD: Wood which does not reveal open pores when it is dry.

COLD-WATER PUTTY: A composition of dental plaster, wood dust, with casein or dextrose as a binder; used with cold water for quick repairs on furniture, etc.

COLOR-IN-JAPAN: Pigment colors ground and mixed with japan drier.

COLOR-IN-OIL: Pigment colors ground and mixed in linseed oil.

COPAL: Fossilized gum resins dug out of the ground. The hardest natural resins. A varnish made from copal gums is called a copal varnish.

CRACKLE FINISH: A novelty finish usually produced by applying a top coat of lacquer designed to shrink, crack, and expose a more flexible undercoat, usually of a different color.

CRACKLE LACQUER: A special type of lacquer used to produce a crackle finish by the rapid drying of the top coat over a slower-drying undercoat.

CRAWLING: A surface failure that causes the material to form waves.

CRAZING: A fine netlike pattern of fine cracks found on aged finishes.

CROCUS CLOTH: An extremely fine abrasive used at the final stages of rubbing a finish, usually with a rubbing oil.

CRYSTALLIZING LACQUER: A baking lacquer which produces a textured effect consisting of numerous small crystals.

CURTAINS: A portion of a finish coat which sags down in folds on a vertical surface, just before becoming set.

CUT: The number of pounds of shellac resin dissolved in a gallon of solvent. For example, 5 pounds of dry shellac in 1 gallon alcohol is a 5-pound cut.

DAMMAR: A gum resin used in making very clear varnishes. Softer than copal gums.

DECALCOMANIA: A method by which decorations are transferred from a paper base to a prepared surface.

DENATURED ALCOHOL: A solvent for paint, shellac, etc., which is made by denaturing grain alcohol.

DEWAXED SHELLAC: A superfine bleached and dewaxed shellac commonly used as the basis for various types of French varnish.

DIPPING: The method by which articles are immersed in clear or colored coating and slowly withdrawn to produce a high-grade finish.

DISTRESSING: The art of selectively damaging wood or its finishes to achieve the appearance of age. Also applied to spattering of dark glaze spots on finishes.

DRIER: Any catalytic material which, when added to the finishing material, accelerates the drying or hardening of the film. Driers are usually in the form of organic salts of lead, cobalt, manganese, and zinc, such as naphthenates, resinates, and linoleates.

DRY COLORS: Dyes in powder form, dissolved in water, alcohol, or mineral spirits to form stains.

DRYING: The solidification of a film. The drying or hardening of a film goes through several stages. The first is known as "dust-free" and is the time required for a film to reach the condition where, if any dust settles on it, the dust will not become embedded, but can be wiped off after the film has hardened. The second stage is known as "tack-free" and is the time required for a film to reach the condition where it may be touched with light vertical pressure of the finger. The third is "hard-dry" and is the time required for the film to become thoroughly hard so that it may be rubbed or polished. Drying may be due to evaporation of volatile solvents, oxidation of oils containing double bonds, or to polymerization.

DRYING OILS: Any oily liquid material, always of an organic nature, which when applied as a thin film will dry or harden within 48 hours upon exposure to normal atmospheric conditions, with or without the required amount of drier. Drying oils are usually derived from natural sources such as vegetable or marine animal matter but also may be obtained by synthetic processes.

DUSTING: The method of antiquing a finish by applying rottenstone powder to a wax coating. Also, the presence of dry particles on a lacquer film left by improper or careless spraying methods.

DUTCH METAL: An artificial gold leaf that is produced from thin leaves of bronze or brass.

EARTH PIGMENTS: Pigments mined from the earth. Ocher, umber, sienna, Vandyke brown, etc.

EGGSHELL: An indefinite term often used by the layman to describe the appearance of a film which has little or no gloss. The use of this term is discouraged, since it is ambiguous. Also a term applied to an off-white color.

ELASTICITY: That property of a film which permits it to stretch or change in size and shape, returning to normal condition without breaking or rupture during the distortion. The term elasticity should not be confused with toughness, tensile strength, or elongation, which have different meanings.

ENAMEL: A broad classification of free-flowing pigmented varnishes, treated oils, or lacquers which usually dry to a high-gloss or semigloss finish. Enamel films are characterized by the absence of brush marks. Actually, the line of distinction between enamels and paints is very indefinite.

EPOXY: A tough, hard synthetic resin noted for its amazing adhesive powers; found in many modern finishes.

ETHYL LACTATE: One of the most powerful solvents for nitrocellulose and various gums and resins.

EXTENDER: A cheap pigment, usually of an inert type, used to extend or increase the bulk of a paint, thus reducing its unit cost. Extenders are also used to adjust the consistency of a paint and to give colored pigments of greater tinting strength. The use of an extender in a paint does not necessarily mean that the resultant products will be inferior. In fact, extenders sometimes improve certain characteristics of a film.

FAT EDGE: Unsightly and deterioration-prone overthick layer of a finish at any edge, caused by allowing the brush to fly or fall over the edge.

FEATHERING: The method of lightly stroking the finish coating with the brush bristle tips only, to produce a thin, blending action.

FILLER: An inert or extending pigment such as china clay, barytes, powdered mica, silica, or whiting. Filler is also a product used to fill or level the pores of wood before applying lacquer, varnish, or shellac.

FLAT FINISH: A finish without sheen, the result of rubbing or because of pigments and flatting oils in the formulation.

FLINT: An alternative name for what is commonly called sand when used to make sandpaper or flint paper.

FLOCK: Shredded cloth fibers. Applied over a tacky substance to form a soft, clothlike finish.

FLOW: The property of paint, varnish, or lacquer film which enables it to level off, free of brush marks or orange peel.

FRENCH POLISH: Refined shellac. Finishing with French polish, which is rubbed on the surface with a cloth, is called *French polishing.*

GLAZING: The process of applying transparent or translucent pigments such as raw sienna, burnt sienna, viridian green, alizarin or crimson, usually on a painted surface, to produce certain blended effects. The glazing paint is reduced to a thin consistency and spread over a ground color with the object of producing a translucent quality which could not be obtained by the use of an opaque paint.

GLAZING PUTTY: Paste finishing material for filling imperfections in wood or metal.

GLOSSY FINISH: A smooth, glass-like surface of varnishes and enamels which are not formulated with de-glossing materials.

GLUE STAIN: Used to sponge new cabinet wood previous to finish sanding. One-quarter of a cup cabinetmaker's hot glue to 2½ quarts of hot water.

GRAIN: The pattern produced in a wood surface by the fiber structure of the wood.

GRAINING: A method of imitating wood grain with color paint coats and tools manipulated to form wood-grain lines and figures.

GRAIN RAISING: The objectionable roughness of wood caused by the application and absorption of stains or other materials. The roughness is due to the short broken fibers of wood which more or less stand up because of the swelling or raising action of the liquid coating. There are nonraising stains and varnishes now on the market which eliminate this disturbing condition.

GROUND COAT: A colored base on which a translucent top coat is later manipulated to imitate other woods, etc.

HAIRLINES: Fine lines in the paint film. These are really a

form of incipient checking and are usually caused by sudden temperature changes or by weathering. Hairlines that are not visible with the naked eye can be detected by the use of a microscope of low magnification.

HAND RUBBING: Use of felt rubbing block and pumice by hand, as contrasted with belt or machine methods.

HARDWOOD: A term designating wood from nonconiferous (non-cone-bearing) trees.

HIGH BOILERS: Ingredients in a lacquer thinner which slow down the evaporation rate. Boiling points range from 150 to 200° C.

HIGHLIGHTING: A coloring or sanding process, by which those portions that naturally reflect the light are accented to increase this effect, forming a stronger contrast with adjacent darker areas.

HIGH SOLIDS: Lacquers having 27 percent or more solids. The average lacquer is 21 percent solids.

HUE: The difference of colors in quality (same as tone in music).

INERT: Inactive materials which have no hiding or tinting value and which have no effect on finishing coats.

INFRARED: Rays that are longer or stronger than visible red light rays and are felt as heat. Infrared heat produced by electric lamps is used to bake enamel.

JACK FROST: A novelty lacquer which dries like frost on a window pane.

JAPAN: A general misnomer, since it may be a drier used to harden oil films, a baking asphaltum varnish, or a grinding liquid for rubbing colors in varnish.

JAPAN COLOR: A pigment color ground in hard-drying varnish to permit rubbing after drying.

JAPAN DRIER: Varnish gum with a large proportion of metallic salts added for rapid drying. A japan drier for grinding with pigment colors should be thinned with turpentine. This type of japan is grinding japan, or T-Japan Drier.

KNOT: Usually a darker-colored inclusion in wood where the

grain is at right angles to and cuts across the normal grain. The result of budding or branching of limbs in the tree.

LACQUER: A fast-drying finishing material containing an appreciable amount of nitrocellulose in combination with various gum resins and solvents.

LACQUER ENAMEL: Clear lacquer with pigment added for color.

LATEX: Generic term used to cover a variety of paints and wood finishes which use water as the thinner.

LEAFING: The ability of an aluminum- or gold-bronze paint to exhibit a brilliant or silvery appearance. Gold leafing is achieved by using proper coating pigments along with suitable bronzing liquids. (Check bronzing-liquid manufacturer's instruction as to the proper pigmented surface to use.)

LIFTING: The softening and penetration of a film by the solvents of another film which results in raising and wrinkling.

LINSEED OIL: A vegetable oil, pressed from seeds of the flax plant. After this has been heated and filtered, it becomes raw linseed oil. When heated to a higher temperature to admit a small amount of metallic drier, the oil becomes boiled linseed oil.

LIQUID FILLER: Lacquer or varnish with finely divided inert pigments added.

LONG OIL: A varnish with a large percentage of oil. Spar varnishes often have 24 to 40 gallons of mixed oil to 100 pounds of gum.

LOW BOILERS: The fast-evaporating solvents in lacquer thinners, to give a fast initial set to the film. Boiling-point range 70 to 100° C.

LUBRICANT: Any material used between two rubbing surfaces to reduce friction or, as in sanding, to reduce clogging in the abrasive grit.

MARBELING: The imitation of marble effects on any surface, by floating enamel colors on water and immersing the object by a deft, sliding motion, leaving the colors adhering to the base material.

MATTE: A finish texture similar in reflectivity to blotting paper.

MEDIUM BOILERS: The intermediate group, between high and low boilers, in a lacquer thinner, which directly influences flow and freedom from orange peel as the film dries. Boiling-point range, 115 to 145° C.

MINERAL SPIRITS: A petroleum spirit that is used as a solvent for paints, enamels, and varnishes.

MIST COAT: A very fluid coat of lacquer which is fogged or misted on.

MOISTURE CONTENT: The percentage of water in lumber. Should be 7 to 10 percent for furniture.

MORDANT: A chemical, such as dichromate of potash, used to set a dye against fading.

MULTISOLVENT: Cleaners for brushes or surfaces to be painted, formulated of several different solvent materials, each specific for a certain kind of contamination, so that the cleaners are almost universal in effectiveness.

NAPHTHA: A petroleum or coal-tar distillate that is used as a cleaner or solvent for paints, enamels, and varnishes.

NATURAL FILLER: Silex, varnish, oil, and drier, paste base free of color.

NEUTRAL OIL: A light-gravity mineral oil used in finishing rubbed work with pumice stone.

NGR STAIN: Non-grain-raising stains, made of fast-drying solvents that do not swell or raise wood grain.

NIBS: Small conical projections above a finished surface caused by wet finish crawling up fiber or dust particles.

NITROCELLULOSE: Raw cotton cellulose mixed with nitric and other acids. The basis for many lacquers.

NONDRYING OIL: An oil which cannot take up oxygen from the air and lose its liquid characteristics. A thin layer of this oil does not form a tough surface film on standing exposed to the atmosphere. Some good examples of nondrying oils are castor oil, peanut oil, and coconut oil.

NONLIFTING: Nonlifting lacquers are intended for refinishing over varnish. The solvent commonly used has high alcohol content; if reduction is required, a nonlifting (high alcohol) thinner should be used.

OIL: A smooth, greasy, combustible material. Oils are classed as vegetable, animal, or mineral.

OIL COLORS: Colors ground to a paste form in linseed oil.

OIL-MODIFIED URETHANE: Modification of polyurethane varnish formulas which provides natural air drying, without hardener additives.

OIL RUBBING: The process of rubbing a finished surface with oil and pumice or other mild abrasive. Neutral oil, paraffin oil, etc., are commonly used, also crude petroleum.

OIL SOLUBLES: Materials capable of being dissolved in oils, including linseed oil, turpentine, benzol, and naphtha. Colored stains of this type are called *oil yellow, oil red,* etc.

OIL STAINS: Oil-soluble colors in naphtha or similar solvent are oil stains of the penetrating type; oil-soluble colors in naphtha or turpentine but with pigment colors and a binder, such as linseed oil, are called pigment oil stains. So-called wiping stains are pigment oil stains.

OLEORESINOUS VARNISH: A finishing material made of gums or resins and drying oils which hardens primarily by oxidation of the drying oils.

OLEUM SPIRITS: A mineral spirit that is a solvent for paints, enamels, and varnishes.

OPAQUE: Any finish that blocks a view of the wood surface.

OPEN-GRAINED WOOD: Wood which reveals conspicuous pores when it is dry.

ORANGE PEEL: A pebbled film surface similar to the skin of an orange in appearance. It is caused by too rapid drying of the lacquer or enamel after spraying, or failure to exhibit the desired leveling effects.

ORANGE SHELLAC: Unbleached shellac, which is a deep amber in color.

OVERTONE: The color reflected by a surface as distinguished from an undertone.

PADDING: The process of employing a pad or wad of cloth to apply a finish with a wiping motion.

PADDING STAIN: Special stains that are applied with a cloth pad and generally used for touch-up work or for "aging" effects in antiquing.

PASTE FILLER: A filling material in paste form which is diluted with turpentine, naphtha, etc., before using. Usually refers to a filler for wood.

PATINA: A quality of mellowness and surface texture which results from long usage and many polishings.

PEARL ESSENCE: Carefully refined fish scales (quanin) incorporated into clear lacquers to produce pearl lacquers. Special effects can be produced by the addition of spirit-soluble dyes. Pearl essence is also made synthetically from mercuric chloride.

PEARLING LACQUER: Fish scales in suspension in a clear lacquer. In unmixed paste form, pearl essence.

PENETRATING FINISH: Any finish formulated for penetrating oils and resins which sink into the wood, leaving little or no material on the surface.

PENETRATING FLOOR SEALER: A penetrating finish for floors but good for simple finish on furniture. Apply to bare wood only; brush or spray. Low luster. Usually steel-wooled and then waxed.

PENETRATING STAIN: Stain color in oil or alcohol.

PHENOLIC: A synthetic varnish resin made from phenol and formaldehyde.

PIANO FINISH: Considered by many as the most superb of all finishes, produced with varnish or lacquer, rubbed and polished.

PIGMENT: Finely divided insoluble particles added to lacquer and other finishing materials, usually to produce a colored product.

PIGMENTED WIPING STAINS: Stains formed of oils and resins in which pigments are suspended. When brushed on and then wiped off, they leave the coloration of the pigments, plus sometimes soluble dyes as well.

PINHOLING: The appearance of fine pimply elevations on a varnish film caused by moisture in the spray lines, trapped solvent, or insufficient atomization, or breaking up, of material.

PLASTIC FINISH: A stipple coating of whiting, glue, linseed oil, and other materials, which can be easily manipulated while still soft.

PLASTIC VENEER: A ready-made finish that comes in the form of a thin, tough plastic film bearing authentic photoreproductions of wood grains. These films, when removed from their protective paper backing, are cemented to the desired wood surfaces.

PLASTIC WOOD: Residue from filtering lacquers, used as a wood-patching putty.

PLASTICIZER: Materials added to lacquer to increase toughness and flexibility.

PLYWOOD SEALER: Special type of material formulated to seal the pores of plywood, especially those made of fir.

POLISHING VARNISH: A very hard-drying varnish, which, with water, pumice-stone rub, and rottenstone, polishes to a very high luster.

POLYCHROME: A modified stipple-coated finish, in several harmonizing colors.

POLYURETHANE: Often called urethane. One of the principal synthetic varnish resins obtainable in single container airdrying type, in moisture curing forms, and in two-container catalytic materials.

PORES: Small pits or voids in the wood surfaces which are actually the open ends of the tree's sap vessels.

POWDER STAINS: Stains in powder form which are mixed with a suitable solvent to produce wood stains. The three common types are water-soluble, oil-soluble, alcohol-soluble.

PRIMER: The coat of finishing material applied first, that is, on bare wood or metal.

PROOF SPIRIT: Equal parts of water and grain alcohol: 100 proof is 50 percent alcohol by volume; 188 proof alcohol contains 94 percent alcohol by volume.

PULLOUT: The act of inserting bristle tips into a crack or a corner and drawing out excess of finishing material.

PUMICE: A natural stone which is pulverized to produce a soft abrasive extensively used in rubbing finishing coats. Various grades. The finer grades—Nos. ½, O, F, FF, FFF, and FFFF (the finest)—are used in furniture rubbing.

RAGGING OFF: The process of wiping off excess stains with rags or blending color on a surface during a glazing operation.

REDUCER: A more or less volatile compound drying by evaporation and penetration, which is employed to bring coatings to the proper tack and consistency. The use of the term *thinner* is preferred to this word.

REMOVER: A solvent for softening old paint and varnish films.

RESIN: Solid or semisolid, natural or synthetic substance, soluble in ether, alcohol, or some other similar organic solvent, but not in water. Used to designate the various resins and gums used in making finishing materials.

RESIN HARDNESS: Grade of hardness of the resin. Usually graded from No. 1 to No. 6 (the softest).

RETARDERS: Slow-drying solvents added to lacquer to slow or retard the drying time.

ROSIN: A series of gums from pine that are left after turpentine distillation.

ROTTENSTONE: A siliceous limestone with negligible cutting action, but a good polisher. The English and Belgian grades are the only types suitable for furniture rubbing.

RUBBED FINISH: A low luster, extremely smooth finish obtained by rubbing with pumice or extremely fine waterproof abrasive paper.

RUBBING COMPOUND: An abrasive mixture in paste form. Commonly used for rubbing lacquer surfaces. Supplied in various grades of fineness, and in different types for mixing with water or naphtha.

RUBBING OIL: Neutral, medium-heavy mineral oil used as a lubricant for pumice stone in rubbing varnish and lacquer.

RUBBING VARNISH: A short-oil, fairly hard-drying varnish, capable of being water-rubbed.

RUNNING: The condition evidenced when a varnish or enamel sags down in curtains because of temperature or faulty manipulation on a verticle surface.

SAGGING: The slipping of a coating material on a vertical surface.

SANDING SEALER: A special lacquer formula or dilute shellac applied thin to the bare wood to seal the surface and make the final sanding smoother.

SAP: The life fluid of a tree. Often encountered when finishing, as a gummy pitch residue around streaks or knots, especially in pine and fir.

SAP STREAK: Deposits of pitch often exposed in sanding and planing that must be sealed (usually with shellac) since oleoresinous finishes will not adhere or harden over them.

SATIN: A finish texture having a soft sheen.

SATURATED SOLUTION: A solution in which the liquid can dissolve no more of the material being dissolved.

SCARIFY: The process of roughening a too smooth surface just enough to encourage good adhesion for the following coat.

SCREENING: The process of forcing paint through the open mesh of a fabric screen to produce a design. Certain parts of the screen are blocked off and do not print. This produces the desired design.

SCUFF: To roughen a coat of finish so that the following coat will bond better to it; basically the same as scarify. Also, to rub together face to face as with sandpaper.

SEALER: General term applied to any finishing coat applied over another as a sealer, or, on bare wood, to seal the pores and stop suction.

SEEDY: Any liquid finish material that has small, unwanted, hard granules, or particles suspended in the mixture.

SEMIGLOSS FINISH: A finishing material such as varnish or enamel which contains de-glossing chemicals to break up the surface shine.

SET: The initial hardening of a varnish or paint film previous to the body drying to complete hardness.

SHADE: The lightness or darkness of surface colors, the other color characteristics being essentially constant. Primarily, the term *shade* is derived from *shadow* and designates the change in appearance that is produced by a reduction in light. It should, therefore, when strictly used, express only the change toward a darker color. Several authorities have defined *shade of a color* as the mixture of a black with that color.

SHADING LACQUER: A transparent colored lacquer used in shading with a spray gun.

SHEEN: The reflectivity of a finish when viewed from a fairly flat angle. Usually given in a progression from gloss to flat: gloss, semigloss, satin, and flat.

SHELLAC: A natural gum resin soluble in alcohol. The standard mix is 4 pounds of resin to 1 gallon of alcohol and is called a 4-pound cut. The natural color of prepared shellac is orange. White shellac is obtained by bleaching orange shellac.

SHELLAC-MIXING LACQUER: A special type of lacquer which mixes in any proportion with shellac. Ordinary lacquers do not mix with ordinary shellac.

SHIELD: Any material that protects a surface from penetration, softening, or removal by top coats.

SHORT OIL: A varnish with a small percentage of oil. All rubbing varnishes are short in oil and may contain as little as 10 gallons of oil to 100 pounds of gum. Volatile solvents provide the necessary fluidity.

SILEX: A form of silica (quartz rock) used in making paste wood fillers. It is transparent when combined with oil and is chemically inert and nonshrinking.

SILKING: Parallel hairlike striations showing in coated films.

SIZE: A material designed to provide surface sealing and stiffening of wood fibers. Also, in gilding, it provides the adhesive action for the leaf or bronze retention.

SKIN: A tough layer of skin formed on the surface of a paint or varnish caused by exposure to the air, which produces oxidation or polymerization on the surface.

SMUTTING: The operation of dusting rottenstone powder over wax to effect age.

SOFTWOOD: Woods of the coniferous group (cone-bearing trees).

SOLVENT: Any liquid capable of dissolving a certain material is said to be a solvent for that material.

SOLVENT NAPHTHA: A coal-tar naphtha. A more powerful solvent than varnish makers' and painters' naphtha.

SPAR VARNISH: A very durable waterproof varnish for more or less severe service on exterior exposure. Such a varnish must be resistant to rain, sunlight, and heat.

SPATULA: A flexible, thin-bladed knife used to rub out colors, patching, etc.

SPIRIT STAINS: Dyes dissolved in alcohol.

SPIRIT VARNISHES: Varnish gums dissolved in alcohol or similar solvents.

SPRAY: To apply a finish by means of spray guns or aerosol spray cans.

STAIN: Coloring matter which is completely soluble in the liquid with which it is mixed. Differs from paint, lacquer, etc., where the coloring matter is composed of finely divided pigments held in suspension and deposited on the surface of the work.

STEEL WOOL: Fine strands of steel, used for rubbing varnished or lacquered surfaces, removing rust, etc. In six grades, Nos. 3, 2, 1, 0, 00, and 000. The No. 000 is the finest and will not scratch the finest surface.

STENCIL: A perforated piece of material—metal, wood, or paper. When it is placed on a flat surface and the color is applied over it, the paint which is applied through the perforated areas forms the design or lettering.

STICK SHELLAC: Shellac in solid stick form and in a wide variety of colors. Used for filling imperfections in wood.

STIPPLED FINISH: A textured finish obtained by special spraying equipment or by twisting and dabbing a piece of crumpled paper over the finish.

SUBSTRATE: Any surface over which a finish is applied.

SUCTION: The ability of a wood surface to absorb a finishing material. Degree of suction depends on type of wood and structure of the pores.

SURFACE DRYING: A condition whereby a top skin coat forms and allows the body portion of a film to remain soft.

SURFACER: An undercoat material used to build and level the surface. Similar to sanding sealer, but applies specifically to an undercoat used on metal surfaces. Also called *filler*.

SWEATING: A condition which shows on a varnish coat that has been rubbed too soon after application, and which will be noted when polishing by the appearance of streaks on the surface. Cured by allowing more drying time and re-rubbing later.

SYNTHETIC: Applies to any finishing material made wholly or in part from synthetic (artificial) resins.

TACK: The cohesion between particles of paint and the surface to which they are applied. Similar to stickiness or adhesion.

TACK RAG: A piece of cheesecloth or other lint-free cotton rag that has been dipped in thin varnish and then wrung out. It is kept in a container so that the varnish will not harden but will remain tacky. The tack rag is used to wipe a freshly varnished surface to pick up dust, etc.

TACKY: That point at which a sticky surface grabs or pulls at anything touching it, but is not readily removed from the original surface.

THINNER: The general term applied to any material used to reduce the consistency or viscosity of a liquid finishing material.

TIFFANY FINISH: A blended multicolor finish, either smooth or textured.

TINT: A color produced by the admixture of a coloring material, not white, with a white pigment or paint, the white predominating.

TIPPING OFF: The brushing process which involves the use of the tips of the bristles to smooth the applied finish.

TOLUOL: A coal-tar naphtha that is used as a diluent in the formulation of lacquer.

TONE: A modification of a full-strength color (mass tone), secured by blending with other colors to make it less brilliant or more harmonious.

TONERS: Pure dye colors ground into pigment and combined with a clear lacquer. Used to form a translucent base color in wood finishing, combining staining and lacquering in one operation.

TOP COAT: That coat of finish which covers another. Usually refers to the final coat of finish.

TOUCH-UP: A method of repairing off-color damage with shade coats to blend in with the rest of the finish.

TURNED WORK: Any object made on a lathe.

TURPENTINE: Spirits of turpentine. A volatile solvent used in paint, varnish, etc. Made by distilling the gum obtained from living pine trees.

UNDERCOAT: Any finishing material coat used under a final or top coat of finish. Also the process of applying an undercoat.

UNDERCOATER: A fast-drying, high-opacity primer.

UNDERTONE: The base color, generally dark, which appears beneath the overtone.

VARNISH: A finishing material consisting of drying oils and resins or gums which dries partly by the oxidation of its oils and resin ingredients.

VARNISH STAIN: General-purpose interior varnish tinted with dye colors or pigments. All wood colors. Stains and varnishes in one coat. Good for pine; seldom used on quality furniture except as quick refinish.

VARNOLENE: A mineral spirit that is a solvent for paints, enamels, and varnishes.

VEGETABLE OILS: Oils obtained from vegetables. Usually used as drying oils. Includes linseed oil, chinawood oil, and poppy-seed oil.

VEHICLE: The liquid portion of a finishing material.

VENEER: A thin surface layer of wood or other material used to add durability or beauty to an otherwise undesirable surface.

VINYL: One of the many synthetic resins used for paints and varnishes.

V.M.&P. NAPHTHA: The abbreviation for varnish makers' and painters' naphtha.

VOLATILE: Easily evaporated. A volatile solvent is one which dries by evaporation.

WASH COAT: A very thin sealing or shielding coat of any finish material.

WATER-BASE PAINT: A paint that can be thinned with water.

WATER STAIN: Colored dyes soluble in water.

WATER-WHITE: Transparent, like water. Used to describe any exceptionally clear lacquer or varnish.

WHITE SHELLAC: The bleached, creamy-white form of shellac.

WOOD ALCOHOL: Methyl alcohol, methanol. An alcohol obtained from the destructive distillation of wood.

WOOD FILLER: Any material useful in filling open pores of wood.

WRINKLE FINISH: A varnish or enamel film which produces a novelty effect very similar to fine wrinkles or irregular ridges. It is used on a wide variety of products, both wood and metal, and can be had in all colors. When properly baked, the resulting patterns range from coarse to fine wrinkles.

YELLOWING: A term applied to white coating which turns yellow or cream because of some fault of the paint or lacquer.

# Index